MONOGRAPHS OF THE
SOCIETY FOR RESEARCH IN
CHILD DEVELOPMENT

Serial No. 237, Vol. 58, No. 9, 1993

13674 Tho

MODELING GROWTH AND INDIVIDUAL DIFFERENCES IN SPATIAL TASKS

Hoben Thomas
Arnold Lohaus

WITH COMMENTARY BY
C. J. Brainerd

MONOGRAPHS OF THE SOCIETY FOR RESEARCH IN CHILD DEVELOPMENT
Serial No. 237, Vol. 58, No. 9, 1993

CONTENTS

COMMENTARY

THOMAS, HOBEN, and LOHAUS, ARNOLD. Modeling Growth and Individual Differences in Spatial Tasks. With Commentary by C. J. BRAINERD. *Monographs of the Society for Research in Child Development*, 1993, **58**(9, Serial No. 237).

The goal of the present research is to understand individual differences and growth of children's and adolescents' performance on two spatial tasks through a formal model framework.

In Study 1, 579 subjects aged 7–16 years old drew lines to represent their water-level task predictions for eight tilted rectangular vessels. In the verticality task, called the "van task," subjects drew lines representing their predictions concerning the orientation of a plumb line suspended from the ceiling of a van parked on eight different inclines.

In Study 2, 185 subjects aged 9–16 years were presented with video displays on a computer monitor and were instructed to adjust lines on the screen to indicate their predictions for the same stimuli used in Study 1. Later, they responded to a multiple-choice verbal analogies test and answered interview questions concerning their task performance strategies for the van and water-level tasks.

In both studies, responses on the van and water-level tasks were scored as correct or incorrect on the basis of empirically derived scoring criteria that varied with age. The number of correct responses for each subject on the van and water-level tasks was modeled as a binomial random variable. Individual differences, growth differences, and sex differences in task performance were modeled as mixtures of binomial distributions, a model that may be viewed as a latent class model.

Data for Study 1 subjects 11 years and older were combined so that the joint structure of the water-level and van tasks could be studied. This structure was modeled as a mixture of bivariate binomial distributions. On the basis of their task performance, subjects in Study 1 were assigned to their corresponding latent classes. Once classified, the original response distributions of subjects within each latent class were explored in an effort to understand their various response strategies. Additionally, the correspondence between verbal explanations and van and water-level task performance was investigated in Study 2.

Results include the following:

1. A two-component binomial mixture distribution fit well the van and water-level task data for each age and sex group; each binomial component may be viewed as a different latent class. Variance accounted for under the model often exceeded 90%. One binomial component (latent class) modeled the poor performers with poor task success rates, and the second component modeled the remaining good performers who consistently performed well. As expected, the verbal analogies task data showed no evidence of a latent class structure. A four-component bivariate mixed binomial distribution modeled reasonably well the joint van and water-level task data. There were two main components: one component for subjects who performed poorly and one component for those subjects who performed well on both tasks.

2. Between-sex differences in task performance were in evidence at almost all ages. However, when latent class membership was controlled, no sex differences in the original response distributions were detected, at least for individuals 11 years and older. Thus, the commonly observed mean performance advantage favoring males on the water-level task is the result of larger proportions of males who perform well than females at each age.

3. Growth in task performance over age is largely a discrete stage process and is a consequence of some poor performers changing their latent class membership as they mature. Good performance was achieved by late childhood or adolescence for about half the population. There appears to be little likelihood of task improvement by the remaining poor performers thereafter.

4. Two processes appear to determine van and water-level task performance: field effects and rule strategy. Field effects exert a passive influence on response errors and alter the average response of all individuals; however, poor performers are much more strikingly influenced by these effects than good performers. Field effects do not appear to determine subjects' response strategy. After early childhood, poor performers respond according to a constrained random response rule, producing a quasi-uniform response distribution with huge variance. Good performers respond in correspondence with a fixed rule—put the line horizontal (or vertical)—and they produce a symmetrical response distribution with small variance.

5. Good performance on the water-level task appears to precede verbally expressed knowledge of the correct principle; the reverse appears true for the plumb line task.

These results have implications for fundamental issues in child development. For example, many conventional models of data analysis, viewed as behavioral models, can be readily falsified. In particular, shift models such as the t test are inappropriate models for viewing individual differences and growth. Between-task correlations require a new conceptual framework.

I. INTRODUCTION:
A PERSPECTIVE ON MODELING OF BEHAVIOR

A model is a caricature of nature: A good model gives just enough
of nature to show off its personality but exclude the fluff.
—Juan Restrepo

This *Monograph* focuses on the problem of understanding individual
differences in cognitive development underlying performance on two
tasks—the water-level task and a van task that assesses verticality—as well
as a contrasting verbal analogies task.

Our main concern is to construct models of task performance in ways
that illuminate how growth and development take place. These models are
"bottom up" in that, while rooted in and directed by data, they are general-
ized in ways that provide implications for future research. The general
approach can be viewed as an example of the hypothetico-deductive method
(e.g., Brown, 1936) or as representing the interplay of empirical processes
and mathematical reasoning—what Coombs (1983) characterized as the
AMI approach.

There is a long if perhaps sporadic history of such efforts in child
development. Early examples include the work by Thurstone (1928) on the
growth of intellectual function. Piaget's modeling of cognitive processes by
(quasi–) group theoretical structures (e.g., Flavell, 1963) may also be so
viewed. However, a better example might be his work in perception (Piaget,
1969), particularly his probability models of encounters and couplings.
More recent examples include Markov modeling of conservation memory
by Brainerd and his colleagues (e.g., Brainerd, 1979, 1982; Brainerd, Howe,
& Desrochers, 1982); Bisanz, Brainerd, and Kail (1987) provide other recent
examples in the same general spirit.

The empirical bases for our work are two growth studies involving,
respectively, 579 and 185 German children aged 6.5 to about 16 years.
However, because it is easy to demonstrate that the basic empirical facts
about the water-level data falsify many cherished beliefs about how research

is to be viewed, how data should be analyzed, and how findings are to be understood, the issues we felt forced to consider go well beyond the typical focus on questions that are thought to be relevant solely to the tasks under study.

The primary empirical considerations driving our interest are two facts that have motivated the vast bulk of the water-level literature: persistent sex differences in task performance and the apparent inability of a substantial portion of college-age adults to perform well on this task.

As an empirical science, the first things that we have to guide us (or to correct our mistaken thinking) are data. To make any progress, we also must have a suitable conceptual model about the phenomena of interest against which the data may be viewed. Unless this model is a reasonable portrayal of reality, all further efforts are likely to lead us astray.

ADVANTAGES OF A MODELING VIEWPOINT

It is important to understand the rationale for adopting a modeling perspective because of the theoretical advantages that such a perspective bestows. Over the years, these advantages have been articulated by many authors, although sometimes with different emphases. Brown's (1936) paper remains useful in this respect, and the initial section of the Hull et al. (1940) book on rote learning continues to be a classic. More recently, and within a developmental perspective, Brainerd (1985) provides a very readable introduction to modeling emphasizing notions of invariance. Box's (1976) article—a charming piece with many bons mots—addresses many issues that other authors do not; his concern with the all too often uncritical acceptance of commonly used data analytic procedures is one of particular relevance to us. Note that Box does not restrict "models" to formalizations constructed specifically for some phenomena of special interest; rather, all of what we commonly term "data analysis procedures" are viewed by him as potential models of phenomena (such as, e.g., behavior). Box also warns against constructing models for their own sake and with few empirical connections, where problems are simply redefined and no theoretical mileage results. He labels such activities "mathematistry," a gaffe that we do our best to avoid here.

We find Coombs's (1983) perspective, which borrows from Coombs, Raiffa, and Thrall (1954), particularly appealing; its key ideas are represented in Figure 1.

The phenomena of interest are represented by the upper-left-hand box of Figure 1, labeled the "real world." In our case, this world consists of the water-level task and associated variables of interest. Through systematic observation, experimentation, and various other procedures, information

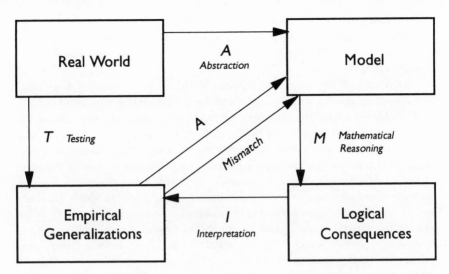

Fig. 1.—A conceptualization of the modeling process (adapted from Coombs, 1983, fig. 1).

about it becomes summarized in certain data relations, or in empirical generalizations, or simply in facts; the process is represented by the path T (for "testing"). For the water-level task, such generalizations include the sex and individual differences among adults in task performance. But there exists no theory that is associated with path T. The modeling process consists of what Coombs calls the *AMI* approach, composed of paths A, M, and I in Figure 1. It begins with abstraction of features of the world into a formal model (denoted by path A), an activity that is uniquely human and that may be difficult to describe. In this abstraction process, the empirical generalizations are almost always the crucial sources of information that guide model construction, so Figure 1 shows two abstraction arrows, one from the real world and the other from empirical generalizations.[1] Different investigators' modeling efforts will often, of course, lead to different and competing models of the same phenomena.

Once a model is constructed, it can be explored analytically to determine its logical consequences; this process is denoted by path M (mathematical analysis) in Figure 1. The most interesting of these formal consequences

[1] Coombs's (1983) fig. 1, from which our Fig. 1 was adapted, does not represent the abstraction process as having a path from empirical generalization. However, many modeling processes begin only when sufficient numbers of well-agreed-on empirical generalizations are available. These generalizations are crucial in guiding model development; consequently, such a path is represented here. The box labeled "model" in our Fig. 1 is labeled "axiom system" by Coombs. Our models start at the level of random variables and probability distributions.

of the model become hypotheses for interpreting data relations in what is hoped will be new and interesting ways. It is at this junction, where model consequences meet data (through path I, i.e., interpretation), that the real interest focuses.

To illustrate by anticipating some results to be presented later, the model that we have constructed leads to some very different interpretations of data. For example, the very meaning of sample means and sample mean differences in water-level task performance receives a new interpretation, which then leads to a different perspective on how the process of development takes place. Thus, the seemingly plausible idea that individuals gradually and incrementally improve in task performance is rejected—that is not the way that development takes place under our model, even though average performance over age often appears smooth and continuous. Such average performance curves should be viewed as empirical facts that require a theory. Our theory predicts the empirical results, but by invoking processes other than incremental growth.

It also turns out that the models that we propose are inconsistent with the large class of familiar models commonly called "additive" or "shift" models, which provide the conventional frameworks for examining performance on the water-level task as well as on most other tasks. Furthermore, when the familiar two-groups t test for group mean differences (a shift model)—which is often regarded as simply a data analysis procedure—is conceived as a model of behavioral process (and not simply as a statistical test), this model is easily rejected as a suitable behavioral model.

Sometimes modeling can lead to connections with issues that would not be thought immediately relevant. The issue of how best to assess a child's cognitive understanding is an example. Is it better to use a child's verbal explanations? Or is it preferable to use our judgments of the child's task performance? Although we cast the issue in somewhat different terms than have been typical (e.g., Chapman & McBride, 1992; Hodkin, 1987), we address the issue by considering whether verbal explanations precede or follow satisfactory performance in the course of development.

As yet another example, in the bivariate setting (i.e., when two variables are being considered), our model forces a rejection of the common "obvious" interpretation of the correlation coefficient and leads to a very different view of how r should be interpreted. None of these uncommon interpretations would have been forthcoming—at least not from the present authors—without a model structure to guide our thinking.

Interest in viewing behavioral processes from a mathematical perspective does not necessarily result in formal modeling. For example, Thelen and Ulrich's (1991) study of treadmill stepping by infants does not qualify as modeling because these authors do not provide a formal model of the stepping process. They do, however, give readers a tantalizing dynamic systems (or chaos theory) perspective on the emergence of stepping. The work that they report would become a modeling effort if a formal model of the stepping activity were specified (path A), its implications studied (path M), and the consequences derived by this process related to the infants' actual stepping behavior (path I).

WEAK VERSUS STRONG MODELS

There are, of course, no "true" models of phenomena, and any search for such models is futile (Box, 1976). The best that can be expected is that the mismatch between model and data (see Fig. 1) will be minimal and that the model proves to be useful. If the mismatch is severe, then the entire model may need to be discarded; if it is not, the model may be retained until a better model is constructed to replace it.

One feature of formal modeling that is not captured in Figure 1 is the distinction between "weak" and "strong" models. "Strong" models are models that are quite vulnerable to, and readily falsified by, specific features of data; most of the models that we present here are of this form. "Weak" models tend to have a looser linkage at the interpretation stage (I), and their implications (the M steps) tend to be more general and less easily falsified by data.

In general, the more complicated a model, the weaker it is. Most theories framed only in verbal language may be regarded as weak in that they are often very difficult to falsify. Furthermore, theories other than those of the formal type rarely specify any clear correspondence between the theory and the features of the data chosen for consideration. Why, for example, is it standard practice to test for mean differences? In fact, there is usually no clear conceptual basis for doing so. When a formal theory is rooted in probability theory, as here, there is typically no question as to which features of the data are relevant. The features of the probability structure of interest are identified through step M, which concurrently makes it clear what inferences (statistics) are necessary for the model to meet data through path I.

MODELING INDIVIDUAL DIFFERENCES

An intriguing aspect of the empirical findings from the water-level task is that they reveal just how blushingly wrong our conventional views concerning data and models can be. In subsequent chapters, we provide an abundance of data, both univariate and bivariate, to reinforce this point.

One fact that needs stressing is the magnitude of individual differences in water-level task performance: some elementary school children are able to perform just as quickly, efficiently, and accurately as some college-age adults, whereas some college students appear so perplexed and perform so poorly that they may resemble children many years younger. Individual differences of this magnitude can create severe conceptual problems. In our view, however, the first problem to consider is not that of identifying possible causative variables for manipulation in experiments or for entry in correlational studies; rather, it is to find a suitable model for the data. Once this step has been achieved, the modeling process of *AMI* may suggest which avenues are fruitful for investigation and which are not. As a result, the search for causative factors may be usefully narrowed.

In a sense, the entire field of child development is the study of individual differences along a growth continuum. The way in which such individual differences have traditionally been handled is by stratification. Because of our developmental penchant, researchers typically stratify on variables thought to covary with performance—usually age, sometimes socioeconomic status—or on variables such as the subjects' sex. However, these conventional procedures are effective only when the variables on which to stratify are readily apparent and observable. Because individuals' water-level task performance cannot be identified beforehand, we obviously cannot stratify prior to data collection. In sum, we view the problem of understanding the development of water-level task performance as roughly analogous to that of trying to construct growth curves for height when the children who were measured had not been coded for sex. What we need therefore are models that allow for objective stratification or clustering of subjects after the data have been collected. Once this goal has been accomplished, the serious questions regarding differences between individuals in the different clusters or strata can be addressed.

To put the problem in somewhat different terms, conventional, normal theory–based data model frameworks have no room for individual differences if the data have not been stratified on critical variables; in such instances, individual differences become residual error variance. However, this problem is not the only problem that we find with conventional perspectives. We also think that there has been an overemphasis on measuring individual differences in terms of means and variances. At the first stage of our own analyses, we measure individual differences in terms of rates and proportions that are represented as specific parameters in our models. This approach is different, but it has been forced on us by both conceptual and empirical reasons: there is a severe mismatch (see Fig. 1) between data and existing data analytic procedures when the procedures are viewed as behavioral models. We shall document this assertion in subsequent chapters.

A modeling framework that we find particularly useful for modeling individual differences is the theory of mixture distributions. This theory, which is intuitively congenial as well, may be viewed as similar to latent class, clustering, or stratification perspectives. Recently, a mixture model was constructed by Thomas and Turner (1991) for modeling water-level task data first reported years ago (Thomas & Jamison, 1975). The simple model proved quite useful in describing the data; variance accounted for under the model generally exceeded 90%, so, by this measure, there was little data-theory mismatch.

One consequence of this first effort (Thomas & Turner, 1991) was the emergence of a coherent picture of individual differences. This picture is basically a simple one: between-sex differences are the result of pooling different within-sex "stratas" together. One implication that follows from this model-based formulation of individual differences is that, to understand between-sex differences, one need study only *one* sex. In other words, there should be no contributions to between-sex differences that are not consequences of within-sex differences. This prediction is the kind of falsifiable prediction that we like.

Whether the reader prefers to view the present work as developmental theory or as developmental methodology is unimportant to us. We like to have it "both ways" and view it from either perspective, when it suits us to do so. Our preference is for formal theory that has as many natural psychologically substantive interpretations as possible. Because our theory has natural ties to specific statistical methodology, the hazy theory-methodology distinction is, desirably, blurred even further.

COMMENT ON THE CONTENT OF THE FOLLOWING CHAPTERS

As a way to orient the reader, we provide here a brief commentary on the contents of the following nine chapters. Chapter II reviews relevant Piagetian theory and summarizes the findings from Thomas and Turner (1991), the forerunner of the present study. Chapter III consists of a sequence of sections concerned with methodology and theory. We first review methodology problems of existing studies, problems that motivate our own model and method. Then the theory of mixture distributions is introduced, and the univariate binomial mixture model that we employ heavily throughout is developed. The chapter ends with a discussion of several statistical procedures that are often used but that are generally unfamiliar. Some readers may wish to skip Chapter III, except perhaps for the section on binomial mixtures—the basic intuition is developed in the section titled "Method and Theory"—and then refer to the appropriate sections when the need arises.

Our empirical effort begins with Chapter IV, which describes the basic methodology and reports the main results. Chapter V is concerned with understanding the response strategies that individuals employed in the water-level task. Chapter VI, like Chapter IV, reports the basic findings concerned with the van task. Chapter VII considers models for the joint distribution of the water-level and van task scores. The unusual bivariate data demand models with special features. Chapter VIII describes Study 2, which is in part a replication of Study 1 but which extends the investigation to the verbal domain and incorporates a verbal analogies task. A model for the joint structure of the spatial tasks and the analogies task is proposed. Chapter IX explores verbally expressed understanding of the task principles and spatial task performance in Study 2.

The final chapter first summarizes the main findings and then discusses the implications of the findings for a variety of issues of theory and methodology. Following an evaluation of the general binomial mixture model framework, the procedure is developed as a general analytic framework for evaluating a variety of task situations where latent classes might be suspected.

II. THE ACQUISITION OF THE CONCEPT OF HORIZONTALITY AND VERTICALITY

PIAGETIAN THEORY

Regardless of one's perspective, Piaget's writings on the water-level task cannot be avoided. After all, he started it all. More important, Piaget's theory remains, arguably, the only integrative perspective on the problem. Liben (1991b) has provided a review of the water-level literature from a Piagetian perspective; we draw on it here and begin with a short review of Piagetian theory as we understand it.

Most of the applicable theory appears in Piaget and Inhelder (1967), where the general development of both verticality and horizontality understanding is argued (chap. 13). As Liben (1991b) has emphasized, the tasks selected by Piaget—the water-level task and the plumb line, for example—were chosen with an eye toward understanding the child's developing horizontal-vertical coordinate system, which is a construct in Piaget's theory.

Piaget proposes three primary stages in the development of the horizontal-vertical coordinate system, with the last two having two substages each. We focus on the broader picture. In Stage I, which lasts until about age 4 years or "a little later" (Piaget & Inhelder, 1967, p. 384), the child lacks the idea of lines, surfaces, planes, dimensions, and so forth. Consequently, with respect to the water-level task, the child's characterization of the liquid's position is a scribbling or the like. For Piaget, this kind of response reflects topological representation, not the Euclidean structure of later development. Research that has focused on the very young child's responses (e.g., Dodwell, 1963) leaves little reason to doubt that children of this age perform in agreement with Piaget's expectations.

Stage II spans the ages from approximately 5 to 7 years. In Stage IIA, the child has learned to abstract the notion of surface or plane but still fails to understand that the growth of trees is vertical independent of the hill's slope or that the liquid in a vessel is not always parallel to the vessel's bottom. In Stage IIB, the child's reproduction of the horizontal and vertical remains the same as in Stage IIA; liquid is understood to remain parallel to the bottom of the vessel, "just as in Stage IIA" (Piaget & Inhelder, 1967, p. 392), and plumb lines suspended from the top of a bottle will likely be understood to be perpendicular to the bottom of the vessel. What distinguishes these two substages is that, in Stage IIB, the child is presumably groping "through a persistent trial and error," suggesting awareness of a problem, and this random groping "provides the key to his subsequent construction of operational systems" (Piaget & Inhelder, 1967, p. 392). Stage IIB is thus subtly different from Stage IIA and cannot apparently be recognized in most research that simply considers children's drawings scored by some criterion.

We think that Piaget's suggestion that the child's behavior can indeed be stochastic is particularly noteworthy: behavior can display a random trial and error quality at some points during development. This feature of Piaget's theory seems to have been largely ignored; we return to this idea much later, when it becomes a formal component of our own theory. Of course, there are other clues that Piaget has used in his interviews to diagnose subtle changes, such as the child's gestures and responses to questions, but for most group-based research such clues are not recorded and hence are not available for evaluation.

There seems little doubt that the main features of Piaget's second stage have found support in the literature: older children do draw lines and surfaces correctly, and success in responding to vessels that are upright or upside down is seen among even young children (e.g., Thomas & Jamison, 1975). The failure of substantial proportions of older individuals to demonstrate similar successful water-level task performance is, of course, a driving force behind the continuing interest in the water-level task.

Stage III, the concrete operational stage, represents the discovery of the vertical and the horizontal. The very words "vertical" and "horizontal" suggest, if not imply, the existence of external reference points that lie beyond the dimensions of the stimulus array itself.

Piaget distinguishes three substages here. The shift from Stage IIB to Stage IIIA marks an entry into an intermediate stage of discovery—in the case of the water-level task, of water's horizontality for vessels on their sides. Stage IIIA is interesting because it is marked by "trial and error construction of vertical and horizontal axes for all positions" (Piaget & Inhelder, 1967, p. 401). Here, again, Piaget stresses the stochastic quality of responses at some stages as a precursor to a more advanced understanding. The high point, however, is the entry into Stage IIIB, which results in the "immediate prediction of horizontal and vertical as part of the overall system of coordinates." This development is said to occur "about age 9" (p. 384), with, Piaget adds parenthetically later, "a few laggards at 12" (p. 408). The onset of Stage III is about 7–8 years, "but not earlier" (p. 379). Thus, Stage III has a window of about 2 years; consequently, it is to be expected that the probability of acquiring Stage III maturity would be very small prior to 7 and after 9 years.

CHALLENGES TO PIAGET'S FORMULATION

On the surface at least, Piaget and Inhelder's (1967) theory would appear to be in trouble with respect to development in this third stage. Significant proportions of college students and adolescents fail to understand the water-level task; for example, an overall estimate of the proportion of high school and college students demonstrating poor water-level task performance is 46%; this figure is based on seven independent studies of a total of 849 individuals (Thomas & Jamison, 1981). Individuals who perform poorly do not provide accurate predictions of their responses, nor, when interviewed, do they give much of a hint that they understand the principles of the task (Thomas, Jamison, & Hummel, 1973). Furthermore, college-age adults who have difficulty with the task do not readily understand the principle even when given self-discovery learning trials in which prediction errors are compared with the real water surface after each trial. Their task performance is resistant to improvement, and they give no verbal evidence of understanding either before or after their experiences (Thomas et al., 1973). Studies by Liben (1978), Liben and Golbeck (1984), and Robert and Chaperon (1989) have obtained very similar results.

Although it may seem sacrilegious to consider the idea, we suggest that Piaget may have been unaware of the difficulty of the water-level problem for subjects older than 12 years and of the potential implications of this observation for his theory. Because it is common to see some college students having great difficulty with the task, it seems that Piaget must have observed such difficulties among older children himself but perhaps dismissed them as unimportant. Furthermore, the apologetic tone with which he develops the ideas so "obvious" to adult readers suggests that this is indeed the case: "Now it may seem to more than one reader rather naive to raise the problem in this way. As adults we are so accustomed to using a system of reference and organizing our empirical space by means of co-ordinate axes which appear *self-evident* (like the vertical provided by the plumb-line and the horizontal given by a water level), *that it may seem absurd to ask at what age the child acquires these ideas*" (Piaget & Inhelder, 1967, p. 378; emphasis added). Using the estimates provided earlier, the odds are roughly one in two of finding readers of this *Monograph* who would fail to succeed on the water-level task. Thus, it seems most unlikely that Piaget would have written in the way that he did had he been aware of this fact.

Whether or not Piaget failed to observe such task difficulties, we think

11

that the empirical fact that not small numbers of older children and college-age adults have difficulties with the water-level task has important implications for his theory. One clear theoretical problem is that, as Larsen and Abravanel (1972) noted, development of a horizontal-vertical coordinate system is for Piaget a prerequisite for successful measurement of length. Thus, failure on the water-level task implies an absence of the Piagetian Euclidean coordinate system.[2] Yet there is no evidence that failure on the water-level task means that the individual is incapable of measuring lengths, something the individual should be unable to do if—as water-level task failure implies—there is a lack of a spatial system.

More generally, a theory that presumes that a spatial system is available by about age 9, and makes later cognitive developments contingent on it, is certainly compromised by the frequency with which adults fail on the water-level task.

We leave it at that, except for noting that some researchers would probably disagree with this conclusion. Liben (1991b) writes "that despite the relatively extensive empirical literature using the water-level task, relatively little of it is ideally suited to addressing the questions of fundamental concern to Piaget and Inhelder" (p. 132). Although the present research was not designed to test features of Piagetian theory, we believe that our data do speak to certain Piagetian issues, and, when we think that our data address such issues, we will consider them.

BACKGROUND AND MOTIVATION FOR THE PRESENT RESEARCH

Thomas and Turner (1991) constitutes the immediate background for our far more extensive current work. The general model structure and the conceptual rationale for the data reduction methodology are issues considered in subsequent sections below. Here, we consider the study's basic findings, the issues that were addressed, and the study's shortcomings that, in part, motivated the present investigation.

Overview of the Thomas and Turner (1991) Study

The subjects of this study ranged in age from 6.5 years to college age; they totaled 387 in all. However, at most elementary ages, there were only 10 children of each sex. The data collection procedures are described in the original source (Thomas & Jamison, 1975). The basic data consisted of predictions that subjects made on eight water-level task items, in which the

[2] Formally: If *no* water-level understanding, then *no* spatial coordinate system. An equivalent statement: If a spatial system, then water level understanding.

vessels were placed at clock orientations of 10, 11, 1, 2, 4, 5, 7, and 8 o'clock. Using what have become standard conventions (e.g., Kalichman, 1988), each subject received an integer-valued performance score (ranging from 0 to 8) based on the accuracy of each of the individual's eight responses. For purposes of analysis, subjects were stratified by age and sex; each subgroup was analyzed separately.

The number of correct responses made by each subject was the dependent variable of interest. Although this procedure is common, what is new about our approach, however, is the assumption that the responses were binomial in distribution, with a performance success probability θ for each of the m task items. At any given age, and for a given sex, subjects were regarded as having "come from" either a binomial distribution with low performance success probability, θ_1, or a binomial distribution with a high probability of success, θ_2. Such a model is called a "two-component binomial mixture distribution." Two binomials are needed because there are very large differences in success probability; they are much larger than could be accommodated by one binomial distribution.

While θ_r ($r = 1, 2$) reflects the individual item success rates, another probability parameter, π_r ($r = 1, 2$), reflects the proportions of individuals who "come from" each binomial distribution. Thus, there is a proportion, π_1, of low-probability responders with a θ_1 success rate and a proportion, $\pi_2 = 1 - \pi_1$, of high-probability responders with a θ_2 success rate, with $\theta_1 < \theta_2$. These two success rate groups are the latent groups or strata. For much of what follows in this *Monograph*, these parameters (or their estimates) carry most of the ideas that are needed. At each age, and for each sex at each age, there are thus three independent parameters of interest (remembering that $\pi_2 = 1 - \pi_1$). It is the magnitudes of the differences in these parameter values, both within groups and between groups, or the course of change in the parameter values over age, that capture the developmental process. Specifically, the main developmental issues that we address concern growth of understanding as indexed by parameters: (1) the patterns of change over age in the θ_r parameters for each sex and (2) the changes in proportions of subjects in the two latent classes, indexed by changes in the π_r parameters over age and for each sex.

In Thomas and Turner (1991), the graphs of the θ_r estimates over age were basically negatively accelerated growth functions that showed some change in early childhood but that became relatively age invariant by ages 9–11. The difference between the estimates θ_1 and θ_2 within each sex were substantial, usually about .6. In general, there appeared to be no important between-sex differences in θ_r estimates at any given age. Sex differences were in evidence at all ages. These differences were reflected in the between-sex π_r proportions, with larger proportions of boys in the better-performing (θ_2) groups, at all ages.

There were increasing proportions of subjects entering the better-performing (θ_2) group over age within each sex until about 13 years or so, with little increase in the proportion of good performers thereafter. This age roughly coincides with the upper age limit of 12 years suggested by Piaget (Piaget & Inhelder, 1967, p. 408), but it is later than the 9 years by which, according to Piaget's theory, most children should have acquired an understanding of horizontality.

In summary, the main findings of Thomas and Turner (1991) are as follows. First, at almost all ages, and for both sexes, there were in evidence two distinct groups of performers. Second, developmental differences seemed largely indexed by changes in the relative proportions of good performers. Third, sex differences were in evidence at almost all ages. These differences reflect the differing proportions of good and poor performers, with larger proportions of good performers seen at all ages in the male group. At any given age, the item success rates within each class or stratum were similar for both sexes.

Considerations in Designing the Present Study

Several goals motivated the present efforts. One of these was to extend the model to another task where it might reasonably be expected to hold as well as to a third task where it would *not* be expected to hold. Of course, we also wished to replicate the model's applicability to the water-level data again.

With regard to replication, one important area of concern focused on the nature of growth as indexed by the model parameter changes over age. Replicating the course of cognitive growth charted by this index would permit ruling out certain broad classes of models concerning how growth might be expected to progress. In particular, the earlier effort suggested that growth was not a smooth and gradual progression but instead similar to a discrete state-like process resembling descriptions provided by Brainerd (1979) for conservation tasks.

The main purpose of including two additional tasks was to achieve an understanding of how these tasks covary with each other and with development. Note, however, that our notion of how best to investigate covariation differs considerably from conventional correlational or regression procedures: when possible, we empirically construct the joint space and model it directly. To do this, however, requires a larger sample of subjects than has been used in previous studies (e.g., Thomas & Turner, 1991); creating such a sample was a major goal of the present effort.

Another major goal was to explore features of the model so as to address possible strategies of task performance. An important feature of mixture models in this regard is the possibility of using the model as an optimally efficient algorithm to partition (cluster) subjects into disjoint subgroups or strata. Once partitioning has been achieved, differences in behavioral strategies can be investigated within the different groups; of particular interest here were the performance strategies of those relatively mature but poorly performing individuals.

III. A BRIEF METHODOLOGICAL PRIMER

THE PROBLEM OF DATA REDUCTION AND GROUP COMPARISONS

In any area of empirical research, questions always arise when deciding what to observe, how to measure or code the responses, and which type of analysis to use; these issues become especially interesting in dealing with the water-level and other related tasks. Here, we discuss problems that exist with conventional approaches to the analysis of water-level type data because these problems motivate the modeling approach that we have selected. (Another perspective is to view what follows as an application of the *AMI* process shown in Fig. 1 above.)

Response Variable Definitions and Data Transformations

In the conventional assessment procedure, each subject is asked to draw a line on a picture of a tilted vessel or adjust a line on a psychophysical apparatus so that it corresponds to the respondent's belief as to the orientation of the water surface. The line's angular deviation is usually measured in degrees from the horizontal, which is defined as zero. There are typically several stimuli or vessel angles to which the subject must provide a response, and these responses must be coded or scored in some way. Formally, we can view this process as follows.

Regard the m responses of subject i to the m stimuli as a response vector $\mathbf{X}_i$. That is, let $\mathbf{X}_i = X_{i1}, X_{i2}, \ldots, X_{im}$ ($j = 1, \ldots, m$) be a vector of m responses for respondent i; $\mathbf{X}_i$ could be, for example, m water-level item responses, and each value of $X_{ij} = x_{ij}$ would be the observed response.[3] All

---

[3] The notation is conventional. Uppercase Roman letters denote random variables, lowercase the values they take on. Parameters are given as Greek letters. Densities and discrete distribution mass functions are denoted for random variable X as $f(x)$. Note that a function's argument distinguishes between different functions. For example, $f(x)$, $f(y)$, and $f(x|y)$ can all be different functions. An estimate of θ is denoted as $\hat{\theta}$; viewed as a

investigators use some rule to decide how best to amalgamate these responses for further analysis; this process may be more formally viewed as the problem of defining a transformation function $g(\mathbf{X}_i)$. In most research, each individual contributes several responses, each to a different item, and the usual goal is to reduce this vector of responses to a scalar (i.e., single number) that is then used in some analysis. Thus, the vector $\mathbf{X}_i$ is transformed to a scalar, Y_i. Most studies have utilized one of two transformations, which are then followed by a data analytic methodology. As noted earlier, the methodology implies a model of performance. For purposes of comparison and contrast, we consider three transformations, denoted g_1, g_2, and g_3; they all have familiar verbal descriptions. Each has been used in published analyses. It is not uncommon to find two different transformations used in the same study, often followed with quite different analytic methodologies; the main point of what follows is to indicate that some commonly used transformation procedures can lead to analyses and results that may be very misleading.

To begin, define each transformation: g_1 is the ordinary mean of each subject's responses; g_2 is the within-subject mean of absolute deviations; and g_3 is the number of correct responses for each subject. Thus,

$$g_1: \quad Y_i = g_1(\mathbf{X}_i) = (1/m) \sum_{j=1}^{m} X_{ij}, \tag{1}$$

$$g_2: \quad Y_i = g_2(\mathbf{X}_i) = (1/m) \sum_{j=1}^{m} |X_{ij}|, \tag{2}$$

$$g_3: \quad Y_i = g_3(\mathbf{X}_i) = \sum_{j=1}^{m} I(X_{ij}), \tag{3}$$

where $I(X_{ij}) = 1$ if $|X_{ij} - r_j| \leq c$ and 0 if $|X_{ij} - r_j| > c$. When $r_j = 0$, g_3 is simply the familiar scoring rule, "If the response is within $\pm c°$, it is correct, so count the number correct of the m responses for subject i." Here, c denotes angular tolerance in degrees for successful responses. In the past, r_j has always been zero, but it can assume different values depending on the goal of the analysis. It will be altered in certain of the analyses reported below and thus is introduced here.

Function g_3 constructs a random variable associated with being correct or incorrect. The outcome probability depends on the distribution associated with each response and, of course, the value of c. Suppose that the probability distribution of a response X is $h(x)$, where X takes on both posi-

---

random variable, one might be inclined to write $\hat{\Theta}$, but this distinction was not preserved here.

tive and negative values. Or, if the absolute value of the response is considered, then regard $|X| = W$ as having the distribution $f(w)$. The probability of a success (i.e., $I = 1$) is then simply the probability that the response falls in the interval from $-c$ to $+c$, in the case of signed responses, or from 0 to $+c$, in the case of unsigned responses. That is (when $r_j = 0$),

$$P(I = 1) = \int_{-c}^{+c} h(x)dx = \int_{0}^{+c} f(w)dw, \qquad (4)$$

and $P(I = 0) = 1 - P(I = 1)$. Usually, c is set to $5°$ or so (Kalichman, 1988) and is constant within a study.

Once g has been specified, the problem is to decide on a model for the resulting scalars Y_i, $i = 1, \ldots, n$, so that data analysis can proceed. The results of transformations g_1 and g_2 are regarded as continuous random variables, so Y_i is also regarded as continuous; thus, the conventional candidates for data analysis are analysis of variance or t test procedures, under normal theory assumptions on the Y_i. Transformation g_3 results in integer data of summed frequencies; two methodological approaches have been used for g_3 transformed data. One of these views the integer data as (approximately) normal and proceeds with conventional analyses; the other considers the Y_i as observed frequencies and proceeds with count frequency analyses such as contingency tables and the like.

Because interest in comparing two groups is typically the purpose of constructing statistical tests, we next consider the implications of using each of these three transformations within an additive model framework.

Conventional Comparisons in Additive (Shift) Model Designs

To remind the reader of the conventional two-group methodology, recall that two different sets of assumptions govern such procedures: namely, assumptions concerning the distribution of random variables that are required for evaluating test statistics and structural model assumptions, that is, that, if two groups differ, they do so only by an additive constant.

Let each Y_i random variable be regarded as having the same distribution as either Y^C or Y^E, two random variables that denote two groups for comparison: E and C might be experimental and control groups, or two different age samples, or a between-sex comparison. Let $\mathscr{E}(Y^E) = \Delta + \mathscr{E}(Y^C)$, where $\mathscr{E}$ denotes expectation, and Δ is a fixed unknown constant. Under t test or analysis of variance assumptions, it is assumed that $\mathscr{V}(Y^E) = \mathscr{V}(Y^C)$, where $\mathscr{V}$ denotes variance, and, of course, Y^C and Y^E are assumed normal in distribution. The null hypothesis tested in the t test, for example, is that the additive shift constant $\Delta = 0$. That is, the *only* group difference is an additive constant difference. Thus, in the additive or shift model, additivity has a precise meaning: the *distribution* of Y^E is the same as the *distribution* of $Y^C + \Delta$. Besides the t test, other shift models include the Wilcoxon, the Mann-Whitney, and, by extension, the analysis of variance.

Transformation g_1

The problem with using g_1 (i.e., the mean of the signed responses) is that different groups can have very different response strategies but similar mean vectors of responses. Thus, there is an inherent indeterminacy with such data.[4]

Transformation g_2

There has been general recognition that using the signed scores as in g_1 and then following with some conventional normal shift model procedure is not appropriate, although such procedures have been used (Walker & Krasnoff, 1978). However, taking absolute values of the error responses and then proceeding with conventional procedures is very common (Abravanel & Gingold, 1977, 1982; Barna & O'Connell, 1967; McAfee & Proffitt, 1991; Morris, 1971; Myer & Hensley, 1984; Wittig & Allen, 1984). Unfortunately, there are serious problems with this strategy because all the normal distributional theory and additive shift theory structure needed for conventional inference collapses. In fact, taking absolute values of random variables (or observations) almost always results in seriously nonnormal data.[5]

[4] Suppose that $m = 2$ and that the two water-level items are rectangular bottles positioned at the 11 and 1 o'clock positions (tilted 30° left and 30° right). Consider four strategies: (a) reproduce a line randomly; (b) put the line parallel to the vessel's bottom (or top); (c) put the line parallel to the vessel's side; (d) always put the line horizontal. Letting X_{i1} and X_{i2} denote the random variables associated with the responses to the left-oriented and right-oriented vessels, respectively, under not implausible assumptions, $Y_i = (X_{1i} + X_{2i})/2$ has expectation zero, i.e., $\mathscr{E}(Y_i) = 0$, for each strategy. Thus, for the first random response strategy, assume that the X_{1i} and X_{2i} have mean zero (in degrees from horizontal). Models for the other three cases are similar: in each case, assume a response distribution with mean zero to which is added the "correct" response magnitude under the strategy. For example, for the third strategy, for a vessel at 1 o'clock, the model would be $X_{2i} = 30 + E$, and, for one at 11 o'clock, $X_{1i} = -30 + E$. E denotes a mean zero random variable. Again, $\mathscr{E}(Y_i) = 0$. Thus, two very different performance groups can have the same expected outcome; consequently, t test procedures are not useful. Shift models are not appropriate models in such cases.

[5] Let X be a normal random variable with mean μ and variance σ^2. $|X|$ is the absolute value of X, called a "folded normal variable" (the negative part is folded into the positive part), and is not normal. However, the larger the mean of X, the more the distributions of X and of $|X|$ are similar. If $\mu/\sigma > 2$ or so, X and $|X|$ are similar in distribution. If the mean of X is close to zero, then the distribution of $|X|$ is far from normal and is roughly triangular in shape. Whether normal theory–based analyses on $|X|$ will lead to sensible results depends therefore in part on the size of the probability mass of X below zero that is folded.

The fact that absolute values are taken *bounds* the distribution of possible scores and causes additivity to fail.

To illustrate empirically, and in what we hope is an intuitive way, how normality fails, consider some data from the present study. These data are water-level responses of children aged 11–16 to each of eight different vessel settings. Their signed error scores, measured in degrees of error about zero (i.e., the horizontal), were recorded. First, we consider the histogram of data defined by g_1, the mean of signed error responses; this histogram is shown in Table 1 and is the histogram of values of $Y_i = \Sigma_{j=1}^{8} X_{ij}/8$, for $i = 1, \ldots, 405 = n$, the sample size. Under the assumption of the approximate normality of the X_{ij}, each Y_i is normal; if it is assumed that the X_{ij} have about the same distribution, then the histogram in Table 1 should appear about normal. In fact, it is at least roughly symmetrical.

Now consider the same data with Y_i defined by g_2 (i.e., $Y_i = \Sigma_{j=1}^{8} |X_{ij}|/8$, the average of the absolute error responses), displayed in Table 2. It is obvious that nothing approaching normality appears here. Furthermore, there exists no simple transformation, such as a square root or logarithmic, that helps very much in restoring normality. From a distributional perspective, the use of any t test, analysis of variance application, or similar procedures such as nonparametric tests of the Wilcoxon variety that require the assumption of symmetry of the parent distribution appears grossly inappropriate.

A second problem with g_2 is that the distribution of any test statistic is

TABLE 1

HISTOGRAM OF OBSERVED FREQUENCIES FOR 11–16-YEAR-OLD
SUBJECTS, TRANSFORMATION g_1, WATER-LEVEL TASK
($n = 405$), STUDY 1

```
−32 2
−28 0
−24 1
−20*7
−16*5
−12**10
 −8****19
 −4***************74
  0*************************************195
  4***********55
  8***14
 12*7
 16*8
 20*5
 24*3
 28 0
 32 1
```

NOTE.— − 12**10 denotes 10 observations with value − 12.

TABLE 2

Histogram of Observed Frequencies for 11–16-Year-Old
Subjects, Transformation g_2, Water-Level Task
($n = 405$), Study 1

```
 2********************************124
 6******************66
10***********42
14**************57
18*********31
22****18
26**9
30**8
34***10
38***10
42*5
46***13
50*4
54 2
58*5
62 1
```

Note.—46***13 denotes 13 observations with value 46.

unknown because the distribution of Y_i under g_2 is unknown. Consequently, test statistics cannot be sensibly referenced to any table of significant values. The only hope for statistical hypothesis-testing theory is to resort to large sample theory, essentially central limit theory.

A third problem is that there is no sensible effects model. That is, how is the performance of one group (e.g., boys) related to that of another group (e.g., girls)? In the t test situation, the distribution of one population is the distribution of the other population plus an additive constant. But what is the statistical model structure in the case of absolute values? It is unclear what hypothesis is being evaluated when t tests are applied to such data, even if the distribution of Y_i based on g_2 were known.[6]

In sum, it is difficult to know how to evaluate the results of studies that have used absolute values because distributional (normality) and structural (additivity) assumptions fail.

[6] Suppose that X is normal, with mean μ and variance σ^2; then

$$\mathscr{E}|X| = \mu_f = \sigma(2/\pi)^{1/2} \exp[-(\mu^2/2\sigma^2)] - \mu[1 - 2\Phi(\mu/\sigma)],$$

where Φ is the standard normal lower-tail distribution function. μ_f shows little resemblance to μ and involves the mean, variance, and tail area of the distribution of X. The variance of $|X|$ is $\sigma_f^2 = \mu^2 + \sigma^2 - \mu_f^2$, which is not simply related to σ^2. Note that these analytic results refer to *one* X, not the average Y_i under g_2. Considering differences between two group means, each based on the g_2 transformed data, does not help. Let Y^E and Y^C be two random variables that are means, each based on g_2 transformed data. Then each is distributed on zero to infinity, i.e., $[0, \infty)$. Suppose that $\mathscr{E}(Y^E) = \Delta + \mathscr{E}(Y^C)$. $Y^C + \Delta$ is distributed on $[\Delta, \infty)$ and thus cannot have the distribution of Y^E.

Transformation g_3:
Normal Additive Effects Analysis

Under g_3 ("the number correct" transformation), continuous data are converted to frequencies or counts. This strategy is perhaps the most commonly used transformation strategy; Kalichman (1988) lists 12 studies of adult samples that have used it. After employing g_3, two general approaches have been used. One is to apply conventional normal theory procedures on the counts, and the other is to proceed with count-based analyses, most typically χ^2 analyses. Some studies report both kinds of analyses. The normal theory–based analysis is considered first.

To proceed with analyses such as represented by the t test requires two things: first, that the data be at least roughly normal in distribution and, second, that the populations being compared be additively related.

Unfortunately, neither assumption holds. Additivity fails because, whenever two different distributions (with different means, say) have outcomes distributed on the same values, they cannot be additively related.[7] That is, the distribution of one random variable plus a nonzero constant cannot have the distribution of the other random variable. This result is an elementary fact, but, because the assumption of additivity is so often violated, it is useful to summarize it in the following theorem:

[7] Suppose that U and V are normal random variables with unit variances; let U have mean zero and V mean one. The distributions of U and V are additively related. That is, the distribution of V is the same as the distribution of $U + 1$. If there were independent observations on U and independent observations on V, the data would be perfectly suited for analysis with the two-sample t test. Consider the count data transform g_3 for U and V with c, the critical value that defines success or failure on the task, set at 1. Let the new random variables be denoted I_u and I_v; each can take on two values, 0 or 1. With $c = 1$, $-c = -1$,

$$P(I_u = 1) = P(-1 < U < 1) = .68,$$

$$P(I_v = 1) = P(-1 < V < 1) = P(-2 < V - 1 < 0) = .48.$$

I_u and I_v have different means: I_u has mean $.68 = (1 \times .68) + (0 \times .32)$, and I_v has mean .48. Define $\delta = \mathcal{E}(I_u) - \mathcal{E}(I_v)$, so, for this example, $\delta = .2$. Unlike U and V, I_u and I_v are not additively related to each other. That is, there exists no additive constant δ ($\neq 0$) such that the distribution of $I_u + \delta$ has the distribution of I_v: both I_u and I_v are distributed on 0 and 1, while $I_u + \delta$ would be distributed on $0 + \delta = .2$ and $1 + \delta = 1.2$.

Similarly, consider two subjects, one with six observations on I_u and another with six observations on I_v, and, as is the common convention, the 0 or 1 outcomes are summed over the six observations for each subject. This, of course, is the number correct transformation g_3. One subject would now have observations on Y_{iu}, the other on Y_{iv}. Both are distributed on the integers $0, \ldots, 6$. But there does *not* exist a constant δ such that $Y_{iu} + \delta$ has the distribution of Y_{iv} because, of course, $Y_{iu} + \delta$ ($\delta \neq 0$) would have a distribution on $0 + \delta, 1 + \delta, \ldots, 6 + \delta$, and this distribution is, of course, not a distribution on the outcomes $0, 1, 2, \ldots, 6$.

THEOREM 1.—Let G and P be two nonidentically distributed random variables, with outcomes distributed on the same discrete values. There exists no constant δ such that the distribution of $G + \delta$ has the same distribution as P. That is, G and P cannot be additively related.

Proof.—The proof is trivial but illuminating. $G + \delta$ means that δ is added to each outcome of $G = g$. It suffices to observe that, if both G and P have outcomes distributed on the same values, then, if a constant $\delta > 0$ is added to, for example, the largest outcome of G (or if $\delta < 0$ is added to the smallest outcome), the distributions G and $G + \delta$ can no longer be distributed on the same outcomes. Consequently, $G + \delta$ and P are also not distributed on the same outcomes. If $G + \delta$ and P are distributed on different outcomes, they obviously cannot have the same distribution.

There are two important points to be made here. First, as was said before, discrete random variables with different distributions on the same outcomes are not additively related.[8] Second, transformations often destroy certain familiar and desirable properties needed for data analysis and conceptual interpretations.

It might be argued that it is common practice to consider frequencies or counts as continuous data; classroom tests, IQ scores, and the like are usually so considered. Fair enough—but there are two problems with such a position.

First, the problem with water-level data is that there are typically very few items, so that scores are distributed over a very narrow range of integers. For example, the outcomes for Robert and Chaperon (1989) were distributed on $0, \ldots, 3$ or $0, \ldots, 4$. Golbeck (1986), Liben (1991a), and Liben and Golbeck (1984) have used $0, \ldots, 6$, while Witters-Churchill, Kelley, and Witters (1983) have used $0, \ldots, 4$ or $0, \ldots, 8$. Just how many integer-value outcomes are needed before a discrete distribution behaves in a sufficiently "continuous-like" manner is a matter of judgment, and it would probably need to be resolved with simulation studies. However, note that, for the normal distribution to approximate the binomial distribution (with binomial parameters m and $p = 1/2$), m needs to be about 10 or so for reasonable accuracy to be achieved.

The continuity-discontinuity problem and the additive constant prob-

---

[8] A similar theorem can be given for continuous random variables that are bounded from above or below (for an example, see n. 6 above). In general, additivity works for normal distributions (with common variance) because they are unbounded distributions. The point is not a minor technicality. For example, in the rod-frame task, it has been standard practice to consider absolute values of setting errors and to treat such errors in conventional data analytic models. Doing so can only obscure our understanding of the phenomena.

TABLE 3

Histogram of Water-Level Task Performance
of Eighth-Grade Children

Boys		Girls
**********	8	****
*****	7	*
*****	6	****
*****	5	***
*****	4	****
***	3	*****
********	2	**************
***	1	*********
***	0	*
$n = 48$		$n = 45$

Source.—Signorella and Jamison (1978).
Note.—Each * denotes 1 individual.

lems are not the only concerns. A further concern is whether, apart from continuity considerations, the distribution of the Y_i is roughly normal in shape. We doubt that it ever is, and we will provide abundant evidence in subsequent chapters to support this assertion. In fact, good evidence for it is already available in the literature. Liben (1991a) and Liben and Golbeck (1984) have been forthright about publishing their frequency histograms of outcomes ranging from 0 to 6. For virtually all their conditions, the *modal* frequency correct in their studies was six, and by a wide margin! This results in a large spike at the end of the empirical frequency histogram, leaving it hardly symmetrical and very far from normal.

Alternatively, consider some water-level data on which the g_3 (number correct) transformation was applied. Table 3 shows the number of correct responses on eight water-level items for eighth-grade children. The data are from Signorella and Jamison (1978).

These histograms appear far from normal in distribution. Does it make sense to apply normal theory–based procedures to such data? We think not. Furthermore, does it make sense to consider the parent distribution of the boys' scores as additively different from the parent distribution of the girls' scores? We think that it does not, and, of course, there exists no additive constant that allows the parent distributions to be additively related, as the simple theorem given above asserts.

In conclusion, to view the water-level or similar data obtained under count data transformation g_3 as satisfying the normality and additivity of effects assumptions that are required for t tests or analysis of variance requires making importantly false assumptions. In the language of Figure 1 above, there is a glaring mismatch between data and model; nonetheless, normality-based additive methods have been commonly employed in pub-

ional convention that we adopt is that $0 < \theta_1 < \theta_2 < \ldots < \theta_k < 1$.
restrictions on the π_r weights are that $0 \leqq \pi_r \leqq 1$ and that $1 = \Sigma \pi_r$.
e k component binomial mixture model, there are $2k - 1$ free parame-
k values of θ, and $k - 1$ free values of π, the last π being obtained by
raction.

d) The idea of latent classes, in which a group or population is thought
ntain subgroups or subpopulations, is familiar in many areas of psy-
ogy (e.g., Coombs, 1964; Lazersfeld & Henry, 1968). Suitable data are
subjected to different kinds of clustering routines. As already noted,
ures and the solution of the mixture problem—generally regarded as
ure decomposition whereby the observations are separated into their
tituent components—can be viewed as similar to the clustering prob-
In fact, some authors (McLachlan & Basford, 1988) think that the
ering problem should be viewed from the perspective of mixture the-
An important reason for this perspective is that, when the clustering
lem is so viewed, there is a clear probability model as the foundational
ture and statistical analysis can consequently follow in a natural way.
y clustering approaches do not share this advantage.

A major way in which individual differences are represented in the
ure model is by considering different "subgroups," "latent classes,"
ters," or "subpopulations"; all these terms mean the same thing here,
we will use them interchangeably. Basically, the strategy is to cluster
ther subjects with similar responses; clustering can be achieved with
ure decomposition, a statistical procedure. A nice feature of binomial
ures is that the parameters of the model have very natural intuitive
pretations. Once individuals with similar responses are clustered to-
er, responses of those within the same cluster can be explored to deter-
e how their responses or strategies differ from those of individuals in
r clusters. Furthermore, by examining how these clusters and the associ-
model parameters vary over age and between sex, it is possible to
lop a much clearer understanding of the pattern of growth and change.

idual Differences and the Response Model

The responses of each individual to the van and to the water-level task
s were each modeled as a binomial distribution using transformation
he "number correct" transformation) to define a response variable Y_i
each subject. Thus, each individual's response to each stimulus item is
rded as independent with the same success probability, θ. This means
the indicator random variables I of Equation (3) have probability $\theta =$
$= 1$). To allow for individual differences in performance, the model
expanded to a mixture of binomials in which the responses of individu-

lished studies (e.g., Barsky & Lachman, 1986; Golbeck, 1986; Kelly, Kelly,
& Johnson, 1988; Liben, 1991a; Liben & Golbeck, 1980; Meehan &
Overton, 1986; Randall, 1980).

Transformation g_3: Count Data Analyses

An approach that regards Y_i under g_3 as a frequency and employs
frequency-based models for analysis appears to be the most conceptually
sound procedure, and it has been used by us as well as by many others (e.g.,
Kalichman, 1989; Kelly & Kelly, 1977; McAfee & Proffitt, 1991; Myer &
Hensley, 1984; Thomas & Jamison, 1975). The main but critically important
difference that nevertheless distinguishes our approach from that of all
other researchers is that we provide an explicit probability model for the
data. Through the path AMI (Fig. 1), this model implies in a natural way
the form of the data analysis and the questions that are of particular interest
to consider.

The use of frequency counts, and modeling the frequencies by an explicit probability distribution, is motivated at this juncture largely by the
apparent *failure* of other data analytic frameworks to reflect reasonable behavioral models. It will also be argued later (in Chap. X, and from a more
general perspective) that our approach can provide considerable power as
a framework for the study of large classes of problems.

All is not sweetness and light, however, and there are problems with
this approach as well. One issue concerns the specifications of c in Equations
(3) and (4), which determines the basic scoring assignment; we discuss this
issue below and describe how we approached it in the present study. Later,
in our enriched theory, it will be argued that the value of c is largely
irrelevant.

Liben (1991b) has suggested that measuring outcomes in degrees of
error represents measurement on a ratio scale and that information is lost
by defining a "number correct" random variable. One might argue that
there is some difference in precision between these two approaches, but it
is erroneous to argue that measurement in degrees (or some other unit)
provides either a ratio or an interval scale of measurement. In fact, determining whether one is measuring with a ratio, an interval, or an ordinal
scale is not simply a problem of intuitively reflecting on the nature of the
recorded units and deciding the matter. It is generally extremely difficult
to argue rigorously that one measures psychological phenomena on anything but an ordinal scale, a message that results from many years of research in representational measurement theory. To argue convincingly that
interval scale measurement is achieved requires that certain conditions be

satisfied, and these conditions are rarely, if ever, satisfied in most psycholog-ical data (cf., e.g., Krantz, 1972; Roberts, 1979; Thomas, 1985).

In summary, we have argued that conventional continuous-variate data analytic models should be viewed as theories of task performance. When so viewed, simple consequences of the models are found to be strikingly at odds with important features of the data that they are intended to model. Frequency-based analysis, based on the "number correct" transformation g_3, appears to be the best alternative for eschewing critical problems.

METHOD AND THEORY

Because of the close connection between our theory and method, and because many of the data analytic techniques that we use are probably not familiar to many readers, most of the essential features of the theory and methodology that we employ in the following chapters are summarized here in a sequence of subsections. We first introduce the terminology and basic concepts of mixture distributions that are extensively used in the analysis and theory that we develop. We then consider the related issues of estima-tion, model selection, and measures of model fit as well as some other proce-dures that we utilize subsequently. In each instance, we try to provide a loose verbal description of the concept or procedure; some less technically inclined readers may wish to focus on these descriptions.

A Binomial Mixture Distribution

Consider the binomial distribution. Let it be denoted by $b(y; \theta, m)$, where

$$b(y; \theta, m) = \binom{m}{y} \theta^y (1 - \theta)^{m-y}, \quad 0 < \theta < 1, \tag{5}$$

with success probability θ and number of outcomes m. Consider a random sample of $n_1 = 10$ observations from $b(y; .4, 8)$. One realization is

$$3, \ 2, \ 6, \ 3, \ 3, \ 2, \ 2, \ 2, \ 5, \ 4.$$

Consider another random sample of $n_2 = 10$ from $b(y; .9, 8)$. The sequence

$$8, \ 7, \ 7, \ 6, \ 8, \ 8, \ 8, \ 7, \ 8, \ 8,$$

is a realization from this distribution. Now consider the combined sample of $n_1 + n_2 = 20 = n$ observations. This sequence

$$3, \ 2, \ 6, \ 3, \ 3, \ 2, \ 2, \ 2, \ 5, \ 4, \ 8, \ 7, \ 7, \ 6, \ 8, \ 8, \ 8, \ 7, \ 8, \ 8,$$

is a realization of a random sample from a two-componen ture. That is, it is a random sample from

$$f(y) = \pi_1 b(y; \theta_1, m) + \pi_2 b(y; \theta_2, m).$$

In $f(y)$, the two binomial distributions are now termed with their corresponding success parameters $\theta_1 = .4$ and θ_2 $m = 8$. The parameters π_1 and π_2 are usually called "weigl reflect the proportion of observations that have "come from sponding components; thus, $\pi_1 + \pi_2 = 1$. In the present sim because each component distribution contributed the same nt servations, 10 each, both π_1 and π_2 are 1/2.

Should it have been the case that the first (component) contributed 5 observations and the second 10, the total sample be 15, $\pi_1 = 1/3$, $\pi_2 = 1 - \pi_1 = 2/3$. Although in these ex proportion of observations from each component corresponds π_2, in most applications the proportion of observations in each sa each component is a random variable and thus will vary from sample even though the values of π are assumed fixed in the po

In practice, of course, the parameter values of the model mu mated from data because they are unknown. For the artificial d above example, using estimation methods described below, the were $\hat{\theta}_1 = .38$, $\hat{\theta}_2 = .92$, and $\hat{\pi}_1 = .46$, with $.54 = 1 - \hat{\pi}_1 = \hat{\pi}$ estimated values are seen to be very similar to the population val

Comments on Mixture Distributions

a) We use mixture distributions because the theory naturall observations that are unlabeled. Should it be known beforehand observations have arisen from one binomial distribution and another binomial distribution with the observations suitably observations from each distribution can be treated separately.

b) There is no need to restrict attention to two compone notion of mixtures extends naturally to k components. There is to restrict focus to binomial mixtures; normal distributions are most commonly used components of mixture distributions (Hand, 1981; Titterington, Smith, & Makov, 1985). Neither to restrict attention to univariate mixtures; in fact, mixtur binomials will find application below.

c) Note that a binomial mixture model is interesting or all different. For example, if $\theta = \theta_r$ ($r = 1, \ldots, k$), the ord distribution results. By convention, the larger r, the larger t

als with different θ success parameters are modeled by different binomial components. Each component differs from every other component in its θ parameter. Conceivably, there could be as many different values of θ as there are individuals in the sample; however, the data do not support such a speculation.

Within a population, the proportions of individuals with particular success probabilities θ differ; within the mixture framework, these population proportions are modeled by the mixture weights, the π_r. Thus, the number of different subgroups ($r = 1, \ldots, k$), the task success probabilities of each (θ_r), and the population proportions of each subgroup (π_r) are all captured by the mixture model.

An additional level of individual differences is also reflected in the model. This is the difference in outcome scores (i.e., number correct) among individuals within the subpopulation defined by success probability θ. Thus, within-component variability can be regarded as analogous to the use of variability as a measure of individual differences in familiar models, much as in conventional normal theory models.

Consider individual i who provides m responses on a task. From g_3, Y_i is defined. In general, each Y_i has an unknown distribution. However, under the assumptions noted above—namely, equal probability of success for each item and independence of responses—Y_i has a $b(y; \theta, m)$ distribution with mean $m\theta$ and variance $m\theta(1 - \theta)$.[9]

Model Assumptions

The assumptions of constant θ within subjects and of item independence are perhaps strong model assumptions. However, such assumptions have been usefully made before (e.g., Lord, 1969). More important, the assumptions may *seem* strong, but in fact there is little evidence to suggest that such assumptions are inappropriate, and thus they may not be as implausible as first imagined. Furthermore, the tenability of the assumptions underlying the model is not a matter that can be easily resolved by intuitive reflection (Thomas & Turner, 1991).

One clear advantage of a formal model structure is that the assumptions can be clearly set down for scrutiny. In the more casual approaches reported in the literature, it is rare to find assumptions underlying models and meth-

---

[9] Note that the distribution of each individual's X_{ij} in Eq. (3) need not be assumed to be the same for each individual i on each trial j, nor need X_{ij} have the same distribution for different individuals on different trials. A slightly lighter condition is required. What needs to be assumed is that θ remains the same over trials for an individual. Thus, the probability mass in the interval from $-c$ to c in Eq. (4) is assumed to remain constant, should the response distribution of the X_{ij} change over trials.

ods systematically considered, and it is rarer still to see them evaluated in data. For instance, of all the studies cited in the earlier section concerned with the data reduction problem, none reported any systematic attempt to assess the suitability of the model assumptions for the data at hand.

In our final discussion chapter, we consider more carefully the assumptions of our model. We show that the assumptions of our model *are* violated, but we also argue that the violations are not critically important ones and thus that our model violations do not appear to jeopardize the findings that we report. In addition, the numerous examples of model fit indices that are included throughout the *Monograph* provide a kind of running account of the appropriateness and plausibility of our approach.

Statistical Estimation in Binomial Mixtures

The k component mixture of binomials distribution is defined as

$$f(y; \Theta, \Pi, m) = \sum_{r=1}^{k} \pi_r b(y; \theta_r, m), \tag{6}$$

where

$$\Theta = \theta_1, \theta_2, \ldots, \theta_r, \ldots, \theta_k, 0 < \theta_r < \theta_{r+1} < \ldots < \theta_k < 1,$$

$$\Pi = \pi_1, \pi_2, \ldots, \pi_r, \ldots, \pi_k,$$

and $1 = \sum_{r=1}^{k} \pi_r$ with $\pi_r \geq 0$. Θ is a vector of success probability parameters, and Π a vector of component weights interpreted as subpopulation proportions.

The mean of Y is

$$\mu = \sum_{r=1}^{k} m \pi_r \theta_r. \tag{7}$$

The variance Y is

$$\sigma^2 = \sum_{r=1}^{k} \pi_r [m\theta_r(1 - \theta_r) + (m\theta_r)^2] - \mu^2. \tag{8}$$

There are $2k - 1$ parameters to estimate in Equation (6): k values of θ and $k - 1$ values of π. These parameters were estimated in standard ways, using the iterative EM algorithm (Dempster, Laird, & Rubin, 1977). The form of the estimation equations is given by Everitt and Hand (1981). Once initial trial values of the estimates are specified, maximum likelihood estimates of the parameters are usually obtained in a few iterative trials. Problems of estimation in mixtures and concerns about parameter identifiability are all discussed elsewhere (e.g., Everitt & Hand, 1981; Titterington et al., 1985). It is sufficient to note here that none of these problems appears to be of critical concern in any of our applications.

When $k = 1$, the maximum likelihood estimates of Equation (6) are familiar. The estimate of θ is $\hat{\theta} = \bar{y}/m$, $\bar{y} = \Sigma_{i=1}^{n} y_i/n$. $\hat{\theta}$ is a random variable with $\mathscr{E}(\hat{\theta}) = \theta$ and $\text{var}(\hat{\theta}) = [\theta(1 - \theta)]/(mn)$, so an estimate of the variance of $\hat{\theta}$ is

$$\hat{v}\text{ar}(\hat{\theta}) = [\hat{\theta}(1 - \hat{\theta})]/(mn). \tag{9}$$

Model Selection

In Equation (6), the number of components k must be estimated. This problem is usually regarded as a model selection problem rather than an estimation problem. In this sense, a model with $k = 3$ components is regarded as a different model than one with $k = 4$ components.

The issue of model selection remains an active research topic, and there are as yet no generally accepted standard methods for deciding which among a sequence of models is the best (McLachlan & Basford, 1988). An overall consideration in matters of both model selection and science generally is the selection of the simplest model possible. All model selection procedures have in fact this same ultimate goal. A procedure that has theoretical appeal and may be the most commonly used selection criterion is Akaike's information criterion (AIC) (Bozdogan, 1987); we use it as one of our model selection criteria. However, AIC is not an intuitive measure, and, although it is useful in helping decide which among a family of models is the best, it is not useful in evaluating just how good or how poor the selected model might be. Consequently, we additionally report two other measures, the ordinary Pearson χ^2 goodness-of-fit statistic and the proportion of variance accounted for (VAF). Each of these three criteria is briefly considered next.

AIC.—AIC is a $-2 \log L$, or minus two log-likelihood-based, criterion. As k increases, model complexity increases, and so does the number of model parameters to estimate. As model complexity increases, $-2 \log L$ decreases, signaling a better fit of data to the model. It is easier to fit a more complicated model than a simple one because there are more parameters available for "fiddling."

The idea behind AIC is that it adds a "penalty factor" to $-2 \log L$, for choosing a more complicated model. This penalty is twice the number of free parameters estimated from the data. Consequently,

$$\text{AIC}(k) = -2 \log L(k) + 2(2k - 1). \tag{10}$$

The AIC model selection criterion is to select the model with k components for which $\text{AIC}(k)$ is smallest.

Under a wide variety of circumstances, $-2 \log L$ has, in large samples, approximately a χ^2 distribution with suitably chosen degrees of freedom (Wilks, 1938). Unfortunately, the conditions necessary for this theorem to hold fail in the mixture settings (Everitt & Hand, 1981), so readers who desire a statistical test to decide between two values of AIC for different k will be disappointed. Often, however, there is little need for such a test since the difference in $-2 \log L$, or AIC, between alternative models is typically dramatic and pronounced.[10]

χ^2.—χ^2 procedures measure the departure of the expected values, computed under the model of interest, from the observed values. In most applications presented here, these values serve simply as a rough index of fit: the smaller, the better. The values cannot usually be referenced to a table so as to provide p values because in many cases there will be one or more cells with small (sometimes very small) expected values that can cause the value of χ^2 to explode. Normally, expected cell frequencies need to be about five or more for χ^2 tests to be approximated meaningfully by the χ^2 distribution. Consequently, in many cases, the test statistic with its associated degrees of freedom but without a p value will be reported.[11]

Variance accounted for (VAF).—This measure is the ratio of the variance under each model to the total variance. The ordinary sample variance, S^2, measures the variance of the data and estimates the total population variance. Variance can also be computed under different fitted models. To estimate VAF under the binomial, form the ratio $[m\hat{\theta}(1 - \hat{\theta})]/S^2$, that is, the ratio of the estimated variance under the binomial to the sample variance. Correspondingly, under the mixture model, construct the ratio $\hat{\sigma}^2/S^2$, where $\hat{\sigma}^2$ is the variance of the mixture given in Equation (8) but where the parameter estimates replace the parameter values. These ratios, incidentally, can exceed one owing to sampling variation; when they do, they are truncated at one, or 100%.

---

[10] Marsh, Balla, and McDonald (1988) have expressed concern that AIC as well as many other fit indices are sensitive to sample size. This fact is not surprising because sample size sensitivity is almost a defining feature of any statistic. Our concern here is not to try to resolve the controversy but to observe that AIC remains a widely used statistic in the mixture setting partly because it has attractive properties (Bozdogan, 1987). We use two other indices as well, however, and, in most cases, we also present data histograms. Whatever index the reader might prefer, we think that the main issue concerns the replicability of the data structure from sample to sample, and that evidence, we think, will be compelling.

[11] It may be useful to note as a rough benchmark that, if the assumptions are satisfied for Pearson's χ^2 test to be asymptotically χ^2 in distribution, the degrees of freedom are determined by the number of cells minus one, minus the number of parameters estimated from the data.

What Happens When the Model Does Not Fit?

We fit many different kinds of models in the following chapters. In many cases, the models we propose fit the data quite well, and thus the theory that generated the model gains additional credibility. Sometimes, however, the models fit poorly. What does one do? Where we can, we provide alternative, more complex models, and these typically fit better. Sometimes we still prefer the simpler model, usually because the more complicated one does not appear to provide sufficient conceptual advantage, as, for example, when the gain in VAF is very small. Furthermore, it is our penchant to select simple models even though certain fit indices suggest that a more complicated model might be preferable. In addition, fit indices taken in isolation can be poor guides. They do not, for example, reflect larger conceptual issues such as growth and change, indexed by the number of mixture components (k), the relative size of these components (π_r), or the changes in item success probability (θ_r); nor do they reflect the fit of the models at adjacent ages.

However, when a model fails and no ready alternative seems evident, the ultimate question must be asked: Is the model pointed in the correct direction? We would like to think that the answer is yes.

Isotonic Regression: Estimating Growth Functions

In the analysis of growth data, there is always the problem of providing a sensible growth function over age while faced with fluctuations of estimates at different ages.

It seems preferable to us to report data without pooling at adjacent ages and then smoothing the estimates (unless sample sizes are too small for meaningful estimates to be obtained). Isotonic regression, which perhaps might be more intuitively called "monotonic regression," is an especially attractive procedure, although apparently it is seldom used.

Many growth functions are quite properly regarded as increasing or decreasing over age, but rarely is there theory to guide the choice of a suitable parametric family for fitting a growth function. A linear function is typically the default option, but most growth processes cannot be linear over broad age ranges. Isotonic regression, which is a generalization of linear regression, seems to us a sensible compromise procedure. It is used often here. Like linear regression, isotonic regression is based on a least squares criterion, but, unlike conventional regression, the abscissa values play no role in the construction of the monotonic curve. In the case of monotonic increasing functions, isotonic regression seeks a unique monotonic nondecreasing function. If the data (here, parameter estimates over age) to which the monotonic curve is to be fitted increase with age, then the isotonic regression is a segmented curve connecting the estimates. In cases in which the estimates are not so aligned, the regression often appears as a segmented curve, with segments of typically nonincreasing (flat) slope. (Examples of such will be seen in Figs. 5 and 6 below, which depict regression curves fitted to estimates of θ and π over age.) Although such functions often appear as step functions, there is no more reason to regard them as suggesting that the true (unknown) growth function is a step function than taking a histogram to suggest a discrete step function distribution. They are best viewed as an approximation to the true unknown function, which might be a smooth function or some other function.

The pool-adjacent-violators algorithm (Barlow, Bartholomew, Bremner, & Brunk, 1972) was used here with sample size weights, with the result that the points at the ages for which there are more data influence the solution slightly more.

Posterior Probabilities: Classifying Individuals into Classes (or Components, or Clusters)

One of our goals was to use the mixture model as a tool for partitioning the sample into discrete groups so that features of the different subgroups can be separately examined. Consequently, once a mixture model is accepted as a plausible model, the problem becomes one of deciding which component of the model has given rise to a particular individual's score. In other words, given an individual's score and the existence of two or more subpopulation mixture components, from which component does the individual most probably "come from," and thus to which component does the individual probably belong?

A key idea in viewing clustering from the perspective of mixture distributions (McLachlan & Basford, 1988) is the notion of posterior probability. The posterior probability of a score y coming from the qth component is defined as

$$P(\text{component } q|y) = \frac{\pi_q b(y; \theta_q, m)}{\sum_{r=1}^{k} \pi_r b(y; \theta_r, m)}. \tag{11}$$

Thus, it is the ratio of the weighted ordinate height at the point y in component q over the mixture distribution. From this definition, it is clear that

$$1 = \sum_{r=1}^{k} P(\text{component } r|y).$$

When allocating individuals (or their scores) to a component, we use the following rule: Assign the score to the component for which the posterior probability is largest.

If the parameters of the model are known, that is, if the θ_r and π_r are known, then this classification rule is the Bayes optimal decision rule. This means that it minimizes the number of wrong classifications (Anderson, 1984, p. 224); hence it is very attractive. In practice, the rule of letting parameter estimates replace the parameter values in Equation (11) is the commonly used method of allocation (McLachlan & Basford, 1988). It is optimally efficient in large samples and is used here.

Once maximum likelihood estimates of the model parameters have been obtained, the estimates are inserted in the above expressions, and the posterior probabilities for each $y = 0, 1, \ldots, m$ are determined. In practice, this is very easy to do because the computation of the posterior probability estimate is an explicit step in the EM algorithm.

Empirical Distribution Functions (edf's):
Estimating the Distribution of Responses

Let X be a random variable, with a cumulative distribution function lower tail $G(x)$. For example, if X were a standard normal random variable, and if $x = 1.96$, then $G(x) = P(X < x) = .975$.

In continuously distributed data, where the distribution function G is usually unknown, if there are sufficient data, the data can be used to estimate G in a very natural way. To estimate $G(x_o)$, compute

$$\hat{G}(x_o) = \frac{\text{the number of observed } x \text{ below } x_o}{\text{total sample size}} \tag{12}$$

and subsequently for increasing values of x_o. The graph of the coordinate pairs $(x_o, \hat{G}[x_o])$ provides an edf plot. It is the shape of the corresponding edf graph that can be revealing. If the data are normal, or at least approximately so, then the graph will be a familiar normal ogive; however, since judging curves can be difficult, such plots are generally transformed so that, if the data are normal, the graph appears as a straight line. The edf can provide interesting clues for understanding certain processes; the procedure was employed below in Study 1.

Standard Errors and Statistical Tests

Our main concern is not with traditional hypothesis-testing procedures. Even if it were, most of the statistical quantities that are estimated here have no known distribution. In such cases, if it were desirable to perform hypothesis tests, it would be necessary to resort to large sample methods.

Nevertheless, it is generally useful to have some estimate of the variability of the estimate, that is, a standard error. Whenever we can really do so, we provide such standard errors. For the parameter estimates of the binomial mixture, estimators provided by Blischke (1964) were used. If they so desire, readers can then construct their own tests. In some situations, however, obtaining standard errors is difficult at best, particularly if the estimates have been obtained from iterative procedures.

In theory at least, one can always provide standard errors for any estimated quantity by using resampling procedures such as the bootstrap (e.g., Efron & Tibshirani, 1986). These procedures replace analysis with brute computation. In practice, however, the bootstrap can be time consuming and might take hours or even days for other than very fast computers when the desired solution requires an iterative routine. Even for moderately large data sets, one iterative solution might take several minutes, and the bootstrap typically requires 200 or more such solutions to construct one standard error. Consequently, we use bootstrap procedures very sparingly.

IV. STUDY 1:
PERFORMANCE ON THE WATER-LEVEL TASK
FROM CHILDHOOD THROUGH ADOLESCENCE

GENERAL METHOD

Subjects

The subjects were students at an elementary, a junior high, and two high schools located in and around the city of Muenster, Germany.

Muenster is a prosperous city of about 266,000 inhabitants located in northern Germany in the state of Nordrhein-Westfalen. There is industrial activity located there, but it is not primarily an industrial city. Although Muenster has a large working-class population, it probably contains a larger proportion of professional residents than most other German cities of comparable size, mainly because of the large sprawling university that is located there. No specific socioeconomic status measures were obtained from the subjects; however, an effort was made to sample schools that would represent a fairly broad spectrum of the socioeconomic classes residing in the area.

The subjects' participation required their parents' permission. For those school classes that were targeted as samples, a letter was sent to the parents informing them of the general nature of the project and asking permission for their children to participate; there were few refusals.

Table 4 reports the children's ages, their sex, and the number sampled at each age. Most of the children ranged in age from 8 to 16 years, with almost the same number of boys and girls represented in the total sample of 579 children. Because entire classes were tested on the prearranged testing days, the sample sizes and proportions of boys and girls in each class were random variables over which there could be no control.

TABLE 4

NUMBER OF SUBJECTS IN TOTAL SAMPLE, STUDY 1

Age (Years)	Boys	Girls	Total	Age (Years)	Boys	Girls	Total
6	10	6	16	13	47	42	89
7	9	16	25	14	33	29	62
8	32	26	58	15	28	39	67
9	14	21	35	16	24	19	43
10	21	12	33	17	2	3	5
11	24	39	63				
12	44	39	83	Totals	288	291	579

Procedure

Data were collected from each participant on a single occasion; subjects were tested in groups, in their classrooms. The size of the groups varied; at younger ages, sometimes as few as six children were tested in a session, whereas, at older ages, the class sizes were about 25. All data were obtained from written, subject-supplied responses on a test booklet.

University student research assistants gathered the data. Usually two, and sometimes three, assistants were present in the classroom during data collection. With rare exceptions, data collection was also monitored by one of us (H.T.) as well as by the classroom teacher.

The time needed to complete the data collection varied somewhat depending on the children's age and the setting, but it generally lasted about 30–35 min. There was no time restriction for completing the tasks, and children generally had ample time to finish at their own pace. Most subjects seemed to be interested and motivated to complete the task satisfactorily.

Test Booklet

A standard test booklet was used for all subjects. Each page was of standard European A4 size. Although written instructions for each task were given in the test booklet, the youngest children could not read them; consequently, verbal instructions were provided for all age groups. Subjects recorded their age, their sex, and the name of their school. No personal names were provided so that all information was obtained anonymously.

All booklets were identical, and presentation of the sequence of tasks and items was fixed. There were three main tasks: a water-level task, a van task to assess understanding of verticality, and a third quite different task. This third task, however, proved far too easy for most subjects. Consequently, there was little variation in task performance. The task will not be considered further.

Water-level task.—The water-level task was administered first. There were eight items, each displaying the same vessel at a different angle. The vessel was a rectangularly shaped bottle 6 cm in diameter and 10 cm tall. Each item appeared on a separate page. The vessels were positioned at 1 (30°), 2 (60°), 4 (120°), 5 (150°), 7 (210°), 8 (240°), 10 (300°), and 11 (330°) o'clock. (The numbers in parentheses denote the angles in degrees referenced clockwise, with 12 o'clock defined as zero.)

Figure 2 shows the vessel in the 2 o'clock position. Note that a horizontal reference surface was drawn below each vessel item. The fixed order of item presentation (which was determined randomly) was 11, 4, 2, 7, 10, 5, 1, and 8 o'clock. The 12, 3, 6, and 9 o'clock positions were not given since these vessel angles are typically very easy (cf. Thomas & Jamison, 1975) even for young children.

There were written instructions on the page immediately preceding the first item. Below the instructions appeared a picture of the vessel placed on a horizontal surface and in its normal upright position (12 o'clock). The drawing showed the correctly positioned horizontal line; the liquid was distinguished by shading. The instructions called attention to the glass vessel below, noted that it was half filled with "drink," and indicated that the subject's task was to draw the line formed by the liquid when the vessel was tilted to the angles shown on the subsequent booklet pages. The children drew their lines freehandedly with a pencil.

Van task.—This task paralleled the water-level task in general form and structure, with drawings of a van parked on hills of different inclines replacing vessels rotated to different angles. The design of the van's rectangularly shaped cargo area about matched the water-level vessel in size; it was 6 cm high and 9.5 cm long (see Fig. 3).[12]

The eight van items differed in the incline slopes of the hills and thus in the van's slope. The slopes are defined about the horizontal, which was set to zero. They are positively signed if the incline is "positively sloped" (as in regression) and negatively signed if it is negatively sloped. In degrees, the eight slope angles were −60°, −45°, −30°, −15°, 15°, 30°, 45°, and 60°. The presentation sequence (again, randomly determined) was 15°, −30°, 45°, −60°, 30°, −45°, 60°, and −15°. Each item appeared on a separate page of the booklet.

Preceding the first item was an instruction page containing a picture of the van parked on level ground. Inside it was a plumb line about 5 cm long suspended from the eyebolt in the middle of the van roof, hanging vertically. The instructions called the subjects' attention to this picture and asked them to draw a line representing the hanging line's correct position in each subsequent item. Responses were drawn freehandedly with a pencil.

[12] We thank Silke Mehler for designing and drawing the vans.

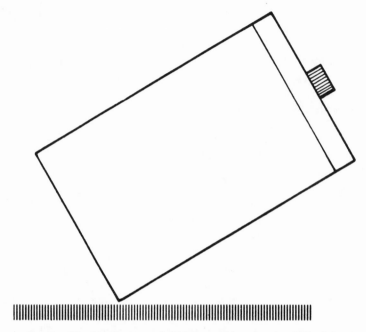

FIG. 2.—Test booklet water-level item positioned at 2 o'clock (60°)

Horizontal line drawing.—On the last page, following the three main tasks (one of which has been ignored), were instructions requesting that the subjects draw a horizontal line. The subjects drew their left-right line starting at a target point positioned on the left-hand side of the page.

SCORING

Water-Level Task

The points of intersection of the subject-drawn water surface line with the periphery of the vessel defined two points. A straight line was drawn through these points, and the angle that it formed with the bottom edge of the booklet page (or the reference surface printed below each vessel) was measured to the nearest degree with a protractor. Lines of 0° were, of course, perfectly correct and parallel to the reference surface; other values were signed according to the slope of the drawn line. Responses that were perfectly vertical (90°) were unsigned but rarely occurred (only two times among more than 4,000 responses).

The same student assistants who had responsibility for data collection served as scorers after suitable training. After being scored, each subject's

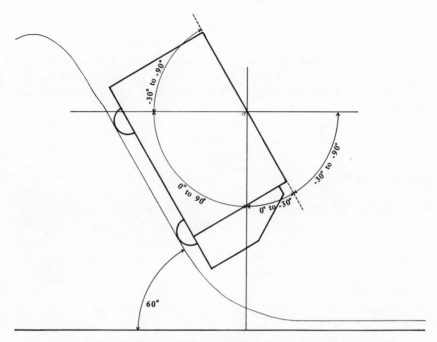

FIG. 3.—Test booklet van item at −60°. For an explanation, see the text

performance was represented by an eight-integer response vector with values generally ranging from −89° through +89°.

Van Task

For the van, two points defined a line: the eyebolt and the end of the subject's drawn representation of the plumb line. A straight line drawn through these points either intersected the horizontal reference axis below the road or was parallel to it. The angle measured was that between a perpendicular dropped from the eyebolt to the road and the line defined by the subject's response. Lines that sloped upward to the right were positively signed; those that sloped upward to the left were negatively signed. All responses were thus confined to the interval from 0° to −90° and to that from 0° to +90°; no one provided a response as extreme as 90°.

Note that, while each response has a unique representation in this scoring scheme, the interpretation of a response can sometimes be problematic. This difficulty is illustrated in Figure 3, which shows the van at −60°. There is no ambiguity about any positively signed angle for the van in this orientation, but two quite different positions are possible for the plumb line with negative slope. For the most common case, a response in the interval from $0°$ to $-30°$ indexes an error pointing toward the van's windshield, but errors in the interval from $-30°$ to $-90°$ put the plumb line facing toward the rear. Similar difficulties can occur in all other van orientations. However, since such responses were extremely rare (only seven times among more than 4,000 responses), they will not be distinguished in the results that we present.

As before, responses were measured to the nearest degree and resulted in a response vector identical to that obtained for the water-level task.

Horizontal Line Drawing

We measured the angular deviation of the horizontally drawn line with respect to the bottom edge of the booklet page. The targeted left-hand starting point and the right-hand end point of the drawn line, or the edge of the paper if the line intersected the edge, defined a line. Scoring otherwise followed the water-level procedure.

Missing Data

A subject's failure to complete one or more items of a task or, on very rare occasions, data that could not be scored (such as the drawing of two plumb lines) led to missing data. Such instances were few; of the 579 children, only 13 failed to complete all water-level items, and eight did not complete all van items. Our procedure was to eliminate subjects' responses from analyses of items that they failed to complete but to include them in the analyses of all other variables. The very minor consequence of this procedure is that the sample sizes vary slightly from one analysis to the next.

RESULTS

Specification of Error Value c

For the water-level task, the value of c in Equation (3) has most commonly been set to $5°$ (Kalichman, 1988). Although its precise value does not seem critical, in the present study c was determined empirically, on the basis of the subjects' drawing of the single horizontal line, the last booklet task.

There are at least two possible sources of error associated with reproducing this line: drawing accuracy and the subject's judgment as to whether the line is "horizontal enough" (given that subjects understood the meaning of "horizontal"). It is assumed that both these sources of error are associated with subjects' drawing responses, and it is also assumed that, under instructions to draw a horizontal line, the expected value of the line's drawing error is zero. That is, it is assumed that subjects have no systematic tendency to draw the line either positively or negatively sloped.

Thus, it is assumed that, at each age and for all subjects, the drawing error associated with instructions to draw a horizontal line is i.i.d. (independently and identically distributed) from an unknown response distribution with mean zero (by hypothesis). Let D_i, a random variable, denote the horizontal line drawing deviation error for subject i, $i = 1, \ldots, n$. Then $\Sigma\, D_i^2/n$ is an unbiased estimate of the unknown drawing error variance at that age. Variances thus estimated are reported in Table 5. The variances are also graphed against age in Figure 4.

Figure 4 suggests that the variances are well described by a function that is linear in age from 6 to 11 or 12 years and constant for subjects aged 12 and older. A least squares function of this form was fitted to the variances. The resulting function, denoted as $\tilde{\sigma}^2$, is defined by

$$
\tilde{\sigma}^2 = \begin{cases} -.893 \times \text{age} + 12.8, & 6 \leq \text{age} \leq 11.75; \\ 2.30, & \text{age} > 11.75. \end{cases} \tag{13}
$$

The value of c was taken as $3\tilde{\sigma}$ at each age. These values (rounded up to integers) are given in Table 5. Thus, for example, for 6-year-old children, a water-level drawing error of 9° or less defined a success and was scored 1, whereas errors larger than 9° were scored 0.

TABLE 5

Estimated Variance, $\hat{\sigma}^2$, of Drawing a
Horizontal Line and Estimated Critical Values
$c = 3\tilde{\sigma}$ from Regression of $\hat{\sigma}^2$ on Age

Age	n	$\hat{\sigma}^2$	$\hat{\sigma}$	$3\tilde{\sigma}$
6	16	7.56	2.75	9
7	25	6.56	2.56	8
8	58	5.48	2.34	8
9	35	4.86	2.20	7
10	33	3.52	1.87	6
11	62	3.14	1.77	6
12	76	2.16	1.47	5
13	67	2.49	1.58	5
14	49	3.27	1.81	5
15	50	1.46	1.21	5
16–17	46	2.11	1.45	5

Note.—The regression equation for $\hat{\sigma}^2$ is $\hat{\sigma}^2 = -.893 \times \text{age} + 12.8$, for $6 \leq \text{age} \leq 11.75$; $\hat{\sigma}^2 = 2.30$, for age > 11.75. $3\tilde{\sigma}$ have been rounded up to integer values. $r(\hat{\sigma}^2, \text{age}) = -.995$, $6 \leq \text{age} \leq 12$.

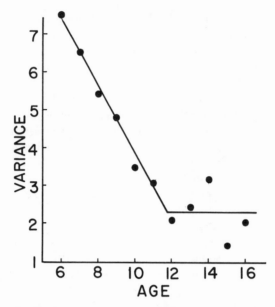

FIG. 4.—Graph of variances of horizontal line drawings at each age. Regression lines are defined by Eq. (13).

An effort was made to set error bounds conservatively so that as many responses would be scored 1 as is reasonable. Thus, the error bound was taken as $\pm 3\bar{\sigma}$, and, of course, the estimate of variance that we used— $\Sigma d_i^2/n$ (where d_i denotes an observed value of D_i)—is larger than an estimate based on the ordinary sample variance. Note that the error bounds for subjects 12 years and older coincide with the conventional 5° value, a happy coincidence.

It is also worth noting that, at all ages, the error variance associated with the drawing task was always relatively small; even the youngest subjects had a standard deviation of less than 3. This fact strongly suggests that young children know and understand what "horizontal" means and that they can reproduce such lines when asked to do so. Consequently, a child's inability to reproduce a correct response on the water-level task cannot be interpreted as meaning that he or she is unable to draw a satisfactory horizontal line.

Water-Level Data

For each age, c was set to the value of $3\bar{\sigma}$ given in Table 5, and a value of Y_i defined by transformation g_3 (i.e., "number correct" from Eq. [3]) was obtained for each subject. Because of small sample sizes, ages 16 and 17 were combined for all subsequent analyses and ages 6 and 7 for most of the analyses.

The water-level data are displayed in histograms in Table 6 for the 566 subjects with complete data. The most striking features of these data are the large individual differences in task performance indexed by each histogram. This is perhaps somewhat less noticeable at the youngest ages, but certainly by age 8 or 9 years, and at all subsequent ages, there are very large task performance differences. Some children perform perfectly or nearly so, whereas others of the same sex and age obtain zero correct. Even by age 16, over 20% of both boys and girls were obtaining at most one correct item.

Another notable feature is that at no age and for neither sex group do the histograms resemble familiar distributional forms. Although the youngest children's performance might suggest a binomial distribution with small θ, nothing even vaguely resembling a normal distribution ever appears.

The data give clear evidence of developmental improvement, but this improvement is not suitably summarized by simply noting the age-related improvement in mean performance. Focusing on means simply fails to do justice to the data: different models are clearly needed in order suitably to describe the data at different ages. While a unimodal parent distribution may be sufficient to account for the data at the youngest ages, it will not suffice for the older ages.

There are sex differences that emerge at most ages, but these differences are more subtle; although the relative proportions of boys with, say, six, seven, or eight items correct typically exceed those of girls, sex differences in mean performance do not portray the important features of the data at any given age.

Model Selection and Model Fits

For each age and sex, the $Y_1, Y_2, \ldots, Y_m$ data were subjected to binomial mixture decomposition. The general goal of the analysis was to determine whether the data were suitably modeled by a k component mixture model. The fit indices in the three right-hand columns of Table 7 summarize the results of these analyses and provide general evidence on the plausibility of the model structure for the data.

For the 6- and 7-year-old girls, a binomial ($k = 1$ component) model was a reasonable fit (e.g., $\chi^2 = .76$, VAF = 78%). Otherwise, a two-component ($k = 2$) model is necessary and fits the data well for most samples. For example, notice in Table 7 that VAF generally dramatically increases as one passes from a binomial ($k = 1$) to a two-component mixture ($k = 2$) while both AIC and χ^2 decrease. For illustration, consider the 9-year-old girls.

TABLE 6

Histograms of Water-Level Task Data Obtained at Each
Age ($n = 566$), Study 1

Boys		Girls	Boys		Girls

Age 6 & 7 | Age 8

Boys		Girls	Boys		Girls
.61***********	0	***************.75	.43*************	0	*****************.68
.17***	1	*****.25	.23*******	1	**.08
.11**	2		.10***	2	**.08
.06*	3			3	****.16
.06*	4		.10***	4	
	5		.03*	5	
	6		.03*	6	
	7		.06**	7	
	8			8	
$n = 18$		$n = 20$	$n = 30$		$n = 25$

Age 9 | Age 10

Boys		Girls	Boys		Girls
.21***	0	*********.43	.19****	0	****.33
.21***	1	***.14	.10**	1	**.17
.14**	2	**.10	.14***	2	***.25
.21***	3	***.14	.25*****	3	**.17
.07*	4	*.05	.05*	4	
.07*	5		.10**	5	
	6	**.10	.14***	6	
.07*	7	*.05	.05*	7	*.08
	8			8	
$n = 14$		$n = 21$	$n = 21$		$n = 12$

Age 11 | Age 12

Boys		Girls	Boys		Girls
.21*****	0	*********.23	.05**	0	******.16
.08**	1	***********.28	.05**	1	**********.26
.13***	2	*******.18	.14******	2	******.16
.25******	3	*******.18	.09****	3	*****.13
.13***	4	**.05	.16*******	4	***.08
.04*	5	*.03	.09****	5	***.08
.08**	6		.05**	6	*.03
.04*	7		.16*******	7	*.03
.04*	8	**.05	.21*********	8	***.08
$n = 24$		$n = 39$	$n = 43$		$n = 38$

Age 13 | Age 14

Boys		Girls	Boys		Girls
.09****	0	******.14	.06**	0	******.22
.11*****	1	********.19	.19******	1	**.07
.11*****	2	******.14	.13****	2	*****.19
.09****	3	******.14	.10***	3	***.11
.11*****	4	****.10		4	**.07
.15*******	5	**.05	.06**	5	*.04
.04**	6	**.05	.10**	6	
.09****	7	***.07	.16*****	7	**.07
.22**********	8	*****.12	.19******	8	******.22
$n = 46$		$n = 42$	$n = 31$		$n = 27$

TABLE 6 (*Continued*)

Boys	Girls	Boys	Girls
Age 15		*Age 16 & 17*	

Boys		Girls	Boys		Girls
.04*	0	**.05	.19*****	0	*.04
.04*	1	****.10	.04*	1	****.18
.11***	2	****.10	.04*	2	*.04
.11***	3	**********.26		3	*.04
.07**	4		.11***	4	
.04*	5	*.03		5	*.04
.07**	6		.08**	6	***.14
.25*******	7	******.15	.15****	7	**.10
.29*********	8	************.31	.38**********	8	*********.41
n = 28		*n* = 39	*n* = 26		*n* = 22

NOTE.—.17*** 1 *****.25 denotes that 17% of the boys and 25% of the girls have 1 response correct; each * denotes 1 individual.

When passing from a binomial to a two-component model, VAF increases from 29% to 86%. Similarly, AIC drops from 108 to 83.2, while χ^2 drops from 303 to 6.35. A two-component mixture model is a good fit to these data.

The expected χ^2 under a two-component model (assuming that the Pearson χ^2 is χ^2 distributed) is 5; the median observed χ^2 over all two-component model fits is 5.73, so the two-component model appears generally satisfactory. Likewise, for all 19 age-sex analyses for which a two-component mixture fits well, the mean VAF is 90%, and VAF ranges from 84% to 100%.

If the χ^2 values could be table referenced to provide probabilities, then, for two components, χ^2 values of 10 or more might be regarded as too large to reflect a satisfactory fit to a model with two components. This could be the case for boys at ages 11, 13, and 16 and for girls at 14 and perhaps 15 years. Four of these samples were satisfactorily fit by a three-component model; the results, parameter estimates, and fit indices are given in Table 7. For the girls at age 15, the data would not support a $k = 3$ solution. The solution iterated to a two-component solution, so no three-component solution is given. For the age groups with three component solutions, the fits to the data are much better, and in some cases it is almost too good when the very small χ^2 values are considered. However, the measurable improvement in VAF is generally small, never exceeding 14%.

In general, then, a two-component mixture model fits the data quite well; at most ages, and for both sexes, it is the best-fitting, simplest model. Only at the very youngest ages are the data satisfactorily modeled by a one-component binomial. In 4 of the 20 instances, the data suggest that three components might be needed, but there is no clear evidence of a

TABLE 7

BINOMIAL MIXTURE MODEL ESTIMATES AT AGES 6–16 FOR THE
WATER-LEVEL TASK, STUDY 1

Age, Sex	n	Range	$\bar{x}$	s^2	$\hat{\theta}_1$	$\hat{\theta}_2$	$\hat{\pi}_2$	VAF	χ^2	AIC
6B	10	0–2	.4	.49	.05 (.069)			78	.76	18.8
6G	6	0–0	0	0	0 (0)					
7B	8	0–4	1.25	2.5	.16 (.13)			42	7.9	30.1
					.0087 (.016)	.31 (.082)	.49 (.18)	93	.60	29
7G	14	0–1	.36	.25	.05 (.055)			100	1.22	22.1
6–7B	18	0–4	.77	1.48	.097 (.07)			48	15.28	54.5
					.019 (.014)	.26 (.065)	.32 (.11)	97	.59	48.6
6–7G	20	0–1	.25	.20	.037 (.039)			100	.75	25.7
8B	30	0–7	1.67	4.92	.21 (.074)			27	1,281	150
					.07 (.019)	.65 (.063)	.24 (.078)	96	5.34	106
8G	25	0–3	.72	1.38	.09 (.057)			47	26.38	69.2
					.0051 (.002)	.26 (.052)	.35 (.095)	100	3.72	58.2
9B	14	0–7	2.29	4.22	.28 (.12)			39	84.9	65.3
					.16 (.042)	.56 (.083)	.32 (.12)	84	4.58	61.6
9G	21	0–7	1.86	5.13	.23 (.092)			29	303	108
					.049 (.021)	.52 (.062)	.39 (.11)	86	6.35	83.2
10B	21	0–7	2.95	4.95	.37 (.11)			38	44.5	106
					.11 (.039)	.53 (.049)	.61 (.11)	86	6.12	94.5
10G	12	0–7	1.75	4.02	.22 (.12)			34	559	54.3
					.16 (.039)	.87 (.12)	.083 (.08)	88	4.42	47.4
11B	24	0–8	2.92	5.3	.36 (.098)			35	175	126
					.25 (.035)	.76 (.065)	.23 (.085)	84	10.48	112
$\hat{\Theta}$ = .01 (.013), .37 (.043), .84 (.069), $\hat{\Pi}$ = .20 (.082), .64 (.098), .15 (.072)								98	1.62	108
11G	39	0–8	1.92	3.76	.24 (.068)			39	9,203	172
					.2 (.023)	1 (0)	.051 (.035)	85	4.64	144
12B	43	0–8	4.81	6.39	.60 (.075)			30	269	250
					.38 (.034)	.92 (.022)	.41 (.075)	93	6.24	107

TABLE 7 (*Continued*)

Age, Sex	n	Range	$\bar{x}$	s^2	$\hat{\theta}_1$	$\hat{\theta}_2$	$\hat{\pi}_2$	VAF	χ^2	AIC
12G	38	0–8	2.66	5.69	.33			31	1,621	206
					(.076)					
					.21	.8	.21	87	7.44	159
					(.026)	(.050)	(.066)			
13B	46	0–8	4.39	7.49	.55			26	476	294
					(.073)					
					.34	.93	.35	85	20.78	210
					(.031)	(.022)	(.07)			

$\hat{\Theta} = .15\ (.0341),\ .55\ (.039),\ .97\ (.017),\ \hat{\Pi} = .29\ (.067),\ .43\ (.073),\ .28\ (.066)$

								98	1.5	206
13G	42	0–8	3.26	7.12	.41			27	848	259
					(.076)					
					.24	.88	.26	90	5.51	182
					(.027)	(.034)	(.068)			
14B	31	0–8	4.32	8.56	.54			23	283	212
					(.089)					
					.2	.87	.51	97	2.56	133
					(.036)	(.03)	(.09)			
14G	27	0–8	3.56	9.49	.44			21	1,016	200
					(.096)					
					.22	.97	.3	89	10.2	119
					(.034)	(.022)	(.088)			

$\hat{\Theta} = .04\ (.025),\ .33\ (.048),\ .97\ (.022),\ \hat{\Pi} = .26\ (.084),\ .44\ (.096),\ .30\ (.088)$

								97	1.84	117
15B	28	0–8	5.5	6.56	.69			26	476	164
					(.088)					
					.33	.91	.62	96	1.11	114
					(.051)	(.024)	(.092)			
15G	39	0–8	4.74	8.41	.59			23	425	267
					(.079)					
					.28	.96	.46	99	10.06	151
					(.035)	(.017)	(.079)			
16B	26	0–8	5.19	10.4	.65			18	4,293	205
					(.094)					
					.18	.93	.62	89	28.81	111
					(.044)	(.022)	(.095)			

$\hat{\Theta} = .02\ (.021),\ .48\ (.08),\ .95\ (.02),\ \hat{\Pi} = .23\ (.082),\ .19\ (.076),\ .59\ (.096)$

								96	4.87	103
16G	22	0–8	5.36	9.1	.67			19	722	157
					(.1)					
					.16	.91	.68	94	5.94	88.6
					(.049)	(.026)	(.1)			
11–16B&G ...	405	0–8	3.99	8.21	.50			24	5,690	2,733
					(.025)					
					.25	.91	.37	93	63.4	1,775
					(.010)	(.008)	(.024)			

$\hat{\Theta} = .1\ (.01),\ .39\ (.013),\ .94 = (.007),\ \hat{\Pi} = .26\ (.022),\ .40\ (.024),\ .33\ (.023)$

								99	2.3	1,728

NOTE.—Estimates $\hat{\theta}_1$ and $\hat{\theta}_2$ are item success rates for each component; $\hat{\pi}_2$ is the proportion of population in the better performing component; VAF is variance accounted for; AIC is Akaike's information criterion. Numbers in parentheses are estimated standard errors. χ^2 under binomial $df = 7$; with 2 components $df = 5$; with 3 components $df = 3$. For samples supporting 3 components, the estimates and their standard errors are given in vectors $\hat{\Theta}$ and $\hat{\Pi}$.

trend toward requiring different numbers of components with increasing age.

Examples of Fitted Models

Table 8 provides an indication of how well the mixture models fit the actual data. The left-hand histogram indicates that the observed and expected frequencies for the 13-year-old girls are in close correspondence. The two-component mixture model fits well.

In the middle histogram are the 16-year-old boys. The data fit the two-component model worse for them than for any other sample. The poorness of fit of the data to the model is indicated by the poor correspondence between expected and observed frequencies, but only for the poor performers. The far-right-hand histogram shows the same boys' data with expected frequencies for the three-component model. The three-component model fits much better, largely because of the improvement of fit for the boys who performed poorly.

Parameter Estimates

θ_r models success probabilities on each trial, while the π_r models population proportions within each component. Consider the estimates of θ_r, denoted $\hat{\theta}_r$, first.

TABLE 8

HISTOGRAMS OF OBSERVED AND EXPECTED VALUES UNDER BINOMIAL
MIXTURE MODEL FOR WATER-LEVEL TASK, STUDY 1

GIRLS AGE 13 YEARS, 2 COMPONENTS[a]		BOYS AGE 16 YEARS			
		2 Components[b]		3 Components[c]	
Frequency	E	Frequency	E	Frequency	E
0**E***	3.5	0*E***	1.9	0*****	4.8
1********E	8.7	1* E	3.5	1*	1
2****** E	9.6	2* E	2.8	2*	1.6
3******	6	3E	1.3	3E	1.2
4**E*	2.5	4E**	.3	4E**	1.3
5E*	1.1	5	.3	5E	1.1
6**	2	6**	1.4	6E*	1.4
7***E	4.2	7**** E	5.3	7****E	4.6
8***E*	4	8********E*	9.2	8**********	9.8

NOTE.—E denotes expected frequency. In the histogram, the relative frequencies are indexed by asterisks and the expected frequencies by E. If the observed and expected heights coincide, no E appears.

[a] $\chi^2(5) = 5.5$.
[b] $\chi^2(5) = 28.8$.
[c] $\chi^2(5) = 4.9$.

θ_r.—The estimates of θ for the binomial model, and of θ_1 and θ_2 for the two-component mixture model, are given in Table 7 above. The two-component estimates of θ_1 and θ_2 over age and within each sex are given in Figure 5. The segmented curves are isotonic regressions of the estimates of θ_1 and θ_2.

The estimates for the poorly performing subjects reveal that $\hat{\theta}_1$ increases with age until 11 years or so but then remains relatively constant at about .25. The graph of $\hat{\theta}_2$ for the better performers shows similar growth in the early years, and, by about age 11, $\hat{\theta}_2$ is essentially constant with a success probability of around .9. For neither $\hat{\theta}_1$ nor $\hat{\theta}_2$ do important sex differences appear to emerge, although the isotonic regression of $\hat{\theta}_1$ for boys consistently exceeds $\hat{\theta}_1$ for girls from 11 years on, a result not found by Thomas and Turner (1991).

If desired, confidence intervals and approximate tests can be constructed with the estimates and their standard errors given in Table 7 above. For example, the mean difference between the θ_2 estimates for boys and girls in the six age groups of 11–16 years is .0285, slightly favoring the girls ($z = 1.806$, $p < .04$), whereas the mean difference between the θ_1 estimates favors boys, .04 ($z = .186$, N.S.).[13] The fact that for both sexes the $\hat{\theta}$ estimates are approximately the same after age 10 suggests that the parameters θ_1 and θ_2 are approximately constant over the subsequent years, largely independent of sex. This reasoning provides the justification (argued in detail later) for pooling the data at these ages for additional analyses.

The differences between the estimates of θ_1 and θ_2 are very large and quite consistent and indicate that there are two quite different groups of performers, a finding consistent with previously reported findings (Thomas & Turner, 1991). The isotonic regression curves for $\hat{\theta}_1$ and $\hat{\theta}_2$ also closely resemble the growth curves presented in Thomas and Turner (1991); the main difference lies in the shapes of the isotonic regressions of $\hat{\theta}_2$ prior to 11 years. Whereas in the previous study that regression was largely constant over age, here it shows an increase over the range of about 6–11 years.

---

[13] Let $\omega_1, \omega_2, \omega_3, \ldots, \omega_r$ and $\nu_1, \nu_2, \nu_3, \ldots, \nu_s$ be two sequences of parameters with estimates denoted by $\hat{\omega}_1, \hat{\omega}_2, \hat{\omega}_3, \ldots, \hat{\omega}_r$, with $\hat{\sigma}^2(\hat{\omega}_1), \hat{\sigma}^2(\hat{\omega}_2), \hat{\sigma}^2(\hat{\omega}_3), \ldots, \hat{\sigma}^2(\hat{\omega}_r)$ denoting estimates of the variances of the $\hat{\omega}$ estimates. Denote the estimates for the ν similarly. Then tests and approximate confidence intervals, based on large sample theory, are easily constructed in natural ways, assuming that the parameter estimates are uncorrelated. For example, an approximate 95% confidence interval for ω_1 is constructed by $\hat{\omega}_1 \pm 2 \times \hat{\sigma}(\hat{\omega}_1)$; to test the (null) hypothesis that $\omega_1 = \omega_2$, construct $(\hat{\omega}_1 - \hat{\omega}_2)/[\hat{\sigma}^2(\hat{\omega}_1) + \hat{\sigma}^2(\hat{\omega}_2)]^{1/2}$, which is about standard normal in distribution under the null hypothesis. Let $\bar{\omega}$ and $\bar{\nu}$ be means of the sequences of estimates, with $d(\omega) = \Sigma_{i=1}^{r} \sigma^2(\hat{\omega}_i)/r^2$, $d(\nu) = \Sigma_{i=1}^{s} \sigma^2(\hat{\nu}_i)/s^2$. Then $Z = (\bar{\omega} - \bar{\nu})/[d(\omega) + d(\nu)]^{1/2}$ is approximately standard normal under the null hypothesis of common means. Consequently, Z may be referenced approximately to a normal table.

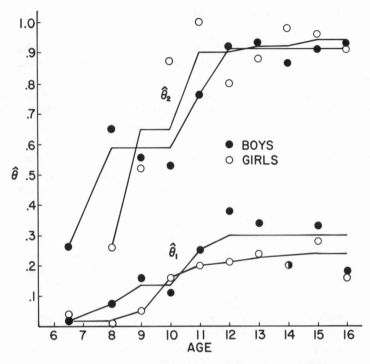

Fig. 5.—Water-level task estimates of θ_1 and θ_2 for boys and girls over age, Study 1. The curves are isotonic regressions of each parameter estimate for each sex.

π_r.—Table 7 above reports the estimates of π_2, $\hat{\pi}_2$, that is, the proportion in the better performing group; these estimates are graphed in Figure 6. For both sexes, the isotonic regressions indicate an increase in the proportion of the better performing population over age, an increase that tends to be rather gradual in the early years, accelerates at around 11–13, and remains relatively constant after about 15 years. Similar findings were reported earlier (Thomas & Turner, 1991).

The isotonic regression curves for $\hat{\pi}_2$ indicate that the proportion of boys among the better performers is larger at all ages, a finding again in agreement with the earlier study. Note that, at age 16, the estimate of π_2 for girls is actually larger than the estimate for boys, but the isotonic regressions for the two sexes do not intersect. This result is due to the sample size weighting that enters into the isotonic regression; there were almost twice as many girls at age 15 as at age 16.

As with the θ estimates, approximate confidence intervals and tests for

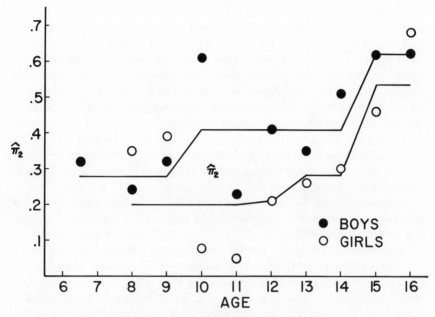

FIG. 6.—Water-level task estimates of π_2 for boys and girls over age, Study 1. The curves are isotonic regressions.

π can be constructed by those who desire to do so, by using the estimates and their standard errors given in Table 7 above.

Pooling Data

A major problem in trying to understand individual differences and growth is that often there are too few subjects available whose responses are sufficiently homogeneous to provide clear patterns in data. In growth studies, this problem is particularly troublesome because of the expected changes in performance over age and, as in the case here, of sex differences as well. An implication of the model that we have applied above provides a basis for ignoring both sex and age differences in the age range of 11–16 years and provides a justification for pooling these samples even though their means and variances differ (see Table 7 above). This suggests that the population means and variances vary as well. How can this pooling be justified?

We argued earlier that from about age 11 to age 16 years, there were no important differences in the θ_r parameter either between sexes or over age. Thus, assume that, within each sex, the mixture components at these ages have the same (or at least quite similar) component binomial distributions, that is, that, for all ages and both sexes, there are common θ_1 and θ_2 parameters. This assumption provides the justification for pooling. The proportions of individuals within each latent class need not be the same.[14]

This interpretation assumes that the three-component solutions obtained at ages for which a two-component mixture provided a less than satisfactory fit to the data should be regarded as sampling error, or at least unimportant variation. Such an assumption is not unreasonable because no evidence of an age trend in increased componential membership was found either in these data or in the earlier study (Thomas & Turner, 1991).

Table 9 shows the histogram of the 405 subjects in the age range 11–16 years. If any doubt that there are at least two distinct groups of performers remained, this histogram should be convincing.

The last rows of Table 7 above provide the parameter estimates for the binomial and mixture decomposition of the pooled data. For the two-component model, the fitted $\chi^2(5) = 63$ is certainly higher than is desirable. Its probability value—which can be meaningfully referenced to a table—is $p < .001$, and by this criterion the model would be rejected. However, the model still accounts for 93% of the variance in the data. A three-component model fits almost perfectly, $\chi^2(3) = 2.3$, N.S., with VAF 99 (see Table 7 above), but it is questionable whether including another component that accounts for only 7% of the remaining variance is justified. We favor the simpler model. In fact, whether a two- or a three-component model is selected will make little practical difference for subsequent analyses.[15]

[14] To argue more formally, let there be t i.i.d. observations from the distribution $.5b(y; .2, 8) + .5b(y; .9, 8)$; here, Y has mean 4.4. Suppose also that there are s observations from $.3b(y; .2, 8) + .7b(y; .9, 8)$; here, Y has mean 5.52. Combining the samples yields a binomial mixture with the same components and with weights $(.5t + .3s)/(t + s)$ and $(.5t + .7s)/(t + s)$ for the first and second components, respectively. Thus, the only consequence of pooling is to alter the component weights, not the θ parameters.

In addition, please note that our goal is not to try to convince the reader that $\theta_r (r = 1, 2)$ is exactly a fixed constant for the years 11–16, independent of age and sex. After all, we did demonstrate, e.g., a slight difference in θ_2 values favoring girls. Our spirit is to formulate the justification clearly and then recognize that the conditions cannot hold exactly but that the violations of assumptions are not likely to cause serious concerns in subsequent analyses (a point that we develop more fully in Chap. X). Using standard large sample procedures, homogeneity tests can be constructed using the statistics in Table 7 above for the 11–16-year age and gender groups of focus. Not surprisingly, given the power of combined sample sizes, both homogeneity tests reject a common θ_r. For θ_1, $\chi^2(12) = 42$, $p < .001$. The larger θ_1 for the 12- and 13-year-old boys with small standard errors caused the difficulty; without them, $\chi^2(10) = 12.45$, N.S. The very large $\hat{\theta}_2$ for ages 11, 14, and 15 for the girls accounts for over half the contribution to the θ_2 homogeneity test, with $\chi^2(12) = 43.2$, $p < .001$. Doubtlessly, there *are* differences among the θ_r, but there appear to be no important age or sex trends in their values, and we regard that as being the most important consideration.

[15] In Table 7 above, for both of the best performing groups in both the two-component and the three-component solutions, the $\hat{\theta}$ estimates are very similar: .91 for

TABLE 9

Histogram of Observed Frequencies of
11–16-Year-Old Subjects ($n = 405$),
Water-Level Task, Study 1

```
0*****************49
1*******************56
2*****************51
3******************52
4***********31
5*********24
6******19
7**************42
8***************************81
```

Note.—6******19 denotes 19 subjects with 6 correct items.

Partitioning Subjects into Distinct Groups

The procedure for clustering individuals uses the estimated posterior probability of component membership defined by Equation (11), with estimates replacing the model parameters.

Recall that, in this method, each score is assigned to the component for which that score's estimated posterior probability is largest. Table 10 gives the minimum number of items required at each age and for each sex for classifying a score as having arisen from the better performing component with parameter θ_2. In the case of a single component, the probability of having arisen from that component is, of course, one.

Table 10 indicates that the criterion values for classifying a score as belonging to the better performing component vary rather widely from sample to sample until about 10 years of age. From 11 years on, however, either five or six correct responses were needed for classification in the better performing group, except for the 11-year-old girls, whose data seem best viewed as reflecting sampling error. The similarity of all the critical values obtained for ages 11 and older provides additional evidence that the components at these ages are relatively homogeneous in their θ_r parameters.

The last line of Table 10 indicates that, for the combined sample over ages 11–16 ($n = 405$), subjects with six or more correct responses were

---

the two-component and .94 for the three-component model. The $\hat{\pi}$ weights of the best performing groups are similar too, .37 for the two-component and .33 for the three-component solution. Because the main goal was to investigate the poorly performing subjects after removing the best performing subjects, the subjects were partitioned on the basis of the two-component solution. Using the three-component solution would mean that about 16 fewer subjects would have been allocated to the best performing group ([.37 − .33] × 405 = 16.2), but, otherwise, the analysis that we provide would change very little.

TABLE 10

Minimum Number of Correct Responses Required for Classification as a
Good Performer in Component 2 for Each Age and Sex Group,
Water-Level Task, Study 1

Age/Sex	n	Criterion	$\hat{P}$(Comp. 2|Crit.)
6B	10	1 component solution	...
G	6	1 component solution	...
7B	8	2	.73
G	14	1 component solution	...
6&7B	18	2	.94
G	20	1 component solution	...
8B	30	3	.66
G	25	1	.97
9B	14	4	.84
G	21	2	.54
10B	21	3	.88
G	12	5	.61
11B	24	5	.72
G	39	8	.99
12B	43	6	.70
G	38	5	.78
13B	46	6	.64
G	42	6	.95
14B	31	5	.88
G	27	6	.84
15B	28	6	.93
G	39	6	.83
16&17B	26	5	.74
G	22	5	.93
11–17B&G	405	6	.95

Note.—"Criterion" denotes number of correct responses needed for component 2 classification. In the case of a single component, the probability of being from it is 1.

classified as good performers and those with fewer than six were classified as poor performers, yielding n's of, respectively, 142 and 263. Note that the ratio 142/405 = .35 is very close to the maximum likelihood estimate $\hat{\pi}_2$ = .37 reported in Table 7 above.

The 263 poor performers (sometimes combined with the poorer subjects from the similarly partitioned age groups younger than 11 years) were the focus of the next several analyses.

Sex Differences in Water-Level Response Distributions

The main reason for sorting individuals into their most probable latent class component distributions is to explore features of the original signed error responses of the subjects in each group rather than to focus simply on frequency counts of correct responses, as has been the case until now.

Arguing that individuals aged 11–16 years have similar binomial mixture structures does not, of course, imply that the original response distributions of signed errors for individuals in the same binomial latent class are identical. The strategy used in addressing this issue is illustrated by considering an important question. Are there sex differences in water-level task performance when latent class membership is controlled? That is, are those males who perform well similar to the corresponding group of females?

Of the 142 11–16-year-old subjects who were better performers, 85 were boys and 57 girls. Of the 263 poorly performing subjects, 113 were boys and 150 girls. Within each performance group, and for each of the eight vessel angles, the response distributions (again, the original signed response scores) for the sexes were compared.

None of the eight t tests, each based on $df = 140$ for the poor group and $df = 261$ for the good group, was significant at any vessel angle; the largest observed value of t was 1.615. Thus, there is no evidence that the boys' and girls' response distributions differ in their means for any of the vessel angles.

A considerably stronger statement may be made, however. Recall that the t test tests only for mean differences, under the assumption of equal variance normality. It is not a general test for distributional differences. Consequently, we also applied the much more general Kolmogorov-Smirnov omnibus test procedure, which tests for any differences in response distribution; this test statistic has an approximately $\chi^2(2)$ distribution under the null hypothesis of identity of distributions (Siegel, 1956). When the better corresponding sex groups were again compared, at no vessel angle did the test reach significance; the largest observed $\chi^2(2)$ was 5.23 ($p = .07$). For the poorly performing group, only one of the eight comparisons achieved significance, $\chi^2(2) = 6.45, p = .04$.

These results provide strong evidence that sex differences in task performance reflect differences in latent class proportions only. When these differences are controlled, sex differences disappear. More generally, when individuals of different age or different sex are compared for each fixed vessel angle, there are no distributional differences among individuals in the range of 11–16 years.[16]

---

[16] The issue is this. Do, say, 12-year-old boys' responses to the vessel at 11 o'clock have the same distribution as, say, those of 14-year-old girls for the same vessel angle? Clearly, evidence against commonality of distributions would be found if any two age and sex groups do not share common distributions for a given vessel angle.

One approach to this problem would be to compare the 528 pairs of sample distributions for good performers and the additional 528 for the poor performers. Any significant differences could be taken as evidence that commonality of response distributions is violated, after adjusting for multiple comparisons.

What we did was to compare all pairs of distributions for one randomly selected

Summary

For both sexes, and at almost all ages, a two-component binomial mixture model fits the data well. These two latent classes have strikingly different success rates on the water-level items, as indexed by their θ_r (item success rate) estimates. Growth changes appear to be largely determined by increases in the proportions of better performing subjects, indexed by increases in the estimate of π_2 over age. Little developmental change appears to take place after age 15 or so. Between-sex differences are primarily determined by differences in the π_2 estimates, with π_2 estimates for males typically exceeding those of females.

Data for both sexes for the age groups from 11 to 16 years were pooled, resulting in a sample of 405 subjects. Pooling can be defended in light of the support given to the model that is assumed to underlie the data. A decomposition analysis again led to a two-component mixture distribution. Using estimates of the posterior probability of component membership, subjects were partitioned into their good or poor "parent" latent classes. Next, sex differences in original responses (not frequencies) within each latent class were explored. There are no sex differences in the distribution of the original responses for any vessel angle. Sex differences appear to be reflected only in the parameter π_2, which is larger for males than for females.

---

vessel angle, the 11 o'clock angle, for poorly performing subjects. There are 6 choose 2 pairs of ages (yearly ages 11–16 years) yielding 15 pairs. For each of these age pairs, there are four possible comparisons (two sexes at each age) and, within each common age, one between-sex comparison, yielding 66 comparisons in all. For eight vessel angles, there would be $8 \times 66 = 528$ comparisons.

The Kolmogorov-Smirnov test of identity of distributions was performed for each of the 66 comparisons for the 11 o'clock angle. The mean of 66 observed χ^2 values was 2.00, exactly its expected value under the null hypothesis. The range was from .11 to 7.13, with two comparisons exceeding 5.99, the .05 critical value.

In some cases, the sample sizes were small, and thus the test may lack power. Still, the evidence suggests that the assumption of commonality of response distribution for different ages and both sexes, within performance groups for a fixed vessel angle, is not unreasonable.

V. DIAGNOSING RESPONSE STRATEGIES IN WATER-LEVEL TASK PERFORMANCE

We turn now to explore some hypotheses concerning the cognitive strategies that subjects may use when they respond to the water-level task. The main interest is in the poorly performing subjects, who lack an understanding of the horizontality rule.

At each age, 7–10 years, subjects were classified using (as before) Equation (11) and the values given in Table 10 above. The procedure defined two clusters at each age and within each sex. Note that, as shown in Table 10, the minimum number of correct responses that were necessary for classification as a good responder typically have high estimated probabilities of componential membership; the higher these probabilities, the more confident one can be about the membership composition of the clusters so formed.

Among the youngest children, all those aged 6 and all 7-year-old girls were included in the latent class of poorly performing subjects; none of these subjects responded correctly on more than two water-level items. The partitioning of subjects aged 11–16 into two classes has already been described; applying this procedure to the entire sample of 566 subjects with complete water-level data resulted in clusters of 185 good and 381 poor performers. The observed frequencies of poorly performing subjects at each age are given in the right-hand column of Table 11.

ASSESSING PIAGET'S "BOTTOM PARALLEL" RULE

An obvious cognitive rule to consider is Piaget and Inhelder's (1967) hypothesis that individuals in Stage II are influenced by a rectangular vessel's bottom and can therefore be expected to reproduce a water line parallel to it.

Recall that the subjects' original water-line predictions were scored using (the number correct) transformation $g_3 (r_j = 0)$ for all eight vessel orien-

TABLE 11

FREQUENCY OF BOTTOM PARALLEL RESPONSES AMONG POORLY PERFORMING SUBJECTS
AT EACH AGE, WATER-LEVEL TASK, STUDY 1

| | RESPONSE FREQUENCY | | | | | | | | | |
AGE	0	1	2	3	4	5	6	7	8	SUM
6	1	0	2	0	0	0	0	5	8	16
7	2	2	0	0	1	2	1	1	10	19
8	10	3	2	0	1	0	5	4	15	40
9	10	5	1	0	0	2	2	1	2	23
10	13	4	1	0	0	0	0	0	2	20
11	46	6	2	0	1	1	0	0	1	57
12	52	3	1	0	0	0	0	0	2	58
13	57	3	1	1	0	0	0	0	0	62
14	27	3	2	0	1	1	0	1	1	36
15	28	2	1	0	0	0	0	0	1	32
16–17	14	1	0	0	0	0	0	0	3	18
Sum	260	32	13	1	4	6	8	12	45	381

NOTE.—Cell entries are numbers of subjects. For example, among age 6-year-old subjects, 5 make bottom parallel responses 7 times on the 8 water-level items.

tations (i.e., $j = 1, \ldots, 8$) under the horizontality rule. But r_j can take on different values for the purpose of evaluating different strategic rules. For this case, the poorly performing subjects' original responses were rescored under the bottom parallel strategy in such a way that correct responses were defined as those that were parallel to the vessel's bottom ($\pm c$, where c is the drawing tolerance specified in Table 5 above).

The number of correct responses under this bottom parallel rule is a random variable. The problem is to distinguish in the observed score distribution individuals who use the bottom parallel strategy systematically from those who produce correct bottom parallel responses occasionally. The problem is solved by assuming that the response distribution is modeled by a mixture of binomials, with one component representing bottom parallel responders and the other representing all other responders. The solution is therefore to decompose the mixture into two components, just as we did before, and to follow with the posterior probability clustering procedure. The poor performers are thus separated into a group that represents those who use the bottom parallel rule and a group of subjects who may be occasionally correct under the rule but who are not systematic bottom parallel responders.

Frequencies of bottom parallel responses are shown in Table 11. The bottom row gives the summed distribution of frequencies over ages. This distribution is U shaped with bimodalities at zero and eight correct—precisely the shape of the distribution that one might hope to find. The parameter estimates for a two-component model are $\hat{\theta}_1 = .02$, $\hat{\theta}_2 = .90$, and $\hat{\pi}_2 = .20$. The minimum number of correct responses for classification as a bottom parallel performer (component 2) was four, with $\hat{P}$(component 2|4 correct) $= .98$. The proportions of subjects who had four or more correct responses and who were thus assumed to use the bottom parallel rule is graphed over age and is shown in Figure 7. The fitted function in Figure 7 is an isotonic regression.

Piagetians should be happy with these results. The proportion of bottom parallel responders is quite high at the youngest ages, when about 80% of the subjects perform in correspondence with the strategy. These proportions show an almost linear decreasing function over age until age 10 years, when it is about 10%; after that age, it drops somewhat more, until it levels off and remains at about 5% from age 13 on.[17] Of the entire sample, however, only about 20% of the subjects are classified as bottom parallel responders, so this rule does not account for the vast majority of those subjects who perform poorly. Nevertheless, among young subjects who perform poorly, the majority, through about age 8 years, do position their responses parallel to the vessel's bottom.

ASSESSING A SIDE PARALLEL RULE

Although not an expected response strategy from a Piagetian perspective, a second natural rule to evaluate is a side parallel strategy, with individuals placing the water-line parallel to the sides of the vessel. The procedures used to evaluate the bottom parallel strategy were applied here as well; the only difference was that transformation g_3 utilized r_j values suitably chosen so that responses parallel to the vessel's side, within $\pm c°$, would be defined as correct.

The results indicated that no subject used this strategy: only nine individuals revealed responses corresponding to this strategy, but none of them were correct on more than two items.

ASSESSING FIELD DEPENDENT-INDEPENDENT EFFECTS

It has long been suspected that performance on field dependent-independent tasks and performance on the water-level task were related. The relation has been explored mainly in conventional ways, by establishing that water-level task performance is correlated with measures of field dependence (e.g., DeLisi, 1983; Liben, 1975; Signorella & Jamison, 1978).

---

[17] Remember that these are conditional estimates (i.e., conditioned on the subjects being poor performers); consequently, the unconditional proportions would be smaller.

FIG. 7.—Proportions of poorly performing subjects who are bottom parallel respond-ers at each age, Study 1. The segmented curve is an isotonic regression.

Recently, McAfee and Proffitt (1991) suggested that individuals who make errors on the water-level task tend to orient their responses in the direction of the tilt of the vessel. They also considered the related question, Are poor performers more biased in their responses or simply more vari-able? They concluded that they were more biased, not simply more variable.

Similar issues are of interest here. We started our analysis by focusing on the original signed responses of the 11–16-year-old subjects.

Table 12 gives the summary statistics for the original signed error re-sponses associated with each vessel angle by both the good and the poor responders. These data reveal several facts about how these two groups differ. In all instances, the subjects who perform poorly have larger mean errors and very much larger variances; furthermore, the magnitudes of the means and variances for the poor performers depend on the vessel angles in particular ways.

Focusing on the means, the means for the group of poor performers are significantly different from zero at each vessel angle, with the smallest observed $|z| = 3.17$, $P(|Z| \geq 3.17) < .001$ (approximately at least, using large sample procedures), except for the 11 o'clock vessel orientation, where $P(|Z| \geq 1.42) \approx .16$.[18] There is also a relation between the signs of the

[18] From a practical perspective, large sample procedures are the same as small sample theory; the difference is that tests and confidence intervals can be constructed only ap-proximately.

TABLE 12

Summary Statistics of Signed Error Responses of 11–16-Year-Old Subjects
(n = 405) for Each Vessel Angle, Water-Level Task, Study 1

	Vessel Angle (O'Clock)							
	10	11	1	2	4	5	7	8
Good performers (n = 142):								
Mean	−.07	.75	−1.58	−1.25	1.29	.15	−1.13	−1.75
Median	0	0	−1	−1	1	0	−1	−2
s	2.77	3.94	3.55	2.98	4.00	2.89	2.71	3.3
s^2	7.70	15.49	12.63	8.90	16.04	8.34	7.35	10.88
Range	−7, 7	−15, 29	−12, 8	−13, 5	−6, 29	−7, 11	−11, 7	−17, 9
Poor performers (n = 263):								
Mean	15.41	1.65	−4.38	−11.96	10.96	6.96	−9.17	−13.39
Median	15	−1	−1	−13	14	1	−3	−15
s	24.86	18.75	22.40	29.21	32.59	23.74	22.83	31.08
s^2	617.9	351.7	501.7	853.2	1,062.1	563.6	521.2	966.2
Range	−83, 90	−38, 73	−81, 54	−88, 90	−85, 89	−43, 88	−81, 37	−88, 89

average angles and their magnitudes that parallels earlier reports (Thomas & Jamison, 1975). The absolute mean errors associated with vessel angles nearest the vertical are smallest; thus, 11 and 1 o'clock have the smallest mean errors, followed by 5 and 7 o'clock, and then by the remaining angles 10, 2, 4, and 8 o'clock. Considering the signs of the errors, note that 1 and 2 o'clock are negative and 10 and 11 positive. However, the signs for 4 and 5 o'clock are reversed relative to 1 and 2, and the same sign reversal occurs for 7 and 8 o'clock, which are negative, and 10 and 11, which are positive. Thus, the means correspond in sign to clock-hour orientations that are 180° apart (compare, e.g., 10 and 4 o'clock or 1 and 7), and there is a rough similarity in their magnitudes as well.

According to McAfee and Proffitt (1991), subjects who make errors are "biased to produce liquid orientations that deviate from the horizontal in the same direction as the tilt of the container" (p. 512). This conclusion is at best incomplete because the 2 and 4 o'clock vessel orientations, for example, may be regarded as being tilted in the same direction yet they have different signed responses. McAfee and Proffitt would not likely have detected such differences, however, because they considered only unsigned (absolute) errors as the variable of focus.

At least from a group means perspective, what appears critical as a factor in the responses of poorly performing subjects and allows for a coherent explanation of the orderings of the mean error values is the dependence on the vertical axis as a response reference point. Consider a vessel at any clock-hour position. Define the signed minimum rotation angle (SMRA) as the minimum rotational movement, clockwise or counterclockwise, required to align a tilted vessel with the vertical axis. A counterclockwise SMRA is negative and a clockwise SMRA positive. For example, a vessel at the 7 o'clock position is $-30°$ SMRA because a 30° counterclockwise movement aligns it with the vertical; 4 and 10 o'clock are both SMRA $+60°$.

A descriptive empirical generalization that corresponds to the ordering of the means and the variances of the poor performers is that the means are proportional to SMRA and the variances proportional to |SMRA|. For example, the smallest (signed) mean angular error is for a vessel in the 8 o'clock orientation, where SMRA is $-60°$; the largest error is for a vessel in the 10 o'clock orientation, where SMRA is $+60°$. Similarly, the larger |SMRA|, the larger the variances. However, SMRA and mean error are not generally monotonically related, as they may appear here, because vessels tilted to 3 and 9 o'clock often result in accurate performance by both poor and good performers (Thomas & Jamison, 1975).

Nevertheless, this descriptive explanation of the sample moment features of the poor performers' data is at best incomplete because it implies no cognitive rule or strategy that subjects might employ to produce a response. It seems highly improbable that subjects would use any conscious strategy that could account for the observed systematic mean tendency to position water-level responses in proportion to SMRA. We think it much more likely that vessel angle exerts a passive but important influence on responses—an influence that is precisely the field effects influences that H. A. Witkin (Witkin et al., 1954) had suggested.

What possible response strategy might those with poor performance employ? Unfortunately, subjects who perform poorly seem unable to articulate what they do, and they may therefore have no explicit set of rule-following strategies such as apparently govern behavior in some other settings (e.g., Siegler, 1989). In an earlier study (Thomas & Jamison, 1975), after having provided a series of water-level task predictions, high school–aged subjects were asked how they knew how to position the water line. Their water-level prediction responses were compared with what they said they did if they provided a specific rule, such as reporting that they placed the water line parallel to the vessel's bottom. However, subjects with large performance errors did not often provide clear rules, and, when they did, their responses did not consistently agree with what they said they did. Consequently, their verbal answers might better be interpreted as responses to the demand characteristics of task: that is, they felt compelled to say *something*.

Before considering an alternative perspective on these response data, consider the same mean error responses for *good* performers. Their data are shown in Table 12. Their means are dramatically different from those of the poor performers; even more dramatic is the reduction in variance. Nevertheless, the general tendency of the mean responses to be slightly biased in the same direction as for the poor performers is evident; only the mean for the 10 o'clock vessel angle is signed differently from the corresponding means for the poorer subjects. Furthermore, with the exception of the 10 and 5 o'clock vessel angles, all the other means for the good performers are significantly different from zero, with the minimum $|z| = 2.27$, $P(|Z| > 2.27) < .025$.

The similarity in the direction of the mean effects of the vessel tilt for both good and poor performers indicates that both groups are affected by vessel orientation, but not to the same degree. It could be that the field effect acts as an additive effect on mean responses and that the effect is much larger for poor performers than for good. However, such an additive effect cannot account for the huge difference in variance that distinguishes the two groups, a group difference that McAfee and Proffitt (1991) apparently did not detect in their study.[19]

Summary.—Both poor and good performers are influenced—and in the same direction—by the vessel's tilt. The greater this tilt is from the vertical, the greater the mean response error (except for vessels on their sides). The two performance groups differ greatly in the magnitude of this influence; poor performers are influenced considerably more. It is inappropriate, however, to focus only on the mean effects of vessel tilt. Doing so ignores a most dramatic feature of the data, namely, the huge variances at all vessel angles for subjects who perform poorly. This variance is many times larger than the variance displayed by good performers. While the influence on the mean response error seems related to field effects, it is difficult to see how differences in variances can be attributed to field effects.

RULES AND RESPONSE DISTRIBUTIONS

Consider next the possibility that poorly performing subjects behave according to a random response rule. Piaget and Inhelder (1967) explicitly proposed that subjects would grapple, in a kind of random way, with tasks such as the water-level task at a time when old rules were abandoned and a new rule had not yet been discovered. However, as far as we know, the possibility that poorly performing subjects might indeed be performing according to a random rule has not been entertained before.

What kind of evidence might be taken as supporting a random response rule? Consider first the error distribution likely to be associated with the original signed responses of *good* performers. These individuals either know the correct rule or at least behave correctly. An approximately zero-centered

[19] One possible reason that McAfee and Proffitt (1991) did not detect the large differences in variance is that they utilized absolute values, which will strikingly reduce the variance when the response distribution has a large proportion of its density below zero.

and perhaps symmetrical response distribution—with, importantly, most of the probability mass of the responses centered near zero—makes sense in this case. Perturbations about the horizontal, defined as zero, can be plausibly viewed as related to motor skills accuracy, perceived horizontality, and subjective criteria such as "that's close enough," among other factors.

Such a distribution of responses is precisely what is provided by the good performers. For each vessel angle, an edf (empirical distribution function) of the signed error responses was constructed using Equation (12). The graphs of these edf's appear in Figure 8 and may be viewed as estimates of the population distribution functions. Each graph is based on the 142 responses of the same subjects in the 11–16-year-old better performing group. Because these edf's were graphed on normal probability graph paper (normal-linear coordinates), they should appear as straight lines if the data are normally distributed. The graphs are generally close to this form, so the data are generally in good agreement with the expectation of a roughly symmetrical response distribution centered near zero and with small variance.

This kind of distribution is not expected when subjects lack a rule to generate consistent responses; instead, response distributions that tend not to favor one response over another would be expected (at least within broad limits). Such distributions are often called "uninformative." The uniform (rectangular) distribution is the distributional form most often considered. If individuals respond according to a uniform distribution, they would be expected to produce an edf that is also a straight line, but in linear-linear coordinates.[20]

If there were no tendency to favor one response setting over another, then the distribution of responses would be uniform on the interval defined by the circumference of the circle. A priori, however, a uniform distribution on the circle can be rejected: the range of responses shown in Table 12 instantly rejects this hypothesis. However, one would expect an approximately uniform-like distribution on some unknown interval if the responses are selected in accordance with a random rule that tends to favor no particular response over another within a broad interval but *avoids* certain extreme response settings such as vertical setting.

For all eight vessel angles, edf's were constructed for the 243 poor performers in the 11–16-year sample. These edf's appear in Figure 9. It is clear that in no instance do these edf's graph a *single* straight line. However, for the bulk of the probability mass (roughly 60%), the middle portions of the edf's are largely linear in form for most vessel angles, except perhaps

---

[20] Let U be uniform on the interval from a to b. Then $f(u) = (b - a)^{-1}$. Its distribution function $F(u) = \int_a^u f(t)dt = (u - a)/(b - a)$ is linear in u, and, consequently, $F(u)$ graphs as a straight line.

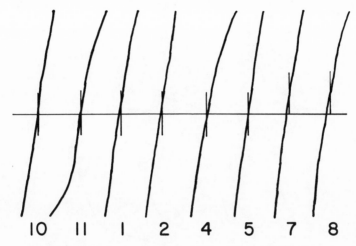

FIG. 8.—Empirical distribution functions (edf's) of water-level task performers who perform well, aged 11–16, $n = 142$, Study 1. Each edf is for the responses at the specified clock-hour orientation. Vertical bars through the edf's indicate abscissa values of 0°. The horizontal line is the 50% point. The graphs are in normal-linear coordinates.

those at 5 and 7 o'clock. Although the bulk of the probability mass appears to be uniform in appearance, the tails of the distribution present another problem, and what model to propose for the tails is difficult to judge. For several edf's, the left- and right-tail portions are largely linear, more so for those at 10, 2, 4, and 8 o'clock than for the other angles. These tails also appear to have approximately the same slopes. What these edf's suggest is a distribution that itself is a mixture of two uniform distributions, with one uniform component spanning the center mass and another component capturing the tail areas.[21]

Figure 10 shows an example of such a distribution (which resembles an inverted T); a distribution of this form was fit to each of the eight clock-hour samples using minimum χ^2 procedures.[22] Figure 10 also shows

[21] It is important to note that, in fitting a mixture of uniform distributions, there was no intention of suggesting that there are two kinds of response processes, each represented by one of the uniform components (although this might be the case). One might just as well call the distribution we fitted an "inverted T distribution." There are equivalent ways of writing expressions for distributions of the same shape, and viewing the problem as a mixture of uniforms provided a tractable approach.

[22] Let $f_L(x) = 1/(t - b)$, $b < x < t$, and $f_S(x) = 1/(d - c)$, $c < x < d$, $b < c < d < t$. Define $g(x) = \lambda f_L(x) + (1 - \lambda)f_S(x)$, $0 < \lambda < 1$. $g(x)$ is a two-component mixture of uniform distributions. The smallest- and largest-order statistics (smallest and largest observed values) are sufficient statistics for b and t, so they are estimates of them. Estimates of c and d can be achieved by direct search, using minimum χ^2 as a fitting criterion. To estimate λ, take $\hat{\lambda} = [(\text{number of observed values outside the interval from } c \text{ to } d)/n]/[\int_b^c f_L(x)dx + \int_d^t f_L(x)dx]$, where n is sample size. To show that this estimate of λ is a moment-like estima-

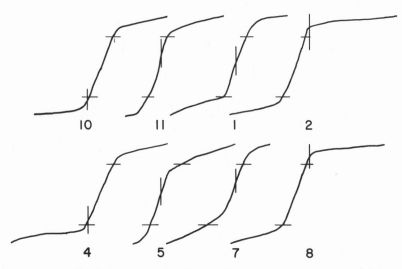

FIG. 9.—Empirical distribution functions (edf's) of poor water-level task performers, aged 11–16, $n = 263$, Study 1. Each edf is for the responses at the specified clock-hour orientation. Vertical bars through the edf's indicate values of 0°. The horizontal bars indicate the 20% (lower) and 80% (upper) points. The graphs are in linear-linear coordinates.

the graph of the 10 o'clock vessel with fitted function, denoted by the straight-line segments. The density at the top of Figure 10 is the best-fitting mixture of uniforms for this vessel angle.

It is clear that a mixture of two uniforms describes the global features of many edf's rather well, but it is also evident that there are serious departures from the fitted model, and this is true for all eight edf's; for example, the lower tail of the 10 o'clock responses is not fit well (see Fig. 10).

Table 13 shows the values of χ^2 for each distribution and the estimated parameters of the uniform mixture distribution as well as the χ^2 fitted value when just the center portion of the edf is fitted, ignoring the observations in the tails. These fitted functions included data within the estimated interval from c to d (Fig. 10), that is, the observations in the middle portion of the uniform. The uniform mixtures were not as well fit to the data as desired. But note again that fit indices can be poor even if the mixed uniform characterizes the main features of the data. This fact is made evident by comparing the $\chi^2 = 35.3$ for the 10 o'clock vessel (see Table 13) with the fitted functions in Figure 10—and this vessel angle was not one of the better-fitting functions.

---

tor, integrate $\int_b^c g(x)dx$. Find that $\lambda = [\int_b^c g(x)dx]/[\int_b^c f_L(x)dx]$; in fact, λ is this ratio for any range of integration outside the interval (c, d). Once b, c, d, and t have been specified, λ may be specified. There are thus four free parameters in the model.

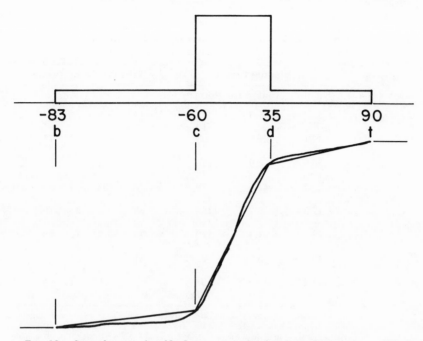

Fig. 10.—Smooth curve is edf of poor water-level task performers, $n = 263$, for vessel at 10 o'clock. Densities at top and segmented curve below are best fitting density and distribution functions for mixture of uniform distributions; b (bottom), c, d (middle), and t (top) denote points of estimated discontinuity and are referred to in the text and in n. 22.

These analyses suggest that a uniform distribution describes the center portions of the response distribution reasonably well for most vessel angles but that the tail sections might be better modeled by some other distribution, perhaps an exponential. A normal distribution is clearly not a satisfactory fit to the response distribution (see the fit indices in Table 13).

In addition to the differences in the form of the distributions that describe the good and poor performers, we already noted that the variances of the poor performers are much larger—in fact, never less than 23 times greater—than the variances of the good performers. Such large variance differences, as well as the very broad range of responses that is evident in Table 12 above, would be consistent with a random rule.

At a minimum, we can conclude that individuals in different subsamples produce very different response distributions. This finding would suggest that different cognitive processes are associated with different response distributions. In fact, when the two performance groups were compared at each vessel angle using the Kolmogorov-Smirnov omnibus distribution test, the $\chi^2(2)$ test statistic was never smaller than 52 ($p < .0001$). This result

TABLE 13

PARAMETER ESTIMATES AND FITS TO THREE DISTRIBUTIONS FOR RESPONSES OF 263 POOR
PERFORMERS, AGES 11–16, TO WATER-LEVEL VESSEL ANGLES, STUDY 1

	DISTRIBUTION			PARAMETER ESTIMATES				
CLOCK ANGLE	Unimix	Uniform	Normal	b	c	d	t	λ
10	35.3	6.0	81 (10)	−83	−6	35	90	.28
11	39.1	21.4	93 (7)	−38	−19	10	73	.35
1	39.9	8.9	138 (8)	−81	−11	21	54	.34
2	26.5	11.5	179 (11)	−88	−33	4	90	.30
4	17.5	2.2	138 (10)	−85	−3	33	89	.37
5	28.3	1.4	119 (8)	−43	−17	12	88	.40
7	40.3	3.7	95 (7)	−81	−10	11	37	.57
8	37.2	12.0	194 (11)	−88	−32	1	89	.36

NOTE.—b and t denote bottom and top bounds of uniform distribution, c and d lower and upper bounds of the center portion of uniform mixture. λ is the weight of the longer tail component. The numbers under "Distribution" are χ^2 fitted values under a mixture of uniform distributions (Unimix) with $df = 7$, $P(\chi^2[7] \geq 14.07) < .05$, a uniform fitted to the observations in interval $c–d$ (Uniform) with $df = 1$, $P(\chi^2[1] \geq 3.84) < .05$, and a normal distribution. The df given in parentheses vary because of the need to combine cell observed frequencies to be 5 or more.

simply reaffirms what a visual comparison of Figures 8 and 9 above reveals. The evidence for a random rule hypothesis for poorly performing subjects seems reasonably good over a broad response range, but the fact that these uniform-like distributions are not centered closer to zero (the correct response) is likely to be the result of passive field effects.

In sum, there appear to be two processes that guide performance on the water-level task. One of these involves passive field effects that influence where the distribution of responses is centered; all individuals are apparently influenced by field effects, but poor performers are influenced considerably more. The second process dictates the form of the response distribution, which is influenced by the apparently different cognitive processes of individuals in the two groups. For good performers, a roughly normal distribution of error seems appropriate, with mean error about zero and with small variance. For poorly performing individuals, a modified uniform distribution appears to be a first approximation. The fact that the *shape* of the response distributions (Figs. 8 and 9) and their *centers* (Table 12) are both different for the two performance groups strengthens the proposal that at least two processes are needed to account for the data adequately.

ASSESSING A RANDOM RULE: CORRELATIONS

Another data implication of the hypothesis that subjects select their responses randomly and independently on each trial is that the correlation among responses for different pairs of vessel angles should be zero. If two random variables are independent, then they are zero correlated. This model implication thus suggests the corresponding natural test in data.

The intercorrelations between all 28 pairs of vessel angles are given in Table 14. The correlation coefficients among the poorly performing subjects ranged from $-.46$ to $.44$ and averaged $-.025$, which is close to the expected value of zero under independence. Using a distribution-free result by Huber (1977), the distribution of these correlation coefficients, under independence, will have variance $1/(n - 1)$. Therefore, most of the values of r should be in a 3-standard-deviation interval of $3(n - 1)^{-.5} = .185$ about zero under the independence hypothesis. Table 14 shows that there are 12 correlations outside this interval, suggesting that the variance of the correlation coefficients is not in agreement with the independence hypothesis. This interpretation is problematic, however, because the 28 correlation coefficients are not independent of each other, and, consequently, Huber's (1977) result would not be expected to hold exactly.

However, there is additional evidence from Table 14 that the responses of the poor performers are correlated from trial to trial in a systematic way. For example, vessel angles 180° apart are generally positively associated. These typically small correlations may reflect field effects, and thus a passive influence on responses, as contrasted with some effort to produce responses in a particular way.

TABLE 14

INTERCORRELATIONS AMONG WATER-LEVEL VESSEL ANGLE RESPONSES FOR GOOD
AND POOR PERFORMANCE GROUPS, AGES 11–16, STUDY 1

CLOCK-HOUR POSITION	CLOCK-HOUR POSITION							
	10	11	1	2	4	5	7	8
10	. . .	−.008	.148	.106	.462	.238	.390	.167
11	.200	. . .	−.074	.095	−.054	.242	.084	.049
1	−.294	−.316	. . .	.131	.189	−.106	.407	.225
2	−.249	−.006	.194	. . .	.155	.112	.306	.308
4	.435	.155	−.137	−.118	. . .	.017	.283	−.051
5	.094	.253	−.406	.036	.022	. . .	.027	.284
7	−.239	−.128	.322	−.012	−.007	−.456	. . .	.153
8	−.241	.008	.019	.312	−.263	.041	.079	. . .

NOTE.—The upper triangle shows correlations for good performers ($n = 142$), the lower one for poor performers ($n = 263$). Means, standard deviations, and ranges of 28 r's are as follows: upper triangle, .15, .15, and from −.11 to .46; lower triangle, −.025, .23, and from −.46 to .44, respectively.

For good performers, there are seven correlation coefficients outside an estimated 3-standard-deviation error band of .253, again suggesting some between-angle response covariance and hence a lack of independence. Because there is little apparent reason to expect correlated responses on the basis of rule strategy considerations, the same source of influence, probably field effects, would appear to be the best candidate for explaining covariation here as well.

GENERAL SUMMARY

The youngest of subjects, through about 8 years of age, appear to perform in correspondence with Piaget's expectation that children will position the water line parallel with the vessel's bottom. However, with increasing maturity, some subjects acquire understanding of the task principle and demonstrate accurate task performance by producing a response distribution with small variance (typically less than 16°) concentrated around the correct horizontal response. These good performers are, nonetheless, influenced by field effects—the tilt of the vessel—because their responses show a small mean performance bias that depends on the vessel angle.

Other subjects, indeed, the majority in the age range from 11 to 16 years, have yet to make significant advances in cognitive understanding. The bulk of their responses at each vessel angle resembles a uniform distribution, with huge variance (350°–1,000°), suggesting that they are selecting their responses randomly from within a broad range of possible responses. Extremely deviant responses of 40° or more in error do occur, but only rarely. These individuals, like the good performers, are also influenced by field effects, but the magnitude of the mean response bias is much larger (see Table 12 above). The magnitudes of the variances are also related to the vessel's orientation. Both groups of subjects also show typically small correlations between their responses at different vessel angles, and this influence seems likely to be a passive field-effects influence.

VI. PERFORMANCE ON THE VAN TASK
DURING CHILDHOOD AND ADOLESCENCE

It will be recalled that one purpose of including the van task in Study 1 was to extend understanding of spatial development to a vertical task. Because the analysis of the van task data follows the same procedure used in the water-level task data, the presentation will be briefer; in general, the results obtained from the two tasks were very similar.

THE VAN TASK DATA

For each age and sex, c was set to the values given in Table 5 above, and the data were transformed by g_3. To maintain adequate sample sizes, data for each sex at the two oldest and two youngest ages were typically grouped together for most subsequent analyses.

Table 15 provides histograms of the van task data for the subjects ($n = 571$) for whom complete data were available. Overall, these histograms resemble the histograms given in Table 6 above for the water-level task data. At each age, there are more boys than girls with scores of six or more correct; within each age and sex, there are large individual differences in task performance. Although by 16 years about 60% of the boys and half the girls were performing perfectly, about 20% of the subjects were still successful on only two or fewer items. As with the water-level task, there are clear trends in improvement over age, but these trends are not well captured by conventional summary sample statistics.

MODEL SELECTION AND MODEL FITS: VAN DATA

Table 16 shows the results of the binomial mixture decomposition. In general, the van data are in even better correspondence with the binomial mixture model than were the water-level data. Starting with the combined

TABLE 15

Histograms of Van Task Data Obtained at Each Age ($n = 571$), Study 1

Boys		Girls	Boys		Girls
Age 6 & 7			**Age 8**		
.32******	0	********.4	.16*****	0	********.31
.21****	1	****.20	.06***	1	*.04
.16***	2	*.05	.16*****	2	****.15
.16***	3	*.05	.03*	3	***.12
.05*	4	****.20	.19*******	4	*****.19
.05*	5	**.10	.19******	5	**.08
.05*	6		.06**	6	**.08
	7		.09***	7	*.04
	8		.03*	8	
$n = 19$		$n = 20$	$n = 32$		$n = 26$
Age 9			**Age 10**		
.14**	0	******.29	.05*	0	**.17
	1	*.05	.10**	1	**.17
.21***	2	****.19	.24*****	2	**.17
.21***	3	***.14	.14***	3	***.25
.07*	4	***.14	.14***	4	**.17
.14**	5	****.19	.05*	5	
.07*	6		.10**	6	*.08
	7		.05*	7	
.14**	8		.14***	8	
$n = 14$		$n = 21$	$n = 21$		$n = 12$
Age 11			**Age 12**		
	0	*****.14	.05**	0	*.03
.08**	1	*****.14	.09****	1	**********.26
.25******	2	********.22	.09****	2	*********.23
.17****	3	*******.19	.14*******	3	**.05
.13***	4	*****.14	.07***	4	*****.13
.13***	5	*.03	.14******	5	**.05
.08**	6	**.05	.11*****	6	****.10
.04*	7	**.05	.11*****	7	*.03
.13***	8	**.05	.21*********	8	*****.13
$n = 24$		$n = 37$	$n = 44$		$n = 39$
Age 13			**Age 14**		
	0	*.02		0	*.03
.09****	1	********.19	.09***	1	*****.17
.13******	2	*******.17	.16*****	2	***.10
.09****	3	******.14	.06**	3	*********.31
.15*******	4	****.09	.19******	4	
.06***	5	***.07	.06**	5	**.07
.01*	6	***.07	.06**	6	**.07
.11*****	7	*.02	.13****	7	*.03
$n = 46$		$n = 42$	$n = 32$		$n = 29$

TABLE 15 (*Continued*)

Boys		Girls	Boys		Girls
	Age 15			*Age 16 & 17*	
	0	***.08		0	**.09
.07**	1	******.15	.04*	1	*.05
	2	******.15	.15****	2	**.10
.04*	3	**.05		3	***.14
.04*	4	*.03	.04*	4	*.05
.07**	5			5	*.05
.04*	6	*.03	.04*	6	
.30********	7	***.08	.12***	7	*.05
.44*************	8	****************.44	.62****************	8	**********.48
n = 27		*n* = 39	*n* = 26		*n* = 21

NOTE.—.21**** 1 ****.20 denotes that 21% of the boys and 20% of the girls have 1 response correct; each * denotes 1 individual.

6- and 7-year-old data, the two-component model fits very well at virtually every age and for both sexes.

There were substantial drops in AIC when passing from a binomial to a two-component binomial mixture in all cases, and this decrease was also reflected in the χ^2 fit index. Overall, the χ^2 fits were excellent; the median value over all two-component analyses was 4.13, a value that compares well with the expected value of 5. The median VAF was 92%; although its range extends from 74% to 100%, there were only four instances in which VAF fell below 91%.

Three values of χ^2 above 10 were obtained. The largest was 13.4, for the 9-year-old boys, which was the only sample to show a measurably better fit with a three-component model. The fit indices for 12- and 14-year-old girls were not noticeably better with three components, and the three-component solutions were generally very slow to converge.

PARAMETER ESTIMATES

θ_r.—The θ estimates are given in Table 16 and are graphed in Figure 11. The patterns of change of θ_1 over age are very similar for both sexes and resemble the patterns for the water-level task (see Fig. 5 above). The estimated values of θ_1 increase from about .1 at the youngest ages to about .3 at age 10 or so; θ_1 then remains roughly constant at about .35 for boys and about .28 for girls. Thus, boys have consistently slightly higher estimated values of θ_1 than girls. It is not clear what the source of such between-sex differences in θ_1 estimates is likely to be, but recall that a similar differ-

TABLE 16

BINOMIAL MIXTURE MODEL ESTIMATES, AGES 6–16, VAN TASK, STUDY 1

Age, Sex	n	Range	$\bar{x}$	s^2	$\hat{\theta}_1$	$\hat{\theta}_2$	$\hat{\pi}_2$	VAF	χ^2	AIC
6B	10	0–5	1.1	2.99	.14 (.11)			32	60.54	39.1
					.014 (.016)	.38 (.093)	.34 (.15)	88	2.07	33.1
6G	5	0–3	1	1.5	.13 (.148)			58	2.91	15.8
7B	9	1–6	2.56	2.78	.32 (.16)			63	8.79	35.1
					.27 (.056)	.67 (.15)	.13 (.11)	100	3.22	37.7
7G	15	0–5	2	4.29	.25 (.11)			35	34.1	71.9
					.034 (.023)	.49 (.066)	.47 (.13)	100	4.94	56.1
6–7B	19	0–6	1.79	3.29	.22 (.096)			42	31.7	79.6
					.079 (.029)	.42 (.061)	.42 (.11)	91	1.69	73.8
6–7G	20	0–5	1.75	3.67	.22 (.092)			37	34.4	88.7
					.046 (.021)	.47 (.062)	.40 (.11)	100	3.33	71.7
8B	32	0–8	3.47	5.67	.43 (.088)			35	111	173.4
					.13 (.033)	.63 (.039)	.61 (.086)	94	6.33	143
8G	26	0–7	2.58	4.89	.32 (.091)			36	71.9	132.4
					.004 (.0073)	.47 (.042)	.69 (.091)	88	3.20	105.7
9B	14	0–8	3.64	6.4	.46 (.13)			31	187	81
					.36 (.049)	1 (0)	.14 (.093)	74	13.4	72

$$\hat{\Theta} = 0\ (0),\ .43\ (.055),\ 1\ (0),\quad \hat{\Pi} = .14\ (.091),\ .72\ (.12),\ .14\ (.093)$$

Age, Sex	n	Range	$\bar{x}$	s^2	$\hat{\theta}_1$	$\hat{\theta}_2$	$\hat{\pi}_2$	VAF	χ^2	AIC
								92	3.04	66.3
9G	21	0–5	2.38	3.65	.3 (.1)			46	32.5	93.9
					0 (0)	.41 (.045)	.73 (.097)	97	3.58	81.1
10B	21	0–8	3.86	6.13	.48 (.11)			33	157	118
					.32 (.042)	.89 (.045)	.28 (.098)	92	2.32	94.9
10G	12	0–6	2.42	3.17	.30 (.13)			53	10.2	50.2
					.067 (.049)	.39 (.058)	.73 (.13)	87	2.68	51.1
11B	24	1–8	4	4.96	.5 (.1)			40	100	120
					.40 (.039)	.93 (.041)	.19 (.081)	91	3.16	104
11G	37	0–8	2.95	5.05	.37 (.079)			37	358	189
					.27 (.028)	.85 (.05)	.17 (.062)	91	4.66	154

TABLE 16 (*Continued*)

Age, Sex	n	Range	$\bar{x}$	s^2	$\hat{\theta}_1$	$\hat{\theta}_2$	$\hat{\pi}_2$	VAF	χ^2	AIC
12B	44	0–8	4.75	6.52	.59			30	267	258
					(.074)					
					.32	.85	.51	91	7.52	200
					(.036)	(.026)	(.075)			
12G	39	0–8	3.46	6.31	.43			31	549	222
					(.079)					
					.26	.85	.29	94	10.8	170
					(.03)	(.037)	(.072)			

$$\hat{\Theta} = .21\ (.161),\ .26\ (.030),\ .85\ (.037),\ \hat{\Pi} = .02\ (.022),\ .69\ (.074),\ .29\ (.072)$$

Age, Sex	n	Range	$\bar{x}$	s^2	$\hat{\theta}_1$	$\hat{\theta}_2$	$\hat{\pi}_2$	VAF	χ^2	AIC
								94	10.8	174
13B	46	1–8	5.22	6.75	.65			27	284	278
					(.07)					
					.38	.97	.46	97	3.21	82.2
					(.035)	(.013)	(.074)			
13G	42	0–8	4	7.07	.5			27	526	255
					(.077)					
					.32	.95	.28	91	8.61	183
					(.03)	(.023)	(.069)			
14B	32	1–8	4.91	6.35	.61			30	147	185
					(.086)					
					.39	.94	.41	95	4.13	136
					(.04)	(.024)	(.087)			
14G	29	0–8	3.97	7.03	.5			28	364	177
					(.093)					
					.31	.94	.3	94	10.7	125
					(.036)	(.029)	(.084)			

$$\hat{\Theta} = .14\ (.113),\ .32\ (.037),\ .94\ (.029),\ \hat{\Pi} = .04\ (.036),\ .67\ (.087),\ .29\ (.084)$$

Age, Sex	n	Range	$\bar{x}$	s^2	$\hat{\theta}_1$	$\hat{\theta}_2$	$\hat{\pi}_2$	VAF	χ^2	AIC
								94	10.6	129
15B	27	1–8	6.55	4.33	.82			27	3,627	125
					(.074)					
					.37	.93	.8	91	7.09	92.5
					(.074)	(.019)	(.077)			
15G	39	0–8	4.9	10.52	.61			18	960	310
					(.079)					
					.2	.97	.54	98	1.45	117
					(.033)	(.013)	(.08)			
16B	26	1–8	6.46	6.18	.81			20	1,308	147
					(.077)					
					.28	.97	.77	98	5.64	54.6
					(.064)	(.014)	(.083)			
16G	21	0–8	5.23	9.49	.65			19	1,095	156
					(.1)					
					.29	.99	.52	91	4.85	79.6
					(.051)	(.011)	(.109)			
11–16B&G ..	406	0–8	4.62	7.59	.58			57	3,534	2,621
					(.025)					
					.32	.94	.42	95	28.1	1,686
					(.011)	(.0006)	(.024)			

$$\hat{\Theta} = .24\ (.012),\ .57\ (.018),\ .97\ (.005),\ \hat{\Pi} = .41\ (.024),\ .23\ (.021),\ .36\ (.024)$$

| | | | | | | | | 100 | 2.1 | 1,666 |

NOTE.—Estimates $\hat{\theta}_1$ and $\hat{\theta}_2$ are item success rates for each component; $\hat{\pi}_2$ is the proportion of population in the better performing component; VAF is variance accounted for; AIC is Akaike's information criterion. Numbers in parentheses are estimated standard errors. χ^2 under binomial $df = 7$; with 2 components $df = 5$; with 3 components $df = 3$. For samples supporting 3 components, the estimates and their standard errors are given in vectors $\hat{\Theta}$ and $\hat{\Pi}$.

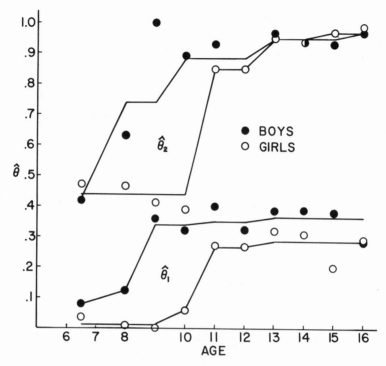

Fig. 11.—Van task estimates of θ_1 and θ_2 for boys and girls over age, Study 1. The curves are isotonic regressions for each parameter estimate for each sex.

ence was also observed in the water-level task, although not in the earlier (Thomas & Turner, 1991) study.

The estimates of θ_2 for the good performers show similar age changes. There are large sex differences between the isotonic regressions in the early years, but this difference is quite probably due to sampling error. From age 11 onward, the estimates of θ_2 for each sex are essentially constant at about .95, and the two estimates almost coincide at many ages from about 12 years on.

As expected, there are generally very large differences between the estimates of θ_1 and θ_2 at all ages, especially if one conditions on sex; starting at age 10 or 11, these differences are very large, about .6, and remain constant over age.

π_2.—The pattern of $\hat{\pi}_2$ over age (see Fig. 12) shows substantial variability in the earlier years; the isotonic regressions are not trustworthy at these younger ages because of the sample sizes, but the overall pattern of change resembles the findings from the water-level data.

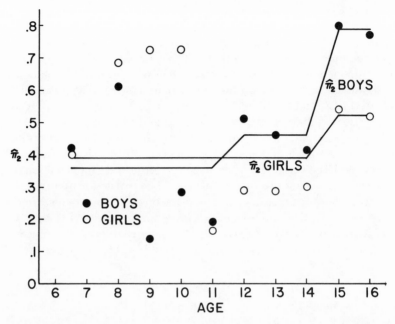

FIG. 12.—Van task estimates of π_2 for boys and girls over age, Study 1. The curves are isotonic regressions.

POOLING DATA AND PARTITIONING SUBJECTS INTO DISTINCT GROUPS

The data for all 11–16-year-olds ($n = 406$) were combined for purposes of further analyses under the same rationale as we detailed in Chapter IV. The histogram of these subjects' scores shown in Table 17 is clearly bimodal, and it resembles the corresponding distribution for the water-level task (cf. Table 9 above). The results of the mixture decomposition for the combined

TABLE 17

HISTOGRAM OF VAN TASK FREQUENCIES OF
11–16-YEAR-OLD SUBJECTS ($n = 406$), STUDY 1

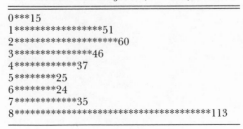

```
0***15
1****************51
2********************60
3***************46
4************37
5********25
6********24
7************35
8*************************************113
```

NOTE.—0***15 denotes 15 subjects with 0 correct.

group are given in the last entry in Table 16 above. The two-component model VAF is 95, and both AIC and χ^2 drop substantially relative to what they are for the binomial, but the $\chi^2(5) = 28.1$ is uncomfortably large. A three-component model accounts for all the variance in the data, but the third component accounts for just 5% of the variance, and this solution was very slow to converge. Thus, a two-component model was again adopted to guide decisions, and this model was used for partitioning the 11–16-year-old subjects into disjoint groups at each age and for both sexes.

The critical values used to partition subjects in the age groups younger than 10 years, shown in Table 18, might seem somewhat problematic because of the large variability in number correct needed for classification in the better performing group at some ages. The worst case occurs at age 9 years, where eight correct were needed for boys but only one correct was needed for girls; the reason for such large discrepancies is evident from the histograms in Table 15 above, which show striking sex differences.

However, the following analyses of possible rule strategies are little

TABLE 18

MINIMUM NUMBER OF CORRECT RESPONSES REQUIRED FOR CLASSIFICATION AS A GOOD PERFORMER IN COMPONENT 2 FOR EACH AGE AND SEX GROUP, VAN TASK, STUDY 1

Age/Sex	n	Criterion	$\hat{P}$(Comp. 2|Crit.)
6B	10	2	.96
G	5	1 component solution	...
7B	9	5	.59
G	15	2	.80
6&7B	19	2	.57
G	20	2	.67
8B	32	3	.71
G	26	1	.78
9B	14	8	1.0
G	21	1	1.0
10B	21	6	.81
G	12	2	.88
11B	24	7	.92
G	37	6	.89
12B	44	5	.59
G	39	5	.53
13B	46	7	.97
G	42	6	.60
14B	32	6	.61
G	29	6	.73
15B	27	6	.92
G	39	6	.96
16&17B	26	6	.91
G	21	7	.99
11–16B&G	406	6	.79

NOTE.—"Criterion" denotes number of correct responses needed for component 2 classification. In the case of a single component, the probability of being from it is 1.

influenced by such fluctuation because at most ages identical or very similar critical values were obtained for both sexes. Consequently, the critical values in Table 18 were used throughout for classification of individuals.

The observed frequencies of the 320 subjects (of 571) who were classified as poor performers at each age are given in the right-hand column of Table 19.

ASSESSING A PRECISE RULE:
PUT THE PLUMB LINE PARALLEL TO THE VAN'S END

One heuristic rule that poorly performing subjects might have used is to align the plumb line parallel to the van's end. To examine this possibility, the original data were rescored using the number correct transformation g_3 with r_j defined suitably for this rule. Thus, for each van angle, r_j was set in such a way that a correct response under this strategy was a line drawn parallel to the van's end, but allowing for a drawing variation of $c°$ (where c is taken from Table 5 above). The frequencies of the so-defined correct responses, shown in Table 19, indicate that substantial proportions of subjects aged 6–8 years obtained from six to eight correct responses under the end-parallel strategy, but consistency in responses is rare after this age. This finding suggests that this strategy was employed only by the youngest of subjects.

This speculation was confirmed when the marginal frequency distribu-

TABLE 19

FREQUENCY OF VAN END-PARALLEL RESPONSES AMONG POORLY PERFORMING
SUBJECTS AT EACH AGE, VAN TASK, STUDY 1

AGE	RESPONSE FREQUENCY									SUM
	0	1	2	3	4	5	6	7	8	
6	1	0	1	0	1	0	1	1	7	12
7	4	3	1	0	0	0	2	3	3	16
8	3	1	2	1	2	1	0	5	6	21
9	11	1	1	0	2	1	1	0	1	18
10	16	1	0	1	0	0	0	0	1	19
11	44	5	0	0	0	0	0	0	0	49
12	50	3	1	0	0	0	0	0	0	54
13	49	3	1	0	0	0	0	0	0	53
14	33	3	1	0	1	0	0	0	0	38
15	20	4	0	0	0	0	0	0	0	24
16&17	15	1	0	0	0	0	0	0	0	16
Sum	246	25	8	2	6	2	4	9	18	320

NOTE.—Cell entries are numbers of subjects. For example, among 11-year-old subjects, 5 made end-parallel responses 1 time among 8 van items.

tion (the bottom row of Table 19) was partitioned into two disjoint clusters. Like the corresponding bottom-parallel strategy of the water-level task (Table 11 above), it is a distribution with primary modes at zero and eight correct, but there also appears a third mode at four correct. This third mode presented fitting difficulties. Although a two-component mixture recorded a VAF of 95%, with scores of three or more correct suggesting membership in the better component (i.e., use of the end-parallel strategy), the $\chi^2(5) = 65.94$ is certainly uncomfortably large. A three-component distribution fit with $\chi^2(2) = 4.5$; the critical value for the best performing end-parallel responders was six or more correct.

Whether to use three or six correct as the criterion value is happily not important practically because only 10 subjects from among the entire poorly performing sample of 320 had from three to five correct (see Table 19). Taking either critical value, the results suggest that about 75% or more children respond with this strategy at age 6, and that about 50% use it at ages 7 and 8, but that essentially no child uses it beyond age 9. The problem, therefore, is to account for the performance of all older poor performers.

The range of possible simple rules to employ in responding to the van task appears sharply constrained. Although it might be thought that some subjects might use complicated rules, the large body of literature on cognitive heuristics (e.g., Tversky & Kahneman, 1974) argues against such a possibility—cognitive heuristics are simple, easy-to-employ principles.

As with the water-level task, we considered two main sources of influence as possibly mediating the behavior of poor performers: field dependent effects and the possibility that these subjects were behaving according to a random rule. The data for the 11–16-year-olds was used to evaluate these possibilities; first, however, we consider sex differences in van task performance shown by this age group.

SEX DIFFERENCES IN VAN TASK RESPONSE DISTRIBUTIONS

Of the 406 subjects aged 11–16, the 172 good performers consisted of 102 boys and 70 girls. There were 234 poor performers, 97 boys and 137 girls. Within each performance group, the response distribution of the boys was compared with that of the girls at each van angle. Testing for any differences in distributions (using the Kolmogorov-Smirnov test as before) revealed a significant sex difference, $\chi^2(2) = 7.68$, $p = .02$, for the van angle of 15° among the good performers and for van angles of $-15°$ and 60° among the poor performers, $\chi^2(2) = 6.16$ and 7.58, $p < .05$, and $p < .02$, respectively. Thus, there were three significant differences among 16 comparisons. As with the water-level task data, the findings suggest that, once subgroup performance differences on the van task are controlled, sex differences disappear.

ASSESSING FIELD DEPENDENT EFFECTS

Table 20 provides summary statistics for both performance groups, for the van at each angle. The data consist of the original signed response settings at each angle. Recall that a $-60°$ angle positioned the van pointing down on a hill sloping from the upper left to the lower right, that is, "negatively sloped."

For the subjects who performed poorly, the mean errors for each angle differ from a zero mean setting; using large sample theory, the minimum $|Z| = 4.26$, $P(|Z| \geq 4.26) < .001$, for all angles except for the van angles $-30°$, $45°$, and $60°$. For the good performers, the means of four vessel angles had $|Z| \geq 2$, while, for the angles $-45°$, $-30°$, $-15°$, and $15°$, the means were close to zero. Comparing the good and poor groups shows that, for van angles $-30°$, $45°$, and $60°$, the poor performers had significantly larger means, with $|Z|$ being 4 or more; the between-group differences on the other angles were not significant at conventional p levels.

Although taken overall these findings are similar to the water-level task, the data are different in two ways. First, there appears to be no pattern of mean differences that covaries with the van angle in a systematic way; second, the between-group mean differences are not as consistently significant.

TABLE 20

SUMMARY STATISTICS OF SIGNED ERROR RESPONSES OF 11–16-YEAR-OLD SUBJECTS ($n = 406$) FOR EACH VAN ANGLE, VAN TASK, STUDY 1

	VAN ANGLE							
	$-60°$	$-45°$	$-30°$	$-15°$	$15°$	$30°$	$45°$	$60°$
Good performers ($n = 172$):								
Mean	.58	$-.05$	.34	.05	$-.49$	-1.40	-2.20	-1.18
Median	0	0	.5	0	-1	-1	-2	-1
s	3.79	2.53	2.59	2.63	3.75	2.55	2.65	2.71
s^2	14.33	6.37	6.71	6.93	14.06	6.52	7.02	7.36
Range	$-7, 21$[a]	$-6, 10$[b]	$-11, 8$	$-8, 7$	$-13, 18$	$-8, 6$	$-11, 4$	$-8, 7$
Poor performers ($n = 234$):								
Mean	9.84	4.20	$-.43$	-3.96	11.10	5.78	$-.73$	-1.48
Median	12	5	-2	-3	11	7	-2	-2
s	18.37	14.95	14.61	14.53	12.67	13.66	14.66	16.63
s^2	337.5	223.6	213.6	211.1	160.4	186.6	215.0	276.6
Range	$-89, 80$	$-38, 86$	$-55, 80$	$-75, 48$	$-49, 71$	$-61, 58$	$-61, 49$	$-59, 81$

[a] An apparent outlier of -73 was deleted; if included, mean is .15, standard deviation is 6.76, median is 0.

[b] One score of 44 was deleted; if included, mean is .21, standard deviation is 4.19, and median is 0.

We think that the mechanisms governing individuals' responses to the van task and to the water-level task do not differ in any fundamental way; rather, it seems to us that two features of the former task distinguish it from the latter task. Unlike the water-level task, in which the vessel appears to be symmetrical about its vertical and horizontal axes (ignoring the vessel cap), the van was symmetrical about no axis. Thus, comparing responses for symmetrical van angles such as −30° and +30° is more problematic. The second difference is that the range of possible settings of the plumb line depends on the van angle (because the plumb line could not exceed the boundaries of the van). The water-level responses were not so curtailed. These two differences could well make the response distributions produced by the two tasks differ in some ways even though the factors influencing subject response and strategy may, as we suspect, be the same for both tasks.

We interpret the degree to which the mean angular settings differ from zero and the differences between the means of the two groups at each van angle as reflecting passive field-effect influences. However, as with the water-level task, there are very large between-group differences in the variances that need explanation. The variance for the poorly performing subjects ranges from 11 (at 15°) to as high as 37 (at 60°) times larger than that of the good performers. We think that these variance differences reflect differences in performance strategies of the good and poor groups.

RULES AND RESPONSE DISTRIBUTIONS

The between-group differences in variances are clearly a more dominant feature of the data than are the mean differences (see Table 20). Furthermore, the variances for the poor performers are related to the absolute van angle: the more inclined the van, the bigger the variance. The good performers show no such ordering of variances; indeed, their standard deviations are essentially constant over van angles and are very similar to those reported for the water-level task in Table 12 above. (The mean standard deviation is 2.9 and 3.45 for the van and water-level tasks, respectively.) Large variances among poorly performing subjects are consistent with the hypothesis that, within broad limits, subjects are producing responses in correspondence with a random rule.

If so, then poor performers' responses should favor no particular response setting over another, at least within a broad range of possible responses. In contrast, for good performers—those individuals who know the precise rule—a roughly symmetrical distribution of responses centered about zero would be expected, just as for the water-level task.

Figure 13 shows edf's of the original signed responses of the 172 good performers for each of the eight van angles. The figure is graphed in nor-

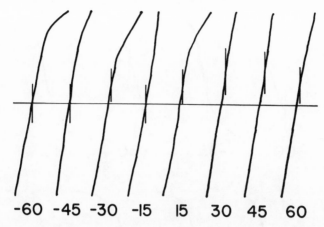

FIG. 13.—Edf's of van task subjects who perform well, aged 11–16, n = 172, Study 1. Each edf is for the responses at the specified orientation. Vertical bars are abscissa values of 0°. Horizontal line is the 50% point. The graphs are in normal-linear coordinates.

mal probability coordinates, and Figure 14 shows the corresponding responses of the 234 poor performers in linear-linear coordinates. The response distributions of the two performance groups are quite different for each van angle. Kolmogorov Smirnov $\chi^2(2)$ procedures applied to these data resulted in test statistics ranging from 37 to 170 with p values always smaller than .0001. This result simply confirms the hypothesis that the graphs in Figure 13 represent a different distribution or family of distributions than the graphs in Figure 14.

For the good performers, the graphs should be linear if a normal distribution is a suitable model. Indeed, the edf's in Figure 13 are in almost all cases generally linear in appearance, and, more critically, the response distributions tend to have mass concentrations in a small region near zero. For the poor performers, Figure 14 shows that, while some edf's appear to graph linear functions over broad regions, some plots appear quite nonlinear in form. These plots obviously do not demonstrate the same configural appearance as the corresponding graphs of the water-level data (see Fig. 9 above). In particular, the tails of these distributions are not as linear in appearance as was the case for some of the water-level edf's.

The same three models that were fit to the water-level data were applied here; the results are shown in Table 21. The mixture of uniforms did not fit well. The uniform distribution fit to each edf with 10% of the observations trimmed in each tail begins to provide a more satisfactory fit, although the χ^2 measures of fit are still too high. The normal distribution generally provides an unsatisfactory fit, although the normal model fit data for two van angles quite well.

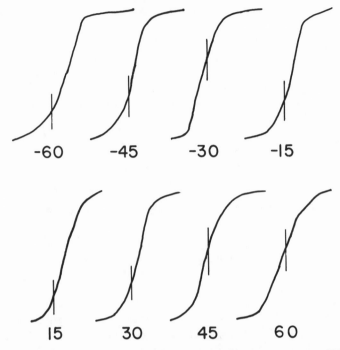

Fig. 14.—Edf's of van task subjects who perform poorly, aged 11–16, $n = 234$, Study 1. Each edf is for the responses at the angular orientation specified. Vertical bars are the abscissa values of 0°. The graphs are in linear-linear coordinates.

We suspect that the main reason why—in comparison to the corresponding results for the water-level data—the edf's differ in form for the poor performers but not the good performers is the difference that we noted above in the properties of the van and water-level stimuli.

CORRELATIONS AMONG RESPONSES AT DIFFERENT ANGLES

Table 22 provides the correlations among van angle responses for the good and poor performers. If the responses were independent from trial to trial, then the correlations would be expected to be zero.

Consider the good performers first. These correlations are generally small, averaging .15 and ranging from −.10 to .46, and their pattern is similar to that found for the water-level task (see Table 14 above). The variance of correlation coefficients under a zero correlation hypothesis is $1/(n - 1)$; for the good responders, eight of the 28 r values are outside a 3-standard-error band of .23, which is evidence against independence.

For the group of poor performers, the correlations averaged .02 and

TABLE 21

Fits of Uniform Mixture, Normal, and Uniform with 10% Tail
Trimming for Responses of Poorly Performing Subjects Aged 11–16
(n = 234), Van Task, Study 1

	χ² Fitted Values		
Van Angle	Uni. Mixture	Uniform	Normal
−60°	60.4	17.9	43.9 (7)
−45°	98.0	24.9	46.0 (4)
−30°	41.5	14.0	46.0 (4)
−15°	46.4	25.7	29.0 (6)
15°	37.9	11.0	11.2 (7)
30°	67.3	23.2	42.9 (9)
45°	73.2	17.2	49.3 (10)
60°	65.1	16.1	12.1 (10)

Note.—df = 8 for uniform mixture; df = 6 for trimmed uniform; df for the normal model vary because of a need to combine cell frequencies so that expected values are about 5 or more.

ranged from −.47 to .68. Most of the values are outside a 3-standard-error band, and there are clear patterns to the values that these correlations take on. Negative angles are always negatively correlated with positive angles, but, for van angles of common sign, the correlations are all positive. In addition, the correlations are highest among van angles that have similar orientations.

TABLE 22

Intercorrelations among Van Angle Responses for Good and Poor
Performance Groups, Ages 11–16, Study 1

Van Angles	Van Angles							
	−60°	−45°	−30°	−15°	15°	30°	45°	60°
−60°	. . .	.132	.118	.058	.217	.210	−.029	.067
−45°	.453	. . .	.167	.153	.023	.154	.115	.148
−30°	.259	.451	. . .	.332	−.092	.123	.251	.247
−15°	.173	.467	.307	. . .	−.161	.106	.109	.237
15°	−.271	−.277	−.342	−.287	. . .	.338	.099	.138
30°	−.188	−.475	−.243	−.287	.492	. . .	.341	.282
45°	−.339	−.398	−.344	−.185	.427	.614	. . .	.324
60°	−.200	−.263	−.303	−.033	.281	.397	.678	. . .

Note.—The upper triangle shows values for good performers (n = 172), the lower triangle for poor performers (n = 234). Means, standard deviations, and ranges of 28 r's are as follows: upper triangle, .15, .12, and from −.16 to .34; lower triangle, .02, .37, and from −.47 to .68, respectively.

These correlational patterns certainly reject any hypothesis of independence among response settings. However, the responses could be conditionally independent—that is, the response distribution might depend on the van's angle, but, once this has been determined, responses at this angle are independently selected. This hypothesis predicts that replicated responses within subjects at each fixed van angle should be uncorrelated. There is, however, no way of testing this hypothesis in these data because no replicated responses within subjects at each fixed van angle were obtained.

SUMMARY

In general, the results for the van task were very similar to the results for the water-level task. The data were again well fit by a two-component mixture; indeed, the data often fit better than for the water-level task data, and age and sex differences reported for the water-level task were similar for the van task. The assessment of response strategies based on the examination of the edf's of the original responses was not as clear cut for the van task as for the water-level task. We think, however, that there are no important differences between these two tasks in terms of subjects' strategies; rather, the source of between-task differences lies in the differences between the stimuli and possible responses to each. Unlike the water-level task, the van stimulus is asymmetrical about every axis, and the plumb line was restricted in movement, depending on the van angle, unlike the water line. These features probably caused the differences in response distributions that distinguish the van and the water-level tasks. In short, the analysis of the van task presented no surprises when compared with that of the water-level task.

VII. THE JOINT STRUCTURE
OF THE WATER-LEVEL AND VAN TASKS

Next, consider the interrelation between performance on the water-level and the van tasks. Such investigations are usually limited to considering task intercorrelations, without regard for what the joint parent distribution might actually be like. Our approach here is to model the joint distribution directly, on the basis of the observed bivariate frequency histogram. To do so requires substantial data, and thus the focus of attention is on the performance of the 399 individuals aged 11–16 years with complete data on both tasks. The data are pairs (x_i, y_i), $i = 1, \ldots, n = 399$, with X denoting the water-level task success scores and Y the van task success scores, so X and Y each range from 0 to 8. The immediate task is to model $f(x, y)$, the joint distribution of X and Y, on the basis of the 399 response pairs.

From the perspective of the joint model, the water-level and van task distributions considered separately are viewed as marginal distributions, $f(x)$ and $f(y)$. At least as a first approximation, we have regarded these distributions as two-component binomial mixture distributions.

Figure 15 depicts the joint frequency histogram for the 399 subjects, and Table 23 provides the corresponding cell frequencies for each of the 81 possible observed outcomes. Figure 15 is quite revealing: it is nowhere near the appearance of the joint bivariate normal distribution commonly pictured in textbooks, and this fact itself has important implications for data analysis and theory.

The form of this joint frequency distribution could have been anticipated, given the form of the van and water-level marginal distributions provided earlier in Tables 9 and 17. Examination of Figure 15 suggests that the joint structure is similar to what was suggested for the marginal distributions: there are primarily two different subgroups of individuals, one consisting of individuals who performed well on both tasks (the persons clustering in the upper-right-hand corner of Fig. 15) and the other (clustering in the lower-left-hand corner) of those individuals who performed poorly on both tasks. There also appear to be two smaller secondary groups

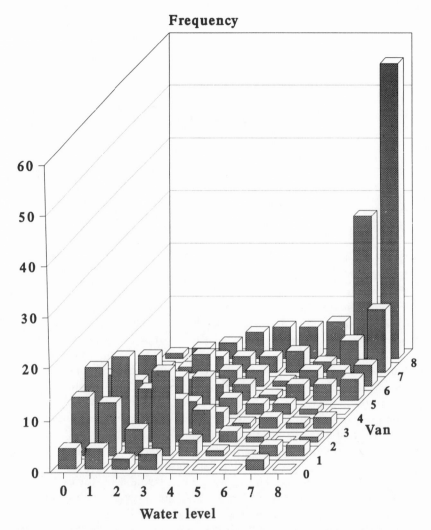

FIG. 15.—Joint distribution of van and water-level task responses, $n = 399$, Study 1

of individuals in the other two corners that reflect poor performance on one task and good performance on the other.

The correlation coefficient between the two tasks is $r = .67$. From a model perspective, one issue is to provide an interpretation for this r. The conventional interpretation of r, indeed, the only interpretation that is ever taught in standard statistical courses (see, e.g., Moore & McCabe, 1993), is motivated by the structure underlying the bivariate normal distribution.

What Figure 15 clearly indicates is that bivariate normality fails. Thus,

TABLE 23

Joint Frequency Distribution of Van and Water-Level Task Responses,
Ages 11–16, Study 1

	OUTCOME: WATER LEVEL								
OUTCOME: VAN	0	1	2	3	4	5	6	7	8
8	1	2	3	5	6	6	7	27	56
7	1	1	3	3	3	4	2	6	12
6	0	1	6	3	3	1	3	3	4
5	3	1	4	3	3	1	3	3	4
4	4	11	7	7	3	2	2	1	0
3	10	9	9	5	3	1	2	1	2
2	14	16	10	8	6	2	1	0	1
1	11	10	5	16	3	1	0	2	2
0	4	4	2	3	0	0	0	2	0

the conventional linear homoskedastic interpretation of r is inappropriate in this case. This fact does not mean, however, that there is no sensible interpretation of r. Just as any sample statistic may have a myriad of interpretations under different models, we provide a very different interpretation of this correlation coefficient that flows from the bivariate binomial mixture model that we develop below.

MODELS FOR THE JOINT DISTRIBUTION

We propose two different models; although the first of these is a special case of the second, it will be treated as a separate model. The models are presented here somewhat informally; the technical details appear in Appendix A.

Both models imply two-component binomial marginal mixture distributions, so both conform with the univariate models that we proposed in earlier chapters. Importantly, both models share a feature called "local independence" that states that performance on the water-level task is independent of performance on the van task when focus is restricted to a particular latent class subgroup of the data. Thus, both models specify that, if the focus is restricted to individuals within a componential cluster (e.g., a component with individuals who perform poorly on both tasks), then, for individuals within that subgroup, performance on one task is independent of performance on the other. This assumption implies that the within-component between-task correlation should be zero. At first glance, such an assumption might seem unreasonable since our conventional assumption is that performance on two tasks should be intercorrelated—particularly for two tasks that seem similar—for almost any group or subgroup of individuals. However, to anticipate the results below, there is both empirical and conceptual justification for the assumption here and in other work (Brainerd & Reyna, 1992; Reyna & Brainerd, 1990). Later, in Chapter X, the general issue of independence is discussed in more detail.

Of course, performance on the van task and performance on the water-level task are in fact correlated, but, under the model proposed, this correlation comes about because different subgroups of individuals are considered together in the overall correlation, not because of within-individual task correlation.

Model 1

This model states that individuals in the poorly performing water-level group are also in the poorly performing van group and that the same holds for the good performers on both tasks. Under this model, a person cannot do well on one task and poorly on the other. Formally, this model specifies that the joint distribution of X and Y is

$$f(x, y) = \sum_{r=1}^{2} \pi_r b(x; \theta_{xr}, m) b(y; \theta_{yr}, m). \tag{14}$$

The local independence condition is reflected in the fact that the two additive terms on the right-hand side of Equation (14) are each products of binomial distributions. This structure is precisely what "local independence" means.

θ_{xr} and θ_{yr} denote the success probabilities for X (water) and Y (van) variables. Under Model 1, the joint mixing weights (the π_r) are also the mixing weights for both marginal distributions: this fact can be made immediately clear simply by summing out one of the variables in $f(x, y)$, leaving the marginal distribution of the other.

A data implication of the model is that the mixing weight estimates, estimated separately for each marginal distribution and denoted $\hat{\pi}_{xr}$ and $\hat{\pi}_{yr}$, should be about the same. In fact, they are very similar—$\hat{\pi}_{x1} = .617$, and $\hat{\pi}_{y1} = .576$—differing by about .04. These estimates differ trivially from the estimates given in Tables 7 and 16 above for the two-component water-level and van task solutions because 399 subjects were used in the present analysis and 405 and 406 subjects, respectively, were used in the separate water-level and van task analyses.

Estimation and fitting of this model is straightforward. The θ estimates obtained from the marginal analyses are used; the only difference is that there are two common π weights. The average of the marginal estimates $\hat{\pi}_{x1}$ and $\hat{\pi}_{y1}$, which is .596, could be used as an estimate of the common π_1;

the maximum likelihood estimate of $\hat{\pi}_1 = .609$, trivially better, was used here.

Figure 16 shows the picture of the fitted model. The extent to which this picture agrees with that of the data shown in Figure 15 gives a first impression of model plausibility. The model clearly captures the main features of the data, but it is also clear that there are some troublesome model inadequacies. For example, the within-component variability on both tasks appears too small; there is insufficient "squashing" of the probability mass into the upper-left-hand and lower-right-hand portions of the outcome space.

Measured by the ordinary goodness-of-fit Pearson χ^2, the model is not satisfactory. Fitting 81 cells and estimating six parameters gives a $\chi^2(74) = 13,277$. This test value cannot be plausibly referenced to a table, huge though it may be, because of the large number of cells with very small expected values. Grouping together cells with expected frequencies less than five reduces 81 cells to 24; the result is that $\chi^2(17) = 171.12$, which, while relatively better, is still not satisfactory with $p < .001$.

Model 2 (Gediga's Model)

Model 2 has four components.[23] Each component is the product of two binomial distributions; two of these components are the same as those of Model 1. Each of the remaining two components represents good performance on one task and poor performance on the other; thus, these two additional components are designed to "pick up" the observations in the lower right and upper left of Figure 15 above, observations that are inadmissible (or at least highly improbable) under Model 1.

The second main difference between the two models is that Model 2 has two transition parameters. One of them, α, is the probability of going from the poor water-level component to the poor van component, and the second one is β. $1 - \beta$ is the probability of being in both the good water-level and the good van components. If $\alpha = 1 = 1 - \beta$, then Model 2 becomes Model 1.

There are eight parameters in Model 2 but seven independent parameters to estimate, so Model 2 has only two more parameters than Model 1. The parameter estimates based on the data shown in Figure 15 are as follows:[24] $\hat{\pi}_{x1} = .62$, and thus $.38 = 1 - \hat{\pi}_{x1} = \hat{\pi}_{x2}$; $\hat{\theta}_{x1} = .25$; $\hat{\theta}_{x2} = .91$; $\hat{\pi}_{y1} =$

[23] We sincerely thank Guenther Gediga of the University of Osnabrueck, Osnabrueck, Germany, for suggesting this model. He also provided some analysis of the model and thus part of App. A. The expression for Model 2 is given by $f(x, y)$ in App. A.

[24] The subscripts $x1$ and $y1$ denote the poor and $x2$ and $y2$ the good performance water-level and van components, respectively.

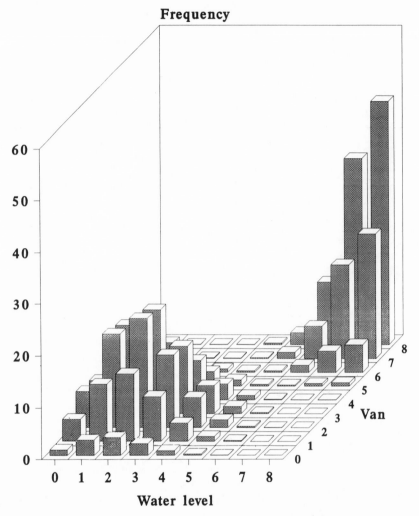

Fig. 16.—Fitted Model 1 of two-component bivariate binomial mixture for the data depicted in Fig. 15.

.58; $\hat{\pi}_{y2} = .42$; $\hat{\theta}_{y1} = .32$; and $\hat{\theta}_{y2} = .94$. The θ estimates are the same as in Model 1. Since $\hat{\alpha} = .85$, most individuals who were poor performers on the water-level task remained so on the van task, and the same held for good performers because $1 - \hat{\beta} = .87$.

Figure 17 pictures the fitted Model 2. It resembles Model 1 (cf. Fig. 16), but it appears to fit the data in Figure 15 much more satisfactorily. There is greater variability within each component than in Model 1, and that model feature allows the model to provide a better fit to the data. It is

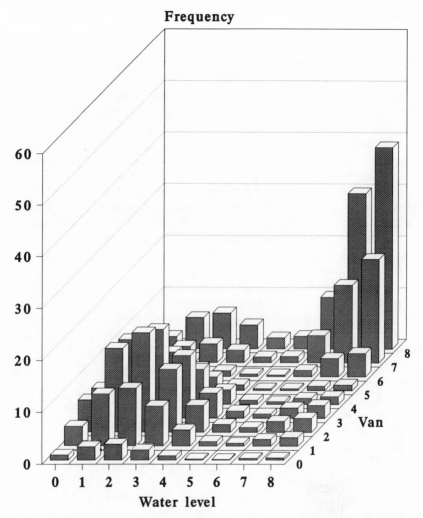

Fig. 17.—Fitted Model 2 (Gediga's model) of four-component bivariate binomial mixture for the data depicted in Fig. 15.

also evident where the model does not fit well. For example, it puts too much probability mass in the upper-left-hand portion of the probability distribution than there should be when compared with the data.

The fitted $\chi^2(73) = 217.65$, based on 81 cells and seven parameters. When cells with expected values of five or less were combined, $\chi^2(16) = 80.92$, $p < .001$, so the model is rejected at conventional significance levels. However, in overall features, it does appear to capture the main features of the data with reasonable fidelity.

Under either Model 1 or Model 2, the *within-component* correlation should be zero; this implication is simply a consequence of the local independence assumption. However, the overall (unconditional) model correlation is not zero. That correlation—obtained in a straightforward manner by computing the model correlation of X and Y using $f(x, y)$ for Model 2—depends on the various model parameters such as the component means and their weights; this model correlation may be given explicitly.[25] Once the model parameters have been estimated, these estimates may be inserted into the model, replacing the model parameters, and an estimated model correlation may be given. If the model is reasonable, there should be a close correspondence between this estimated model correlation and the ordinary Pearson correlation computed from data. In fact, the estimated model correlation is .67 and thus in precise correspondence with the $r = .67$ from the data (the corresponding Model 1 correlation is .84 and is too large).

To assess the within-component correlation, the 399 individuals were allocated, under Model 2, to the component with the highest (posterior) probability of membership (see App. A). The regions of each component and their boundaries are given in Figure 18. Figure 18 also shows the number of observations allocated by the assignment rule to each component and the within-component correlation coefficient r. This correlation is simply the Pearson sample correlation coefficient computed on the data for all individuals within each cluster. For example, in region d (Fig. 18), there are $n = 16$ individuals with van scores from 0 to 4 who have water-level task scores from 6 to 8. The within-cluster $r = -.36$.

The within-cluster r values range from $-.36$ to .17 and average .01. Only the $r = .17$, obtained for the 214 individuals classified as poor performers on both tasks, reveals a value that falls outside a 2-standard-deviation confidence interval under the hypothesis that the correlation should be zero.[26] However, the fact that the two largest clusters had the

---

[25] The model correlation is given in App. A, but it is not intuitively friendly. However, the model correlation for a special case of Model 1 is given explicitly in Chap. X when model assumptions are discussed.

[26] The issue of restriction of range has sometimes been raised as a potentially relevant factor for understanding the reduction of the overall correlation when within-cluster correlations are considered. However, this perspective is not appropriate here. While it is often true that restricting the range of scores on one or both variables typically results in a drop in the correlation coefficient (under some population models, sample correlations will typically rise), the issue of range restriction is meaningful to consider only within the context of the larger question, What is it desired to estimate? Consider the bivariate normal model, with truncation from below on the predictor variable so that scores below some truncation point are not observed; for example, selective schools may reject applicants with scores below some cutting point. This is equivalent to truncating the distribution of the predictor variable at the cutting point. This is the classic truncation or range restriction problem: owing to truncation, the sampled population is not bivariate normal;

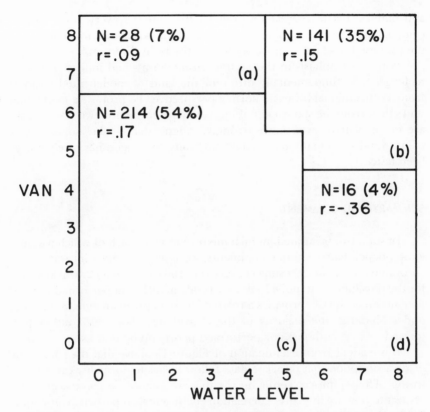

Fig. 18.—Component space and assignment of 399 subjects of Fig. 15 based on fitted Model 2 for data depicted in Fig. 17. Cells represent subjects who perform (a) poorly on the water-level task and well on the van task, (b) well on both tasks, (c) poorly on both tasks, and (d) well on the water-level task and poorly on the van task.

most positive r values (.17 and .15) suggests that the model is not quite correct. That, of course, we already know from the value of the fitted χ^2!

While the model does not fit as well as would be desired, the preceding analysis suggests that the model is a very reasonable first approximation because of (a) the good correspondence of the data with the model in Figures 15 and 17 above, (b) the coincidence of the estimated model correlation

---

there is range restriction, owing to truncation, of the predictor variable. A natural quantity to want to estimate, however, is the bivariate normal correlation coefficient (the population correlation if truncation had not occurred). In this situation, corrections of the sample estimates may be employed (e.g., Thomas, 1989). This situation is not the setting for our model; there is no truncation, and there is no restriction on the range of possible outcomes. Another way to view our problem is to ask the question, What would be the correlation within one latent class if there were no comingling of observations from other latent classes?

and empirical data correlation, and (c) the generally very small within-component correlations. These empirical findings coalesce to suggest that the proposed model is at least pointed in the right direction.

With the emphasis in this section on model fits and indices, it is easy to forget how fundamentally different the kind of model fitted really is from a conventional bivariate normal perspective. To propose a model that states that, from the standpoint of individual performance, two similar tasks are uncorrelated—even more strongly, independent—takes some adjustment. But, like so many research assumptions, the notion has rarely if ever been tested.

SUMMARY AND COMMENT

In sum, two bivariate binomial mixture models, each of which assumes local independence within components, were fitted to the joint water-level and van data for the 399 subjects aged 11–16 years. Model 2, which allows for the possibility that individuals may reside in different performance components on each task, provides a reasonable first approximation to the data; under Model 2, the majority of the individuals, about 90%, either performed well on both tasks or performed poorly on both tasks.

It is evident from examination of Figure 15 above that the commonly made assumption that bivariate data follow bivariate normality can be very wrong. This empirical result means that we cannot be complacent with respect to how we interpret correlation coefficients. In particular, for some tasks, the obtained correlations should be viewed as reflecting different latent groups of subjects. Within each latent group there may be a small between-task correlation, but the major contribution to the overall correlation coefficient is primarily a reflection of the different subgroups and how these subgroups are separated from each other. This interpretation is very much in agreement with the observed data: that the data are multimodal hardly needs a statistical test, as Figure 15 reveals. The overall correlation was .67, but, within each subgroup, the correlations ranged from −.36 to .17.

We note that this perspective on correlation represents a sharp departure from the conventional perspective on how correlations should be viewed, but we challenge the reader to propose an alternative model that accounts as well for the empirical facts.

The implications of these findings for alternative theoretical perspectives is very unsettling, but their impact is not entirely clear at this time. The body of literature concerned with spatial abilities and their development has largely been premised on some very old but standard assumptions about the population structures from which samples are taken. Hypotheses and theory have been constructed largely without questioning these assumptions that are at the very foundations of research. For example, Halpern (1986) notes that, for spatial abilities, two separate factors have emerged from factor analyses, a visualization factor and an orientation factor. However, these results assume that a parent bivariate normal family was the source of the data, not a latent class structure. Consequently, if the present argument is accepted, one is in the very difficult position of trying to assess how these findings would be altered if long-held underlying assumptions are importantly false, and that can be very difficult to do.

It is certainly true that the data base for Study 1 is very restrictive in *task* focus, and it remains possible that the latent structure revealed here will not be replicated for certain other tasks. This seems highly unlikely, however, and, as will be noted in Chapter X, the latent class structure of a number of other spatial tasks is emerging.

As will also be expanded on later, it might be conjectured that there is something special about our procedure and our particular model structure that leads us to our results. Admittedly, the models outlined in this chapter are hardly standard and familiar! In Chapter X, a very general result is provided that says that the structure observed in the count data approach is also the structure underlying the original untransformed observations (at least from a univariate marginal perspective). Thus, the findings that we report are not simply indigenous to our methodology.

VIII. STUDY 2:
REPLICATION AND EXTENSION
TO THE REALM OF VERBAL ACTIVITIES

Study 2 had two main goals. The first was to continue exploring the relation between performance on the water-level and the van tasks as well as to investigate the relation of each task to performance on a conceptually quite different verbal analogies task.

Tasks termed "spatial tasks," such as the water-level task, have often been regarded as being special, but in what way are they special? In all other studies of which we are aware, it has been assumed that the joint structure of spatial tasks with other spatial as well as nonspatial tasks is (approximately at least) jointly normal (e.g., Linn & Petersen, 1985). Consequently, the difference between spatial tasks and nonspatial tasks (however such a distinction might be formally defined) has been in terms of the parameter values of the model of focus (e.g., multivariate normality), not in terms of different *families* of models (bivariate mixtures of any form cannot be bivariate normal). Consequently, we wished to study (for the first time, we think) the bivariate structure of the relation involving a high-level verbal task—for which there is no evidence of a mixture structure—and a spatial task for which there is now strong evidence of a mixture structure.

There were other reasons as well for selecting this particular verbal task as opposed to some other verbal tasks: the analogies test assesses the ability to build logical relations and is included in the most widely used German intelligence test, the *Intelligenz-Struktur-Test* (Amthauer, 1973). Among the subtests in this test, the analogies test correlates most highly with the total score of the whole test ($r = .72$); furthermore, the analogies test is highly loaded on the Spearman general factor (Guthke, 1977). Consequently, the test is much richer in verbal reasoning and abstraction than many other word knowledge or vocabulary tests are likely to be. Thus, it appeared to be an excellent test for exploring the bivariate structure of spatial and verbal reasoning tasks.

Although it is perhaps obvious, it should be noted that the verbal analogies task is not suitably modeled by a binomial-based distribution. One clear reason is that the items are ordered and vary greatly in difficulty, unlike in the water-level and van tasks.

The second goal (to which the next chapter is devoted) was to explore the relation between performance on the two spatial tasks and verbally expressed responses (statements) concerning the correct principle in each task. This issue falls within the province of the debate termed "explanations versus judgments" (Brainerd, 1973) and concerns whether subjects' task judgments or their explanations of what lies behind those judgments should be the primary criterion for assessing cognitive competence. In work involving the water-level task, there have been a number of investigations concerned with task performance and verbal explanations, and all concur in finding an association between the two (e.g., Kalichman, 1989; Liben & Golbeck, 1984; McAfee & Proffitt, 1991; Myer & Hensley, 1984; Thomas & Jamison, 1975; Thomas et al., 1973). However, this conclusion is but a very weak statement, and there has been little attempt to provide more than measures of association between different performance measures.

Our interest in verbal responses focuses on two issues. One of these is whether verbal task knowledge precedes or lags behind task performance. We shall develop a simple model that shows how this question may be answered on the basis of certain data relations in cross-classification tables. The second issue concerns the role that sex may play in the relation between verbalizations and task performance.

A third source of motivation for Study 2 was to explore a computer-based procedure for individual data collection. Although considerably more labor intensive than the group procedure used in Study 1, this method is not susceptible to the kinds of difficulties that can occur in group data collection settings, and, in addition, it eliminates the possibility of scoring errors.

METHODS AND PROCEDURES

Subjects

The ages and sexes of the subjects are given in Table 24; in terms of samples sizes, the useful range is from about 9 through 16 years. A few of the youngest children attended an elementary school, but most came from a single large junior high school. Both schools were located in Muenster, Germany. Other recruitment procedures followed those used in Study 1.

TABLE 24

NUMBER OF SUBJECTS IN TOTAL SAMPLE, STUDY 2

Age	Boys	Girls	Total	Age	Boys	Girls	Total
7	0	3	3	14	18	5	23
8	1	4	5	15	9	10	19
9	10	7	17	16	16	11	27
10	6	9	15	17	5	1	6
11	8	7	15				
12	12	9	21	Total	98	83	181
13	13	17	30				

Procedure

All data were collected by computer; children responded via the keyboard to displays of information presented on the computer's monitor. Task procedures were introduced to the children by a trained university research assistant or by one of the authors (H.T.); each child remained seated next to an assistant throughout the data collection period.

After obtaining demographic information (which included age and sex), each subject responded to the items of the water-level task, the van task, and a verbal analogies test (always presented in that order). After completing the tasks, the child was asked, "What is the principle or idea about where the water goes in the bottle?" A corresponding question was asked for the van task. Responses were recorded verbatim and keyboard entered by the adult assistant.

The Water-Level Task

This task was a computer-adapted version of the psychophysical apparatus used in several early studies (Geiringer & Hyde, 1976; Signorella & Jamison, 1978; Thomas & Jamison, 1975; Thomas et al., 1973; Willemsen & Reynolds, 1973). A line-drawn vessel, identical to that depicted in Figure 2 above, appeared on the monitor. Its size varied somewhat with the monitor's screen size, but typically it was about as large as its 6 × 10-cm size in Study 1. The water surface appeared as a straight line, positioned randomly, but always 10° or more in error. The line always passed through the geometric center of the vessel and thus, if positioned correctly, would appear as a vessel half filled with liquid. The research assistant described the task using standard instructions. The child was told that the vessel contained a beverage and that the line represented the surface of the beverage. She was shown how the water line could be rotated to any orientation by pressing keys on the computer's keyboard and told that her task was to adjust the line to its correct position for the given vessel displayed on the monitor. When the child was satisfied with her response, she pressed another key. This action caused the next item to be presented and in addition recorded the child's response to the previous item.

Four keys controlled the movement of the water line, which could be moved clockwise or counterclockwise and in either fast or slow increments of rotational movement. "Fast" moved the water line in 5° increments with each key press, "slow" in increments of 1°. The four control keys were color coded and marked. The procedure was found to be easily mastered by children of all ages in a few moments.

The first water-level item was the vessel in its upright position. This was a sample item on which the child was encouraged to learn how the keys that controlled the movement of the water line worked. The remaining items were vessel angles in clock-hour orientations of 1, 2, 4, 5, 7, 8, and 11 o'clock. For each child, the order of item presentation was independently and randomly determined. Note that there were seven tilted vessel angles rather than eight as in Study 1: because we were concerned that data collection might not be completed in the time available for testing each child, the water-level task was shortened by one item. There was no time limitation for completing the task; typically, it took the child from 5 to 8 min.

The Van Task

The picture of the van as it appears in Figure 3 above was reproduced on the monitor. The plumb line hung at a randomly chosen incorrect angle, never closer to the correct vertical position than 10° in error. As in the water-level task, four keys controlled pendulum-like movements of the plumb line either clockwise or counterclockwise and in fast (5°) or slow (1°) movements. The child adjusted the plumb line until it was oriented in the position that he thought would be correct for the van parked at the angle displayed, then pressed a key, which recorded his response; the next van item was then displayed. There were eight test items representing the same angles as in Study 1; an additional initial "sample" item showed the van in its normal position on a level road and served as a familiarization trial for the child. The van item presentation sequence was determined randomly for each child.

Analogies Test

This task was adapted from a German version patterned after the Lorge-Thorndike (1964). In the original version, intended for use as a paper and pencil test, there are 56 items grouped into 10 subtests. Items within subtests are ordered in terms of difficulty, as are the subtests themselves, the last items of one subtest corresponding to the first items of the next, more difficult subtest. Normally, only a portion of the items contained in a subtest are administered to the children. Because we wanted a single test that could be used for subjects of all ages, we constructed a single list of items increasing in difficulty by selecting the sequence of two-included/two-omitted items (i.e., the items selected were items 1, 2, 5, 6, 9, 10, 13, 14, . . . , 53, 54). Thus, the list contained 28 items presented in the same increasing order of difficulty. The following fictitious item (very similar to an item actually used) illustrates the test format for all items and the level of difficulty of an easy item:

Glove : Hand ⟶ Shoe : _____
(1) Milk   (2) Foot   (3) Body   (4) Laces   (5) Walk

Each item had five alternatives; children pressed key numbers 1–5 to indicate their selection.

The items spanned a wide range of maturity and/or ability levels. In pilot testing with university students, the last test items were perceived as difficult. To minimize frustration caused by presenting items that were well beyond the children's ability levels, the children were told that some items were intended for much older people and that they would have 7 min to complete the task. In addition, the task terminated after six consecutive wrong responses. The children were not told the correct answer to any item, nor were they told that the test would self-terminate.

Preceding the analogies test, each subject was given three pretest items from which to learn the nature of the task. After the child responded to each of these items, the monitor displayed the correct answer. If this answer differed from the child's answer, the child was told to select the correct alternative; for the younger children, additional clarification by the research assistants was sometimes needed. For the test items that followed, children selected their response alternative without subsequent feedback. The program prompted the child to confirm that the alternative that she selected was the desired one; if it was not, a different choice could be made at that point. After the key confirming the selection was pressed and the child's response recorded, the next item was displayed.

When either termination criterion was reached, and after the current item (or task) was completed, the program moved to the final portion of the procedure in which the child answered questions concerning the water-level and plumb line principles.

Most children seemed motivated and interested in all three tasks, perhaps in part because they offered a novel activity within the school setting, and possibly because, as some children remarked, the tasks resembled video games; in addition of course, it was a break from the conventional school routine. The data for each child were collected within a single session that usually lasted about 25 min.

RESULTS

We first report results relevant to replication of the main findings of Study 1 by briefly describing the corresponding analyses performed on the current data set.

Comparison with the Findings of Study 1

The Water-Level Task

Although the water line could be adjusted so as to be exactly horizontal and thus 0° in error (just as with the psychophysical apparatus used in early studies, e.g., Thomas & Jamison, 1975), many subjects appeared to be satisfied that their response was "good enough" when it was slightly in error; indeed, a number of them spontaneously mentioned that the water line or plumb line was "close enough" when it was a few degrees off. Consequently, the Study 1 criterion values given in Table 5 above were used, via transform g_3 (the number correct transformation of Eq. [3]), to define each response as correct or incorrect.

Table 25 provides back-to-back histograms of the data for each sex. Some ages are combined within sex because of the small sample sizes available for the yearly age points. As expected, these histograms resemble the corresponding histograms of Study 1. Table 26 provides the results of the binomial mixture analysis. Again, these results are quite similar to the results of Study 1 that were shown in Table 7 above. At most of the ages, and for both boys and girls, the two-component binomial mixture distribution fits the data well; in all cases save one, the VAF was 90% or more. At ages for which the χ^2 values exceeded 10, a three-component model was fitted. This model fits better, of course, yielding smaller χ^2 values, but, as indexed by VAF, fit improvement was never more than 10%, indicating relatively small improvements in the fit of the model to the data.

Table 26 provides estimates of the parameters π and θ. Here, again, both the patterns and the magnitudes of these estimates resemble the corresponding estimates from Study 1.

TABLE 25

HISTOGRAMS OF WATER-LEVEL TASK DATA OBTAINED AT
EACH AGE ($n = 181$), STUDY 2

Boys		Girls	Boys		Girls
Age 7 & 8			*Age 9 & 10*		
	0	******.86	.25****	0	*********.56
1.0*	1	*.14	.06*	1	**.13
	2		.19***	2	**.13
	3			3	
	4		.13**	4	*.06
	5			5	
	6		.13**	6	*.06
	7		.25****	7	*.06
$n = 1$		$n = 7$	$n = 16$		$n = 16$
Age 11 & 12			*Age 13 & 14*		
.20****	0	*******.44	.16*****	0	*******.32
.25*****	1	****.25	.10***	1	**.09
.15***	2	*.06	.13****	2	*****.23
.05*	3		.06**	3	**.09
.10**	4	**.13	.10***	4	
.10**	5		.19******	5	**.09
.10**	6	**.13	.03*	6	**.09
.07*	7		.23*******	7	**.09
$n = 20$		$n = 16$	$n = 31$		$n = 22$
Age 15–17					
.17*****	0	*******.32			
	1				
.03*	2	***.14			
.07**	3	*.05			
.03*	4	*.05			
.03*	5	*.05			
.13****	6	**.09			
.53**************	7	*******.32			
$n = 30$		$n = 22$			

NOTE.—.10*** 1 *****.23 denotes that 10% of the boys and 23% of the girls have 1 response correct; each * denotes 1 individual.

The Van Task

Histograms for the van data—scored using the same criteria as in Study 1—are shown in Table 27; as before, the data for adjacent ages were combined because of small sample sizes. These histograms again closely resemble the histograms of Study 1 (see Table 15 above). The corresponding binomial mixture analyses appear in Table 28 (for comparable Study 1 results, see Table 16 above). Two-component mixtures described each age

TABLE 26

Binomial Mixture Model Estimates
at Ages 9–16 for the Water-Level Task, Study 2

Age, Sex	n	Range	$\bar{x}$	s^2	$\hat{\theta}_1$	$\hat{\theta}_2$	$\hat{\pi}_2$	VAF	χ^2	AIC
9–10B	16	0–7	3.44	8.26	.49			21	252.5	113
					(.125)					
					.15	.87	.47	84	12.06	71.6
					(.046)	(.046)	(.12)			
$\hat{\Theta}$ = .002 (.008), .34 (.072), .95 (.034), $\hat{\Pi}$ = .23 (.106), .39 (.122), .37 (.12)										
								94	4.36	70.5
9–10G	16	0–7	1.43	5.20	.20			22	4,221	84.8
					(.10)					
					.07	.81	.19	90	5.14	55
					(.026)	(.086)	(.098)			
11–12B	20	0–7	2.7	6.12	.38			27	189.5	116.8
					(.109)					
					.16	.81	.35	94	.28	84
					(.038)	(.056)	(.106)			
11–12G	16	0–6	1.62	4.65	.23			27	309	79.7
					(.106)					
					.07	.70	.26	96	4.32	54.8
					(.028)	(.085)	(.109)			
13–14B	31	0–7	3.68	6.49	.53			27	279	190.3
					(.09)					
					.17	.81	.56	90	9.75	138.8
					(.039)	(.036)	(.089)			
13–14G	22	0–7	2.45	6.07	.35			26	333.5	129.1
					(.102)					
					.16	.85	.28	92	6.15	92.3
					(.035)	(.055)	(.095)			
15–16B	30	0–7	5.1	7.27	.73			19	7,732	198.5
					(.081)					
					.18	.96	.71	91	12.16	104.5
					(.049)	(.017)	(.083)			
$\hat{\Theta}$ = 0 (0), .49 (.085), .97 (.015), $\hat{\Pi}$ = .16 (.068), .16 (.068), .67 (.086)										
								97	.69	102.4
15–16G	22	0–7	3.59	9.21	.51			19	565	169
					(.106)					
					.13	.92	.48	90	10.95	91.9
					(.038)	(.032)	(.106)			
$\hat{\Theta}$ = 0 (0), .41 (.076), .96 (.025), $\hat{\Pi}$ = .31 (.99), .27 (.094), .42 (.11)										
11–16B&G	141	0–7	3.4	7.28	.49			22	2,123	974.1
					(.042)					
					.15	.87	.47	94	30.6	568.6
					(.015)	(.015)	(.042)			
$\hat{\Theta}$ = .03 (.01), .37 (.027), .92 (.013), $\hat{\Pi}$ = .03 (.038), .31 (.039), .39 (.041)										
								98	7.81	561.5

Note.—Numbers in parentheses are estimated standard errors. χ^2 under binomial df = 7; with 2 components df = 5; with 3 components df = 3. For samples supporting 3 components, the estimates and their standard errors are given in vectors $\hat{\Theta}$ and $\hat{\Pi}$.

TABLE 27

VAN HISTOGRAMS AT EACH AGE ($n = 181$), STUDY 2

Boys		Girls	Boys		Girls
Age 7 & 8			*Age 9 & 10*		
	0		.19***	0	***.19
1.0*	1	**.29	.06*	1	*****.31
	2	***.43	.13**	2	
	3	*.14	.25****	3	*****.31
	4	*.14	.06*	4	
	5		.06*	5	
	6			6	
	7		.06*	7	*.06
	8		.18***	8	**.13
$n = 1$		$n = 7$	$n = 16$		$n = 16$
Age 11 & 12			*Age 13 & 14*		
.2****	0	****.25	.19******	0	*****.23
.10**	1	****.25	.13****	1	***.14
.2****	2	***.19	.10***	2	**.09
.05*	3	****.25	.10***	3	*****.23
.2****	4		.03*	4	****.19
.10**	5		.03*	5	*.05
.05*	6		.03*	6	
.05*	7		.06**	7	*.05
.05*	8	*.06	.32**********	8	*.05
$n = 20$		$n = 16$	$n = 31$		$n = 22$
Age 15–17					
.17*****	0	***.14			
.07**	1	*****.23			
.07**	2	**.09			
.03*	3	***.14			
.03*	4	*.05			
.10***	5	*.05			
.03*	6	*.05			
.03*	7	*.05			
.47**************	8	*****.23			
$n = 30$		$n = 22$			

NOTE.—.19*** 1 ***.19 denotes that 19% of the boys and 19% of the girls have 1 response correct; each * denotes 1 individual.

and sex group reasonably well; VAF was always 85% or higher. There were three age groups for which the χ^2 fitted values exceeded 10; for these groups, three-component solutions are given. Although the three-component model fits better, our previously noted penchant is to select the simpler, two-component model, as being a reasonable model at all ages. Confirming our expectations, the parameter estimates for π and θ given in Table 28 are similar to those reported in Table 16.

TABLE 28

Binomial Mixture Model Estimates at Ages 9–16 for the Van Task, Study 2

Age, Sex	n	Range	$\bar{x}$	s^2	$\hat{\theta}_1$	$\hat{\theta}_2$	$\hat{\pi}_2$	VAF	χ^2	AIC
9–10B	16	0–8	3.56	8.26	.44			24	421.7	107.5
					(.124)					
					.27	.97	.25	86	8.14	74.6
					(.045)	(.031)	(.108)			
9–10G	16	0–8	2.69	7.43	.33			24	1,580	100.2
					(.118)					
					.19	.96	.19	91	10.66	66.4
					(.039)	(.041)	(.097)			

$\hat{\Theta} = .17\ (.041),\ .29\ (.106),\ .96\ (.041),\ \hat{\Pi} = .67\ (.117),\ .14\ (.087),\ .19\ (.098)$

Age, Sex	n	Range	$\bar{x}$	s^2	$\hat{\theta}_1$	$\hat{\theta}_2$	$\hat{\pi}_2$	VAF	χ^2	AIC
								93	2.68	70.9
11–12B	20	0–8	3.00	5.79	.38			32	164.6	109.7
					(.109)					
					.14	.62	.50	88	7.67	93.3
					(.038)	(.055)	(.112)			
11–12G	16	0–8	1.88	3.98	.23			36	164.6	109.8
					(.106)					
					.18	1	.06	91	4.1	59
					(.035)	(0)	(.06)			
13–14B	31	0–8	4.13	10.98	.52			18	1,025	253.2
					(.09)					
					.19	.95	.43	90	8.71	131
					(.039)	(.020)	(.089)			
13–14G	22	0–8	2.63	5.00	.33			33	365.1	112.9
					(.100)					
					.27	.93	.09	76	12.87	100.8
					(.035)	(.063)	(.062)			

$\hat{\Theta} = .03\ (.025),\ .38\ (.046),\ .94\ (.062),\ \hat{\Pi} = .28\ (.096),\ .63\ (.102),\ .09\ (.060)$

Age, Sex	n	Range	$\bar{x}$	s^2	$\hat{\theta}_1$	$\hat{\theta}_2$	$\hat{\pi}_2$	VAF	χ^2	AIC
								100	2.15	106.1
15–16B	30	0–8	5.1	10.71	.64			17	3,043	243.2
					(.087)					
					.26	.98	.53	85	35.28	128
					(.041)	(.012)	(.091)			

$\hat{\Theta} = .08\ (.032),\ .59\ (.065),\ .99\ (.006),\ \hat{\Pi} = .28\ (.082),\ .24\ (.077),\ .48\ (.091)$

Age, Sex	n	Range	$\bar{x}$	s^2	$\hat{\theta}_1$	$\hat{\theta}_2$	$\hat{\pi}_2$	VAF	χ^2	AIC
								96	1.92	113.8
15–16G	22	0–8	3.63	9.29	.45			21	682	161.9
					(.106)					
					.22	.93	.33	90	5.02	98.6
					(.038)	(.032)	(.100)			
11–16B&G	141	0–8	3.61	9.01	.45			22	4,807	1,019
					(.041)					
					.24	.96		89	55.23	621.2
					(.015)	(.011)				

$\hat{\Theta} = .07\ (.013),\ .42\ (.024),\ .98\ (.008),\ \hat{\Pi} = .34\ (.04),\ .39\ (.041),\ .27\ (.037)$

Note.—Estimates $\hat{\theta}_1$ and $\hat{\theta}_2$ are item success rates for each component; $\hat{\pi}_2$ is the proportion of population in the better performing component; VAF is variance accounted for; AIC is Akaike's information criterion. Numbers in parentheses are estimated standard errors. χ^2 under binomial $df = 7$; with 2 components $df = 5$; with 3 components $df = 3$. For samples supporting 3 components, the estimates and their standard errors are given in vectors $\hat{\Theta}$ and $\hat{\Pi}$.

The Joint Structure of the Water-Level and
Van Tasks, Study 2

As in Study 1, the data for children in the age range of 11–16 years were combined. Although age and sex differences in task performance are to be found within this age range (just as in Study 1), these mainly reflect differences in the proportions of subjects within each age group that are members of the subgroups. The success parameter estimates of θ remain largely similar across age range and sex (see the estimates in Tables 26 and 28). Perhaps the one anomaly concerns the θ_2 estimates for the oldest boys and girls on the water-level task, which are a good bit larger than those estimates for the subjects in the preceding age groups. However, since no similar finding emerged in the corresponding Study 1 data, we interpret the finding as sampling variation.

The joint frequency histogram of the van and water-level tasks appears in Figure 19, and the marginal distributions for each task are given in Tables 29 and 30.

There are too few observations satisfactorily to fit the joint frequency distribution as was done in Study 1; however, as can be seen in Figure 19, the general pattern of the response distribution is similar to the corresponding figure (Fig. 15 above) in Study 1. Two relatively distinct components of subjects—those who perform well versus those who perform poorly on both tasks—are again evident, along with two smaller components of subjects who do well on one task but not on the other. However, a striking difference between these two figures is that extremely poor performers on both tasks were much less frequent in Study 1: the joint mode among poor performers in this study with zero correct on both tasks (0, 0) was rarely observed in Study 1.

The marginal distributions shown in Tables 29 and 30 are very similar to each other and to the corresponding marginal distributions for Study 1 (cf. Tables 9 and 17 above). Both these distributions are essentially U shaped, suggesting a mixture of binomial distributions with very different success parameters (θ). A two-component mixture fit to the marginal water-level data accounted for 94% of the variance, although $\chi^2(4) = 30.06$. A three-component solution yielded $\chi^2(2) = 7.81$ and accounted for about 98% of the variance. Similarly, a two-component model fit to the van marginal distribution in Table 30 accounted for 89% of the variance, but the $\chi^2(5) = 55.2$; a three-component model fits virtually perfectly, with $\chi^2(3) = .87$ and VAF of 99%.

In sum, although there are differences in procedure, the major findings of Study 2 with respect to the van and water-level task data parallel closely those findings from Study 1. In particular, the distributional structure and

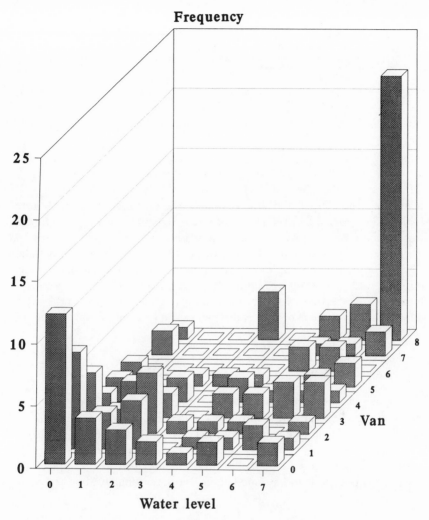

FIG. 19.—Joint distribution of van and water-level task responses, $n = 141$, Study 2

age and sex differences have all been replicated. The model proposed appears to remain intact.

Comparison of the Analogies with Water-Level and Van Task Data

Analogies Test

Since our main interest in this task concerns how the scores on the analogies test relate to the van and water-level score distributions, univariate

TABLE 29

HISTOGRAM OF OBSERVED FREQUENCIES FOR 11–16-YEAR-OLD
SUBJECTS, WATER-LEVEL TASK (n = 141), STUDY 2

```
0*****************35
1*******14
2*********17
3****8
4****8
5******12
6*******13
7*****************34
```

NOTE.—5*****12 denotes 12 individuals with 5 correct.

features will be abbreviated. But, of course, the univariate (marginal) distribution can be used to predict the bivariate structure, just as was the case for the joint van and water-level data. Table 31 provides the means and variances of the test scores for each sex; certain age groups have been combined because of sample size considerations. For each, mean test scores improve with increasing age, and there are no between-sex differences in means at any age; all t tests were insignificant. This fact supports the expectation that there would be no sex differences (at least in means) on this task.

The Joint Structure of the Water-Level Task and the Analogies Test

Figure 20 shows the joint sample frequency histogram of water-level scores with values ranging from 0 to 7 and analogies test scores grouped into six convenient finely meshed intervals of 0–4, 5–8, 9–12, 13–16, 17–20, and 21–24. At each fixed water-level score, the corresponding (conditional) sample frequency distribution of analogy test scores appears reasonably symmetrical and unimodal; it seems reasonable, then, to model

TABLE 30

HISTOGRAM OF OBSERVED FREQUENCIES FOR 11–16-YEAR-OLD
SUBJECTS, VAN TASK (n = 141), STUDY 2

```
0**************27
1**********20
2********16
3*********17
4*****11
5****8
6**4
7***6
8****************32
```

NOTE.—4*****11 denotes 11 subjects with 4 correct.

TABLE 31

ANALOGIES TEST MEANS AND VARIANCES, STUDY 2

AGE RANGE	BOYS			GIRLS		
	n	$\bar{x}$	s^2	n	$\bar{x}$	s^2
7–8	1	5	0	7	5.71	8.24
9–10	16	8.5	5.2	16	8.88	7.17
11–12	20	12.1	13.25	16	10.81	14.7
13–14	31	10.97	15.63	22	13.18	12.54
15–17	30	13.13	14.81	22	13.55	17.69

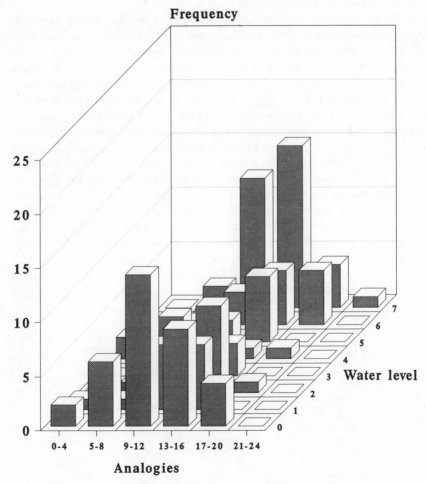

FIG. 20.—Joint distribution of analogies test and water level responses, $n = 141$, Study 2.

these conditional analogy distributions, conditioned on a fixed water-level task score, as normal distributions. The (marginal) distribution of water-level task scores is modeled as a two-component binomial mixture. This marginal distribution is simply the frequency histogram of water-level scores given in Table 29 above.

Letting X denote the analogies scores and Y the water-level scores,

$$f(x|y) = (2\sigma^2\pi)^{-1/2} \exp[-(x - \mu_{x|y})^2/2\sigma^2] \tag{15}$$

models the conditional distribution of analogy scores given a particular $Y = y$ water-level task score, with conditional mean $\mu_{x|y}$ and conditional variance σ^2; under the model proposed, σ^2 is free of Y.

Note that Figure 20 shows a slight tendency for the analogy scores to increase as water-level scores increase; this fact is reflected in the modest $r = .23$ correlation between the analogies test and the water-level scores. Assuming that the regression of the analogies scores on the water-level task scores is linear, then $\mu_{x|y} = y\beta_{y1} + \beta_{y0}$ is the regression of analogies X scores on the water-level Y scores (β_{y1} is the slope and β_{y0} the intercept). With $f(y)$ denoting (as before) a (marginal) binomial mixture distribution, $f(y) = \Sigma_{r=1}^2 \pi_r b(y; \theta_r, m)$, the joint distribution of the analogies test and the water-level task, is given by $f(x, y) = f(y)f(x|y)$. This distribution is discrete on one variable (the water-level task) and continuous on the other (the analogies test). Under this model, the marginal distribution of analogies will generally not be normal in distribution; it will be a mixture of normals distribution, although it may appear reasonably normal in some data. Table 32 gives the marginal frequency distribution of the analogies test scores with the observations grouped into the same intervals as in Figure 20; since this relatively coarse grouping is not very revealing, a second histogram with smaller groupings of the same data is given in Table 33. The data have mean 12.31 and variance 15.49.

TABLE 32

HISTOGRAM OF GROUPED FREQUENCIES OF ANALOGIES TEST
SCORES FOR 11–16-YEAR-OLD SUBJECTS ($n = 141$), STUDY 2

Score Interval
0–4 ***7
5–8 ******12
9–12 *************************53
13–16 *************************53
17–20 *****15
21–24 *1

NOTE.—0–4***7 denotes 7 observations in the interval 0–4.

TABLE 33

HISTOGRAM OF GROUPED FREQUENCIES OF ANALOGIES TEST SCORES
FOR 11–16-YEAR-OLD SUBJECTS (n = 141), STUDY 2

Score Interval
0–1***3
2–3****4
4–5*1
6–7******6
8–9*********9
10–11*******************23
12–13**47
14–15**************************27
16–17*******7
18–19**********10
≧20****4

NOTE.—0–1***3 denotes 3 observations in the interval 0–1.

Fitting the model f(x, y) *to the data.*—Using the method of moments (e.g., Hogg & Craig, 1970), parameter estimates under the joint frequency model $f(x, y)$ of the analogies test and the water-level task given above were fit to the data. Least squares estimates of the regression function of the analogies test scores regressed against the water-level task scores provided estimates of the regression parameters, β_{y1}, β_{y0}, which were then used to estimate $\mu_{x|y}$, $y = 0, 1, \ldots, 7$, and σ^2. The marginal estimates of the binomial mixture distribution, given in Table 26 above, provided the estimates of the other parameters. Using these estimates, it is straightforward to fit the data to the joint frequency distribution.

For a marginal two-component binomial mixture, based on the 48 cells with frequencies grouped as in Figure 20, $\chi^2(35) = 172.6$, $p < .01$. For a three-component marginal mixture, $\chi^2(33) = 116.1$, $p < .01$. Neither model fits as well as desired, although both models do reflect the main features of the data.

Important substantive and methodological implications of this analysis can be obtained by examining the data and the fitted model in more detail. Figure 21 displays the fitted joint distribution, assuming a two-component binomial marginal mixture of the water-level data. Most of the probability mass of the distribution is carried by the components with extreme water-level scores. Conventional wisdom, based on our wide belief in the bivariate normality of most measures, would suggest that the greatest mass of probability would be concentrated in the center region of any data display. Of course, Figure 21 and the original data histogram, Figure 20 (which is based on no model of course), indicate that this conventional assumption of bivariate normality is very wrong. What this fact implies is that the joint structure

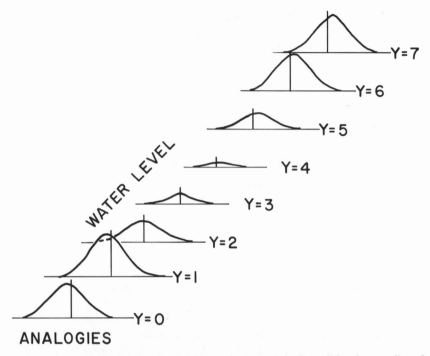

ANALOGIES

Fig. 21.—Estimated joint distribution under a model of conditional normality of analogies scores at each water-level score with marginal water-level scores a two-component binomial mixture, Study 2. The ordinates on each normal curve mark 12 items correct on the analogies test. Y denotes number of water-level items correct.

of a spatial test, at least of the kind reported here, with any other kind of test is likely to be strikingly different from the presumed bivariate or multivariate normality required for the plausible implementation of *most* of our standard statistical methodologies. This fact has important implications for work that attempts to understand spatial data within conventional data analytic perspectives, an issue about which we will say more in Chapter X. What we are saying here is that one of the most basic assumptions required for conventional inference, bivariate normality, is strongly violated.

The Joint Distribution of the Analogies Test and the Van Task

The joint frequency histogram of scores for the analogies test and the van task shown in Figure 22 looks very similar to the corresponding joint analogies test and water-level task histogram (cf. Fig. 20). The marginal frequencies for the van task are given in Table 30 above; the marginal distribution for the analogies test (cf. Tables 32 and 33) remains unchanged. The correlation between the analogies test and the van task scores is .31.

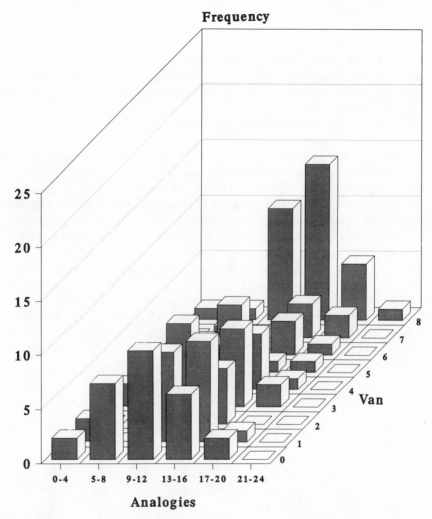

FIG. 22.—Joint distribution of analogies test and van responses, $n = 141$, Study 2

Fitting the model $f(x, y)$ *to the data.*—The joint frequency model fit to the water-level and analogies data was fit here as well. Using the same grouping intervals as before (but note that, because there are eight van items, there are 54 cells to fit), $\chi^2(41) = 133.4$, $p < .01$, for a two-component marginal binomial mixture, and, for a three-component marginal mixture, the fit of the joint frequency data yields $\chi^2(39) = 57.5$, $p < .01$. The structures fit better than in the case of the joint water-level and analogies data, but the fit still remains unsatisfactory even though the model responds to the major features of the data.

Summary and Brief Discussion

The basic findings of Study 1 concerning distributional forms, sex differences, and growth processes were replicated in Study 2 with few surprises. An important but not unexpected finding of Study 2 is that the joint structure of the water-level task and the verbal analogies test, and also of the van task and the analogies test, is fundamentally different from the joint structure of the water-level and van tasks.

In seeking plausible models for the joint distribution of the analogies and the two spatial tasks, we selected a strong model containing as few parameters as would seem possible; the model specified that the conditional distribution of analogies test scores was normal, with constant variance, for each fixed water-level or van score. The marginal distribution of the spatial task scores was modeled as a binomial mixture. We could have obtained better-fitting models by, for example, exploring other forms of the regression functions than the linear function that we assumed it to be. However, given the relatively limited size of the data set, it seemed best not to attempt to do so.

An important analytic implication illustrated here is that, when the joint probability structure of the water-level task or van task is considered in combination with *any* other tasks, the resulting structure cannot be multivariate normal. This potentially limits the range of analytic tools commonly employed for such data.

IX. VERBALLY EXPRESSED UNDERSTANDING OF PRINCIPLES AND PERFORMANCE ON SPATIAL TASKS

We address two related issues in this chapter: first, the degree to which task performance lags or leads verbally expressed understanding and, second, the role of verbal explanations as a factor contributing to an understanding of individual differences in spatial task performance.

Concerning the first of these issues, it was noted earlier that the role of verbally expressed explanations versus task performance in indexing cognitive understanding is an old issue in cognitive development that has generally focused on asking which of these two criteria is the most suitable. Brainerd (1973) reasoned that explanations tend to underestimate understanding and, consequently, argued against their use; recently, however, the presumably resolved debate has been reopened (Chapman & McBride, 1992; Hodkin, 1987). Taking a somewhat different perspective on this issue, we model the relative developmental priority of successful task performance versus verbally expressed understanding. This approach, however, is not unrelated to the issue of which index is the better criterion; for example, if performance appears to precede the ability to provide suitable verbal explanations, then cognitive understanding would be better assessed by performance criteria than by explanations.

Exploring the relation between verbal responses and performance on the water-level task is of course nothing new; it has been studied by a number of investigators (e.g., Kalichman, 1989; Liben, 1978; Liben & Golbeck, 1984; Myer & Hensley, 1984; Thomas & Jamison, 1975; Wittig & Allen, 1984), and Liben and Golbeck (1984) have examined similar correspondences in a verticality task. Collectively, there is general agreement that task performance and verbal expressions of task principles are related (Liben, 1991b); however, the relation may not be strong. For example, Myer and Hensley (1984) reported a contingency table correlation coefficient of .29.

The general expectation seems to be that measures of association between task performance and verbal statements of knowledge *should* be high. What has apparently gone unrecognized is that the expected magnitude of the correlation coefficient will depend on one's conceptual view of the developmental correspondence between verbal responses and task performance: in particular, whether the contingency correlation coefficient is expected to be high or low depends on the lag, or the lead, in the ontogenetic correspondence between performance and expressed understanding. Indeed, in our model, as will be shown later, as the time lag between the emergence of the two abilities increases, the correlation coefficient decreases toward zero.

The second issue concerns the role of verbal explanations in facilitating our understanding of individual differences and, in particular, the degree to which verbalizations may aid our understanding of sex differences in spatial task performance. Sex differences in verbal abilities have been repeatedly established. For example, Maccoby and Jacklin (1974) write, "Females' superiority on verbal tasks has been one of the more solidly established generalizations in the field of sex differences" (p. 75). Because we have presented substantial evidence that there are latent classes within each sex with respect to spatial task performance, our approach uses this fact: a main focus of our approach is to compare sex differences in verbalizations while conditioning on spatial task performance. Thus, one might speculate that girls should show a different distribution of verbal responses than would boys of the same performance group (good or poor). If so, then performance in one domain might mediate performance in the other.

We explored this possibility, even though we did not think it likely that we would find support for it. One reason for this skepticism is that sex differences in verbal skills often reflect fluency, and fluency may bear no relation to the ability or inability to articulate what one is doing when responding to a verticality or horizontality task.

A general approach to the kinds of questions that we are asking is to rely on conventional frequency-table procedures. The construction of such tests is the same for both independence and goodness-of-fit hypotheses, although each assumes a different sampling scheme. However, a difficulty with this general approach that is rarely considered is that conventional χ^2 methodology assumes that all data are perfectly classified in each category. This assumption is probably wrong when behavioral data form the basis for classification, but it is unclear whether it is importantly wrong.

There are at least two sources of classification error in our data. One of these is the classification of subjects as good or poor performers. Although the procedure employed to perform this task is an optimal one, it is by no means perfect—misclassifications are always going to occur. A second likely source of error is the classification of subjects on the basis of their verbal responses since the process is certainly subjective. Either source can also influence the interpretation of the results of analyses concerned with the lag or lead between verbalization and task performance.

The most satisfactory approach to the misclassification problem is to model the error explicitly. However, to do so is not an easy task, and, in the general case, it has no solution: there are more parameters to estimate than there are observations (e.g., Mote & Anderson, 1965). Thus, classification error will not be modeled here. However, the issue can always be explored on a post hoc basis, by considering how slight rearrangements of cross-classification table entries alter the reported test statistic. If perturbations leave matters relatively unchanged, classification error is probably not an important problem.

GENERAL PROCEDURES

2 × 2 Tables and Lag-Lead Correspondence

Consider Figure 23, which defines subjects jointly classified by task performance and verbalized understanding of the task. Let a, b, c, and d denote the observed frequencies in the table, with $a + b + c + d = n$ the total sample size. The sample correlation coefficient in a 2 × 2 table is given by

$$r_c = \frac{bc - ad}{\sqrt{[(a + b)(a + c)(c + d)(b + d)]}}. \tag{16}$$

Conditional probabilities provide information on lag-lead correspondence. There are three possibilities: task performance can lead, it can lag, or it can coincide with verbally expressed understanding. Let G denote good, P poor, Y yes, and N no. These possibilities translate into relations between the conditional probabilities, $P(G|Y)$ and $P(Y|G)$. Read $P(Y|G)$ as the probability of a "yes" given good performance and $P(G|Y)$ as the probability of good performance given a "yes." Estimates of the quantities are simply

$$\hat{P}(G|Y) = b/(b + a), \quad \hat{P}(Y|G) = b/(b + d).$$

The three lag-lead possibilities translate into the following relations on the two conditional probabilities:

    1. $P(G|Y) > P(Y|G)$ when task performance leads verbal expression;

    2. $P(Y|G) > P(G|Y)$ when verbal expression leads task performance; and

    3. $P(Y|G) = P(G|Y)$ when task performance and verbal expressions coincide.

The basic idea is that the event that occurs later in development is the conditioning event in the larger, left-hand probability. For example, if

PERFORMANCE
POOR GOOD

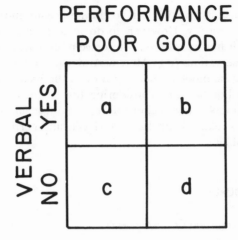

FIG. 23.—Schematic 2 × 2 table of task performance (good, poor) and verbally expressed knowledge of the task principle (yes, no).

satisfactory verbal explanation occurs later in development than good task performance, then, given satisfactory verbal expression (i.e., Y), good performance should be much more probable. That is, $P(G|Y) > P(Y|G)$.

Consider a simple illustration of why this result is so. It is obviously true that

P(a person is at least 2 years old|the person is at least 8 years old) >
P(a person is at least 8 years old|the person is at least 2 years old).

Because 8 years follows 2 years, it is the conditioning event in the larger probability. To see how these possibilities affect r_c (Eq. [16]), suppose that the first of the two inequalities listed above holds. Then

$$\hat{P}(G|Y) = b/(b + a) > b/(b + d) = \hat{P}(Y|G).$$

Now maximize the difference between the left- and the right-hand sides of this inequality; this maximization corresponds to increasing the period intervening between when good task performance is displayed and when the ability to articulate the principle verbally is achieved. The left-hand side, $b/(b + a)$, is maximum at 1 for any $b > 0$ when $a = 0$. Now minimize the right-hand side, $b/(b + d)$. It is monotonically decreasing with increasing d. Now consider r_c (Eq. [16]), with $a = 0$:

$$r_c = \frac{bc}{\sqrt{[bc\,(c + d)\,(b + d)]}}.$$

Clearly, r_c decreases toward zero as d becomes large. Hence, r_c approaches zero as the difference $P(G|Y) - P(Y|G)$ increases. The same result occurs if the second of the listed inequalities holds. Thus, the degree to which one task leads the other is reflected in r_c, which converges to zero as the magnitude of the differences between the onset of the two abilities increases.

As an example, for Myer and Hensley (1984), $a = 5, b = 13, c = 42$, and $d = 25$; $r_c = .29$, which is unrevealing. However, the estimates and their standard errors are $\hat{P}(G|Y) = .72 \pm .048$ and $\hat{P}(Y|G) = .34 \pm .051$, which provides evidence suggesting that good water-level task performance well precedes the ability to articulate a correct rule verbally.

Although this development has assumed a 2×2 table, the conditional probabilities are similarly defined for other tables, and the correlation coefficient behaves similarly as well.

Classification of Verbal Responses

As noted in the preceding chapter, Study 2 subjects were asked two questions after they had finished both the water-level and the van tasks. Responses were recorded and later transferred onto cards that were subsequently used by judges in classifying subjects. The full set of responses to each task was each divided in half; each of the resulting four sets of cards was given to 10 judges for evaluation and sorting.

The cards were sorted according to two separate classification schemes. First, they were sorted to determine whether subjects know the task principle. The three possible categories of responses were "yes" (the subject does understand the principle), "no" (the subject does not understand the principle), and "?" (the verbal responses were so ambiguous that it was not possible to decide the matter). The second classification criterion, and the second sorting by the judges, aimed to specify the source of the explanation provided by the subjects. The six categories were (a) no explanation, (b) explanations relating to the subject's internal images, (c) explanations relating to the subject's internal feelings, (d) external explanations related to distal environmental frames of reference (e.g., the monitor's screen), (e) external explanations related to proximal frames of reference (here were classified explanations concerning features of the bottle's or the van's shape or orientation), and (f) explanations related to the principle of gravity (explicit statements of the principle were classified here).

Introductory psychology students at the University of Muenster served as judges. To ensure that they knew the correct principle themselves, each judge was given an instruction sheet that illustrated the task, specified the correct principle, and illustrated correct answers. In addition, the judges were provided with examples of the kinds of explanations that were required for classification in one of the six categories. All judges, of course, were blind as to the subject's task performance.

The modal category of the 10 judges' evaluations defined the subject's classification. In most cases (91% for the water-level and 89% for the van explanations), a clear modal response category judgment emerged; otherwise, subjects were eliminated from the analysis. Also, procedural errors in the initial data collection prevented recording several subjects' verbalizations. These cases were eliminated as well. Consequently, of the 141 subjects aged 11–16 on whom we focus here, 127 remained available for the analyses related to the water-level task and 125 for the van task.

RESULTS

Task Performance and Knowledge of Principle: Lag-Lead Analysis

Table 34 provides frequencies of subjects classified by knowledge of the principle and task performance. Classification with respect to good or poor task performance used the posterior probability critical values, based on a two-component mixture solution, given in Tables 26 and 28 above. For classification in the better performing group, four or more correct from among seven responses were required for the water-level task, and six or more correct from among eight were required for the van task.

Consider the water-level task data for both sexes combined shown in Table 34: $\chi^2(2) = 41.38$, $p < .001$; the corresponding correlation coefficient $r_c = .50$. An association between verbally expressed knowledge of the principle and task performance is clearly evident here.

TABLE 34

CROSS-CLASSIFICATION OF SUBJECTS BY PERFORMANCE CRITERIA AND JUDGED KNOWLEDGE OF THE TASK PRINCIPLE, STUDY 2

	BOYS			GIRLS			BOTH		
	Poor	Good	Total	Poor	Good	Total	Poor	Good	Total
Water-level task:									
No	14	5	19	13	1	14	27	6	33
Yes	7	37	44	2	13	15	9	50	59
?	7	6	13	13	9	22	20	15	35
Total	28	48	76	28	23	51	56	71	127
Van task:									
No	13	2	15	19	0	19	32	2	34
?	16	5	21	19	1	20	35	6	41
Yes	12	23	35	6	9	15	18	32	50
Total	41	30	71	44	10	54	85	40	125

Note.—No = judged not to know principle; ? = knowledge of principle uncertain; yes = judged to know principle.

More interesting, however, are the conditional probability estimates and their standard errors (for this analysis, it seemed reasonable to include the uncertain "?" subjects in the "no," or lacks verbal understanding, category, as the following example illustrates):

$$\hat{P}(G|Y) = 50/(50 + 9) = .85 \pm .047,$$

$$\hat{P}(Y|G) = 50/(6 + 15 + 50) = .70 \pm .054.$$

The difference between these estimates is significant, $Z = 2.04$, $p < .05$. Thus, $\hat{P}(G|Y) > \hat{P}(Y|G)$, indicating that task performance leads verbal expression of the principle. The same orderings of the estimates are evident for boys and girls separately, although the differences between the probabilities are smaller.

The van task data for the combined sexes (see Table 34) yield a $\chi^2(2) = 39.87$, $p < .001$, $r_c = .49$. As in the case of the water-level task, van performance and verbal explanations are correlated. However, for the van task, $\hat{P}(Y|G) > \hat{P}(G|Y)$ in all cases. As before, for the entire sample of boys and girls,

$$\hat{P}(Y|G) = .80 \pm .063, \quad \hat{P}(G|Y) = .64 \pm .069.$$

Again, the difference between these estimates is significant, $Z = 2.04$, $p < .05$.

With water-level task performance preceding verbal understanding, and with verbal understanding preceding van task performance, the suggestion is that water-level task performance precedes van task performance. This hypothesis can be tested with the van and water-level data from Study 1 using a similar application of the lag-lead model; the corresponding estimates are not in this order. They are, however, similar to each other and are not reliably different from each other either.[27]

Thus, there is the intriguing suggestion that acquisition of verbal understanding and task performance may be differently sequenced in the two spatial tasks and that the tasks themselves may lag one another, although

[27] A lag-lead analysis can be performed directly on the joint water-level and van data. If success in water-level task performance precedes that in van task performance, then $P(GW|GV)$ should be larger than $P(GV|GW)$, where GW and GV denote good water-level and good van task performance, respectively. The relevant data are available in Fig. 18 above. $\hat{P}(GV|GW) = .90$; a 95% confidence interval is .85–.95. $\hat{P}(GW|GV) = .83$, with a 95% confidence interval of .78–.89, but the difference between these estimates is of questionable reliability, $z = 1.78$, $p < .07$.

Note that the lag-lead estimates are simply estimates of proportions, p^*, based on estimates of conditional distributions, so $\hat{\sigma}^2(\hat{p}^*) = \hat{p}^*(1 - \hat{p}^*)/n$, where n is the number of observations on which $\hat{p}^*$ is based. Thus, confidence intervals for p^* are easily constructed. Significance tests between two estimates are easily constructed using bootstrap procedures (cf. Efron & Tibshirani, 1986).

this notion is somewhat sullied by the failure to find evidence that water-level task performance precedes van task performance in Study 1, as would be implied by the findings just reported here in Study 2.

Regardless of what the data might suggest, there appears to be a lack of clear theory on what to expect regarding the sequencing of such tasks. Piaget's position on the time of emergence of the understanding of the two tasks seems unclear. Typically, he describes (Piaget & Inhelder, 1967, chap. 13) the development of vertical and horizontal understanding as if both emerged concurrently. He does observe, however (Piaget & Inhelder, 1967, p. 378), that infants' first awareness of the horizontal comes from their prone position and that primitive understanding of the vertical develops as soon as the infant starts to raise herself, suggesting that horizontality might precede verticality. In other places (e.g., Piaget & Inhelder, 1967, p. 401), he notes that "the vertical is no better constructed than the horizontal," a statement that does nothing to resolve the issue.

Sex Differences: Task Performance and Judged Knowledge

Consider next between-sex comparisons when conditioning (holding fixed) performance level at either good or poor. Recall that the main interest focused on whether the distribution of verbal responses for possessing knowledge of the principle ("yes"), being uncertain ("?"), or lacking knowledge of the principle ("no") differed between sexes. The data appear in Table 34, and there are two relevant comparisons for each task. Each comparison involves two data columns of three cells each, and the null hypothesis of interest is that the data came from the same distribution. The results for the water-level task indicated that $\chi^2(2) = 6.83$ for good performers and that $\chi^2(2) = 4.62$ for poor performers. The corresponding comparisons for the van task yielded $\chi^2(2) = 1.056$ and 3.28, respectively. Only the first of these comparisons is significant ($p < .04$), so, in the main, there appears little evidence to reject the null hypothesis. However, the three-category classification does not reflect possible qualitative differences in responses as well as the source of explanation (which is considered next) might.

Sex Differences: Task Performance and Source of Explanation

The jointly classified judged source of explanation by task performance (good or poor) data are given in Table 35. Before conditioning on task performance, however, consider the results of good versus poor performers for both sexes combined. For the water-level task, $\chi^2(5) = 34.92$, $p < .001$, while, for the van task, $\chi^2(4) = 45.22$, $p < .001$ (note that the "?" or no explanation category was omitted). Thus, not surprisingly, there are quite

TABLE 35

Cross-Classification of Subjects by Performance and Source
of Explanation, Study 2

	Boys			Girls			Both		
	Poor	Good	Total	Poor	Good	Total	Poor	Good	Total
Water-level task:									
a) No expl.	2	0	2	0	1	1	2	1	3
b) In. image ..	8	5	13	5	8	13	13	13	26
c) In. feel.	2	1	3	5	0	5	7	1	8
d) Ex. distal ..	1	10	11	3	2	5	4	12	16
e) Ex. prox. ..	10	8	18	16	3	19	26	11	37
f) Gravity	5	26	31	1	10	11	6	36	42
Total	28	50	78	30	24	54	58	74	132
Van task:									
a) No expl.	0	0	0	0	0	0	0	0	0
b) In. image ..	3	0	3	5	0	5	8	0	8
c) In. feel.	3	0	3	5	0	5	8	0	8
d) Ex. distal ..	5	5	10	11	1	12	16	6	22
e) Ex. prox. ..	19	2	21	19	0	19	38	2	40
f) Gravity	12	23	35	6	9	15	18	32	50
Total	42	30	74	46	10	56	88	40	128

Note.—Classification category definition: a = no explanation; b = internal imagery; c = internal feelings; d = external distal referents; e = external proximal referents; f = gravity.

different distributions of explanation sources for the two performance groups. For both tasks, incidentally, the largest contribution to the χ^2 statistic was made by the gravity category (see category f above), 25 in the first case and 15 in the second.

Conditioning now on task performance, the analysis parallels the analysis just completed above. For the water-level task, $\chi^2(5) = 9.44$ and 8.94, respectively, for good and poor performers. The corresponding results for the van task are $\chi^2(2) = 1.056$ and $\chi^2(4) = 5.079$, respectively. None of these values approach significance, so there is not good evidence that the distributions for the two sexes, with performance controlled, are different.

Besides these formal analyses, we also carefully compared many of the individual statements provided by the boys and girls classified in the same categories. For example, we compared the subjects in category d (external distal source) and category e (external proximal) (see Table 35) for both boys and girls, good and poor performers alike, and we compared subjects in several other categories for which there were sufficient numbers of subjects. Fishing expeditions, such as this one, can be dangerous at best. The most striking difference that we detected was that, among the 10 boys who performed well in the water-level task and who were classified in external distal course (category d), seven emphasized features of the monitor screen;

however, neither of the two corresponding girls did so. This finding might suggest that boys are more likely to use different cues than girls, but the small frequencies make speculation very hazardous.

Summary and Brief Discussion

The correlation between verbal understanding and task performance depends on the degree to which one leads or lags the other in development, and thus its interpretation may be ambiguous without considering certain conditional probabilities. When viewed within the framework of a simple model, the analysis revealed that good task performance precedes the ability to articulate a suitable explanation on the water-level task but that task performance may lag verbal understanding on the van task. There appears to be no obvious theoretical basis for understanding this finding, however, although it is not difficult to imagine that such differences might well be related to the kinds of cues and action patterns required of the developing child as progress is made toward the development of internalized cognitive action systems.

Perhaps one of the more interesting general implications of this analysis is that data analysis that does not consider the dynamic developmental processes may be misleading. It may well be necessary to perform longitudinal analyses in order to resolve basic issues concerning the sequence and timing of different developmental processes.

Both children's verbally expressed knowledge of the water-level and van task principle and the source of their verbal explanation (e.g., gravity or their internal feelings) are related to task performance. However, when sex differences in task performance are compared while conditioning on task performance group membership (good vs. poor), there appear to be no reliable sex differences. Put differently, differences in verbal responses do not covary with task performance when task performance group membership is controlled, and this fact suggests that the search for causative factors contributing to between-group differences should be directed elsewhere.

X. GENERAL DISCUSSION

MAJOR CONCLUSIONS

Having now slogged through what might seem to some readers like endless numbers of charts, figures, and expressions, one might well wonder just what all these results mean. Consequently, we set forth here informally and in abbreviated form what we regard as the most important general conclusions and implications of our studies. We will subsequently expand in a more deliberate manner on many of these points. Also, we rely on certain arguments to follow, so we anticipate some additional theoretical developments that will appear later in the chapter.

Besides the critical role that a model structure plays in guiding our thinking, there are four main points to stress:

> i) Spatial abilities, at least as assessed by our tasks, appear fundamentally different from other abilities. By itself, this conclusion is hardly new. But we think that the wider implications for theory and practice have not been recognized as point ii indicates. Furthermore, we do not think that the differences between spatial abilities and other nonspatial abilities (like the analogies task) are easily captured with simple quantitative indices.
>
> ii) Because the data structures for our spatial tasks are so unusual, they force a rethinking of the mechanisms underlying spatial task performance, how research is conducted, and how data are analyzed.
>
> iii) Within-sex differences are more important than between-sex differences. Between-sex differences are consequences of within-sex differences.
>
> iv) Growth is largely a state-change process.

To elaborate on these points, first, there is something quite special about the water-level task, the van task, and most probably other similar "spatial" tasks. While it has long been believed that there are certain special features about spatial tasks and associated abilities, we do not believe that there have been clear distributional features of data reported before that make the argument compelling. It is not just differences in the summary statistics or estimates of our model but the fundamental distributional forms of our data that make this case. The evidence gleaned from an examination of, for example, Table 9 or Figure 15 above should be convincing. Whatever may be thought of our modeling efforts, these distributions demand new formulations. We doubt that the reader has ever experienced such striking distributional structures before—certainly we have not. It might be thought that there is something special about our particular procedure: for example, the way in which the frequencies were obtained or the focus on discrete rather than continuous data. Rest assured, it is not an artifact of our methodology, as is argued below.

Second, if our conceptualization is accepted as plausible, namely, that the population is a latent class structure, then the entire armamentaria of traditional data analytic methods in common use—t tests, factor analysis, effect size, meta-analysis, and the like—will have to be abandoned (or at least employed selectively and carefully) because they simply do not address issues of relevance to such structures. Put differently, there is a huge mismatch between the probability models underlying most data analyses and the data at hand.

We are calling for no less than a revolution in thinking about research design, how growth and change occurs, and how data analysis should be conducted. This viewpoint is certainly extreme, but the data provided appear convincing.

A third major point concerns the issue of how individual differences are characterized. Within-sex differences should be the focus; these differences imply between-sex differences. The search for between-sex differences has been misdirected.

Finally, although it may take a longitudinal effort to resolve the matter fully, growth appears to be largely a matter of changing states or latent classes.

THE WATER-LEVEL AND VAN TASKS: UNIDIMENSIONAL FINDINGS

Because in both studies results obtained on the water-level and van tasks were quite similar, they will be discussed jointly, with distinctions between them being made when necessary.

Within-Sex Differences: θ Changes

By about 8 years, and probably earlier, within-sex differences in task performance suggest two performance groups. The group differences are measured by θ_r ($r = 1, 2$), the task success probability. These task success rates improve over age until about 11 years, after which time success rates remain approximately constant through at least age 16. These conclusions are supported by, for example, Figures 5 and 11 (Study 1) and the data in Tables 26 and 28 (Study 2); for both sexes, the patterns of θ_r estimates over age for both the van and the water-level tasks are similar. Although the value of θ_r is dependent on the value of c, we will argue below that the particular value of c selected is largely unimportant.

Between-Sex Differences: π Changes

The differences between boys' and girls' performance are the consequence of within-sex differences in the proportions of good and poor responders at each age. Such differences are certainly in evidence by about age 10 years; in the case of the water-level task, isotonic regressions of the $\hat{\pi}_2$ over age indicate that the regression functions for boys are consistently above the corresponding functions for girls (see Fig. 6 above and also Thomas & Turner, 1991, as well as Tables 26 and 28 above). Only the isotonic regression obtained for the van task in Study 1 (Fig. 12), which shows a similar pattern for both sexes for ages younger than 12 years or so, is inconsistent with this result; this inconsistency seems best viewed as sampling error.

The general pattern of changes in π_2 estimates indicates that the proportions of good performers increase between about 10 and 15 years and then remain approximately constant (see again Figs. 6 and 12). No further changes were seen at college age (Thomas & Turner, 1991), and it is probably the case that the proportions remain roughly constant over the life span (Robert & Tanguay, 1990). The magnitude of the between-sex difference between π_2 for boys and π_2 for girls is somewhat uncertain during the early years, but, by late childhood and early adolescence, it is about .3.

The one reasonably consistent between-sex difference to emerge that does not reflect subpopulation proportional differences is the typically smaller $\hat{\theta}_1$ for girls relative to boys that was obtained on both the water-level and the van tasks in Study 1 (see Figs. 5 and 11) and on the water-level but not the van task in Study 2 (see Table 26). This finding contrasts with Thomas and Turner (1991), who reported that the isotonic regressions over age for $\hat{\theta}_1$ were strikingly similar for both sexes.

What Grows?

The patterns of growth exhibited by changes in the model parameters over age are relevant to general issues concerning the nature of developmental change and whether growth should be viewed as a discrete process or as a more gradual, continuous affair. While the pattern of θ and π changes is not forced by any model assumptions, the trajectories taken by the parameter estimates over age can falsify many models concerning how growth occurs.

It is possible to imagine many different patterns of growth trajectories, over age, that the model parameters might take; Figure 24 illustrates several idealized possibilities. For example, one possibility is that the proportion of poor responders remains constant over a broad age range but that performance within this group gradually improves, merging with that of the good performers at some mature age. This pattern is illustrated in panels c and d. Finding support for this pattern of changes would suggest that, at least for the poor responders, growth is a gradual affair because the θ parameters (graphed in panel d) index within-subject improvements. A scenario of this general form was proposed by Flavell and Wohlwill (1979) for the development of conservation. Alternatively, if only π_2 increased with age and the θ parameters remained essentially constant over age (represented in Fig. 24 by panels a and b), then growth would be a discrete affair because changes in π_2 index changes in latent class membership.

Note that such inferences concerning the nature of growth cannot be discerned by simply examining changes in sample means. Except for sample fluctuations, the means for both sexes show gradual improvement over age (for illustrations, see Tables 7 and 16), but such increases do not, by themselves, imply anything about the nature of the growth process. Recall Figure 1 and Coombs's (1983) *AMI* formulation: these mean changes over age are empirical generalizations, awaiting some model interpretation. It takes a theory to distinguish between different growth possibilities.

Not all combinations of possible growth trajectories of the parameters π_2, θ_1, and θ_2 are conceptually plausible from a developmental perspective. Remember that the mean of the (two-component) binomial mixture distribution is $\mu = m(\pi_1\theta_1 + \pi_2\theta_2)$. Because μ (estimated by the sample mean) must increase with age at least during the childhood and adolescent growth years, the combination of panels c and b in Figure 24 is obviously not a possible growth scenario: the means would remain constant over age, and empirical facts quickly falsify any thought that this pattern might be plausible.

For at least the middle to later childhood years, panels a and b of Figure 24 represent a reasonably good match between idealized parameter trajectories and the empirical findings that we have reported. Compare these curves with the isotonic regression functions of, for example, Figures 5 and 6. Alternatively, panels e and f portray a more accurate idealized growth pattern if a broader age perspective that includes performance in the early years is desired.

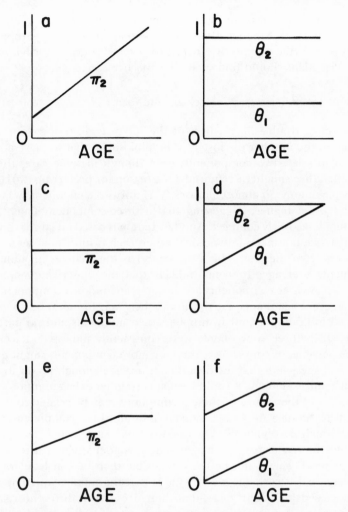

Fig. 24.—Several hypothetical growth trajectories of θ_1, θ_2, and π_2 parameters of binomial mixture model graphed against increasing age.

Under our model, an important feature of growth is change in latent class membership, indexed by π_2, and such changes imply discrete stage growth processes. There is also some improvement within subpopulations, at least during the early growth years, as the θ estimates increase. The main growth change, however, is reflected in the parameter π_2. Because the major growth changes are reflections of changes in the magnitudes of the π_r, the results suggest that growth is largely a discrete stage process.

Thus, the results here are very much in agreement with the discrete state perspective taken by Brainerd and his colleagues on changes in conservation, memory, and class inclusion (Brainerd, 1979; Brainerd et al., 1982; Howe, Brainerd, & Kingma, 1985). They also agree in spirit with Siegler's (1981) discrete rule perspective (which will be considered shortly), and, of course, Piagetians should find such a perspective congenial.

How Many Latent Classes or Components Are There?

The most troublesome aspect of the mixture clustering approach is deciding on the number of clusters. The philosophy that we have adopted has been to select two components, even though in some cases the data suggest that three might be required. One reason for preferring two components is parsimony; in almost all cases, VAF for two components was about 90% and often higher, suggesting that a three-component (latent class) model might be overly complex. Another reason is based on larger considerations that are not taken into account when each distinct data set is examined apart from the rest. This issue concerns the changes in number of components over age. It seems unlikely that the underlying population would display three components at one age point and two components, say, at two adjacent age points. Furthermore, there was found to be no general age trend indicating a shift in numbers of components and no particular ages at which three components were consistently indicated. It certainly remains possible, of course, that three or more components might exist at some or all ages—but that the data do not provide enough power to detect such differences. Finally, it could be that certain model assumptions might be wrong, and the failure of these assumptions may be related to the ease with which the data might occasionally indicate three components rather than two; such possibilities will be discussed in a later section.

While the reader may quite legitimately wonder whether three components (or more) might not be more plausible than two, at least for some situations, what is certainly *not* at issue is that the number of components needed exceeds one. This fact—that there are indeed different, relatively homogeneous subpopulations—is the much more fundamental fact. Deciding precisely how many latent classes there are is certainly important, but it is not the most critical issue.

THE WATER-LEVEL AND VAN TASKS: BIVARIATE CONSIDERATIONS

Hindsight is always better than foresight, so finding that both the water-level and the van tasks displayed bimodal distributions makes the finding that their joint distribution is multimodal seem predictable. Nevertheless, finding clear evidence of such distributions for the kinds of tasks under consideration here is new. Clearly, such a finding has critical implications for methodology. One of these implications concerns how correlation coefficients are viewed and indicates that an overhaul of our thinking is required, at least with respect to certain kinds of tasks and their associated abilities. And, because the familiar interpretation of what correlation coefficients mean is pervasive in our training, changes in our perspective call for a period of digestion.

The conventional road for understanding correlation is the linear homoskedastic model: both regression functions are linear in their conditional means, and the conditional distributions are homoskedastic in their variances. One might regard these features as the minimum required to support conventional interpretations of correlations. Of course, the bivariate normal model possesses these properties (e.g., Hogg & Craig, 1970), and all conventional correlational hypothesis testing and inference are conducted under the bivariate normal model.

Neither linearity of regression nor homoskedasticity of variance hold in the general mixture setting. A cursory glance at Figures 15 or 19, the bivariate histograms of van and water-level task data, suggests that there are at least two modes, but the two-component model (Eq. [14]) was rejected pretty convincingly. Apparently, four modes are required. While the four-component Model 2 did not fit as well as desired, it appears to be a plausible first approximation. Although the overall correlation between the tasks depicted (in Fig. 15) is $r = .67$, the figure hardly portrays the kind of intuitive structure that we usually think about when correlation is the focus.

Figure 18 shows that, when the sample is partitioned into disjoint subgroups, representing subpopulations or latent classes, the within-component correlation decreases dramatically. The overall correlation reflects more the differing subgroups than the correlation within each subgroup, which may be small and often negligible.

The bivariate structure of the analogies test and the van and water-level tasks indicates that care in interpreting sample correlations needs to be exercised in that situation as well. In general, linearity of regression and homoskedasticity fail here as well, as indeed does unimodality (see Fig. 20).

The conclusion is that we can no longer be sanguine about conventional methodologies and conventional interpretations of sample statistics as representing suitable vehicles for understanding certain psychological processes.

COGNITIVE STRATEGIES AND INFLUENCES ON PERFORMANCE

The cognitive strategy of subjects classified as poor performers clearly differed from the strategy of those subjects classified as good performers.

Young children aged 6–8 years and classified in the poor group typically placed the water line parallel to the vessel's bottom (see Table 11), a strategy that appears to conform with Piaget's expectations (Piaget & Inhelder, 1967, p. 367). A similar strategy was employed by those similarly classified 6–8-year-old van task subjects who placed the plumb line parallel to the van's end (see Table 19). However, older poor performers appeared to have no strategy that corresponds with a consistent response rule; rather, they seem to be behaving according to a constrained random rule. If they indeed are, then they would appear to be responding in correspondence with Piaget's expectations that subjects who are between stages will exhibit the groping and uncertainty that marks his Stage IIIA (Piaget & Inhelder, 1967). The problem with Piaget's view is that substantial numbers of subjects appear unable to make the transition to full understanding, as would be expected under his theory. Perhaps 40% of the girls, and roughly 20% of the boys, apparently remain locked in this transitional stage.

The evidence for this interpretation is twofold. First, subjects performing in correspondence with a random rule would be expected to display much larger variance in their responses relative to the variance evidenced by their better performing peers. In fact, the variances (and ranges) of the responses of those who perform poorly are huge: for no vessel angle is their variance ever less than 23 times the variance of good performers (see Table 12), and a similar result holds for the van task (see Table 20) as well.

Second, if subjects tend to favor one response over another, the probability mass of the responses would tend to cluster around a preferred value. This expectation occurred for good performers, and their typically symmetrical and normal appearing response distribution falls off around a zero mean, the correct water-level response (cf. Figs. 8 and 13). The response distribution for poor performers is not of this form. At least over a broad range, the response distribution tends to favor no response over another (see Figs. 9 and 14). Evidence for this response style is better for the water-level than for the van task, but, as was noted, the van task is peculiar in that the van itself is asymmetrical and the range of possible movement of the plumb line is constrained by the physical boundaries of the van. Poor performers appear to avoid grossly wrong responses—even though responses of 40° or more in error do occur—but they apparently cannot decide among responses within a broad interval. Thus, the response distribution is roughly uniform for the bulk of the responses, although the tails of the distribution are more difficult to model suitably.

Another influence that affects both response groups, although to different degrees, is what Witkin et al. (1954) call "field effects." It has long been suspected that such effects contribute to water-level task performance, but to date the evidence has been correlational (e.g., Abravanel & Gingold,

1977; Myer & Hensley, 1984; Signorella & Jamison, 1978). Here, a different source of evidence is provided. Both good and poor performance groups are influenced by such effects, as the means given in Tables 12 and 20 indicate. In particular, the means of the poor performers are not the same as they would be expected to be if only a random rule were influencing their performance. The response distribution for good performers is also systematically altered, but the field effect influence is much more pronounced for the poor performers. Field effects appear to be largely an additive constant effect reflecting the degree to which the vessel is tilted away from the vertical. This influence is proportional to the signed minimum rotation angle (SMRA), the degree of movement necessary to rotate the vessel into its vertical orientation. Thus, while we interpret response variability as being the result of active random rule behavior, we view the mean response error as a passive, largely unconscious influence.

In sum, the two major influences that appear to affect both good and poor performers on both tasks are rule behavior and field effects. The two groups use different rules and hence generate different distributions of responses. Everyone is influenced by field effects, but poor performers much more so than good performers.

To be sure, some data suggest that the emerging picture cannot be quite this simple. One dissonant fact is that, under our random response generation hypothesis, each response is assumed independent of every other. In fact, contrary to this assumption are the consistent although usually small correlations that we obtained between responses at different angles (see Tables 14 and 22). However, an alternative hypothesis mentioned earlier might well hold, namely, that the responses are conditionally independent given any fixed stimulus angle. Thus, a response, and, consequently, the response distribution, depends on the orientation of the stimulus presented. Supporting this hypothesis is the fact that responses are indeed dependent on the stimulus angle; however, whether within-subject responses replicated for a given angle would be independent of each other remains to be tested.

RELATION OF CURRENT FINDINGS TO OTHER RESEARCH

There are a number of points of contact between the research reported here and other research that has focused on rules or strategies underlying children's cognitive processes. Examples include applications of information integration theory (e.g., Anderson & Cuneo, 1978; for critical evaluations, see Lohaus, 1989, 1990) or the growing body of literature concerned with issues of domain specific versus general knowledge rules (e.g., Siegler, 1989).

In spirit at least, our work shows some important similarities to Siegler's (1981) rule assessment approach. Siegler's work is motivated largely from a Piagetian perspective. His approach is to construct a series of different versions of Piagetian concrete operational tasks. The goal is to identify which from among a small set of possible rules children of different ages may use when responding to different tasks. Like our own work, his has focused on individual differences in rule strategies, but he makes no attempt to model the response process. Thus, his decision rules and methodology for classification are quite different from ours. It would appear, however, that his data would be amenable to a modeling approach. While he does find some individual differences in task performance, he does not report the striking within-sex differences that we report. Of course, the tasks that he has used are much more varied than the ones that we have—they include number conservation and balance beam and shadows tasks. Although the nature of the joint structure between the kinds of tasks that he has used and our tasks remains an open question, those that Siegler employed may well require quite different kinds of abilities from what is required by the water-level and the van tasks.

In the original studies that used the psychophysical water-level apparatus (Thomas & Jamison, 1975; Thomas et al., 1973), the vessel was rotated by the experimenter to a fixed clock-hour position in the frontal plane. Subjects rotated a disk with a pretend water line to predict the position that the water would take in the tilted vessel. As a variation on this procedure, imagine a vessel tilted to a particular position with the water therein subsequently frozen; now, if the vessel is rotated, the solid mass remains in the same position relative to the container. McAfee and Proffitt (1991) had subjects rotate pictures of such container systems to the "correct" position, assuming that the container contained liquid water. When the task was altered to the "ice" condition, previously poor performers performed much more satisfactorily. However, in a subsequent assessment using the standard water-level task, these same subjects again performed poorly. McAfee and Proffitt (1991) add, however, that "subsequent verbal questioning showed that most of these subjects explicitly know that a liquid surface remains horizontal" (p. 511), but they provide no data. The authors argue that poor performers misrepresent the problem but that they do not lack knowledge of the process, adding that poor performers are no more variable than good performers.

The data presented here appear to present a serious challenge to some of these ideas. For example, the huge variability of poor performers relative to the very small variability of their better performing peers is a key finding (see Table 12). One reason that McAfee and Proffitt (1991) may not have obtained such differences in variability is that they used absolute deviation scores in their analysis; the problems with such measures were discussed in

Chapter III. Their claim that poor performers understand the principle that a liquid remains horizontal also does not agree with the findings reported here. For example, in the present study, the joint estimated probability of failing on the task and displaying an understanding of the task principle was only .05 (6/132) in the water-level task and .14 (18/128) in the van task (see Table 34). Furthermore, in Thomas et al. (1973), where error-corrected feedback was given after many incorrect response trials, subjects remained unable to answer correctly the probe question, "What is the principle or idea behind where the water goes in the bottle?"

Some Additional Issues for Cognitive Development

There are some fairly obvious extensions of the present work to related tasks and other ages. We mention here what we regard as some of the more interesting issues that remain open.

a) An assumption that underpins much of the age-related growth differences that are reported here is that individuals who are poor performers either remain so or change stage and become good performers; if they do change, it is assumed that they then remain in this mature stage. While this assumption appears reasonable, it is untested, and testing would require a longitudinal research design.

b) An intriguing question concerns the nature of the interrelation between field dependence and rule behavior. Poorly performing subjects are clearly much more field dependent, but how does this relate to rule behavior? Does field dependency act as a kind of inhibitory mechanism blocking acquisition of knowledge about the principles of the task?

c) The fact that the original distributions of the 11–16-year-old boys' and girls' error responses on the two tasks were indistinguishable when task performance was controlled (i.e., girls who perform well are indistinguishable from boys who perform well, as are boys and girls who perform poorly) raises interesting questions as to whether *any* important between-sex differences remain when latent class membership is controlled.

d) What contributes to the within-sex subpopulation differences in the first place? Any satisfactory explanation must specify in some coherent way a mechanism or process by which such population differences could arise.

Although it remains an unpopular hypothesis and is infrequently mentioned in the literature, it has been proposed that sex differences in performance on the water-level and certain other tasks have a biological foundation; specifically, task performance may be *facilitated* by an X-linked recessive gene. There are some explicit predictions that may be derived from the theory (cf. Thomas, 1987). In fact, the theory predicts that the data will support the hypothesis that a two-component mixture distribution generated the data. Of course, there are other factors that might cause a mixture distribution, but there exists no alternative theory. Furthermore, finding evidence of a mixture does not imply that the biological theory is correct.

General Methodological Implications

Additive (Shift) Model

The linear additive model that underlies fixed-effects analysis of variance and the two-sample t test has dominated thinking about issues of research design and data analysis for decades. This model carries with it not only a perspective on how data should be analyzed but also one on how "effects" are to be viewed. Focusing on mean differences between groups— be it in experimentally randomized studies or in observational ones— remains a most common research strategy. For many domains of investigation, such models will no doubt continue to be very useful; however, at least for research questions that are at the intersection of "sex and space," we think that conventional methods must be reevaluated.

There is now considerable evidence that subpopulation differences contribute in important ways to between-group differences on a number of what are often called "spatial tasks" other than those on which we have focused here; these include the rod-and-frame task (Thomas, 1982, 1987), the embedded figures task (Turner, 1991), and mental rotations tasks (Thomas & Kail, 1991; Turner, 1991). These subpopulation differences must be considered in research designs if progress toward understanding group differences is to be achieved. If the latent class perspective is perceived as useful in this regard—and we know of no alternative framework that works as well—then, as a general research model, the shift model is wrong and inappropriate. This is because, in general, latent class models are not additive models. Consequently, additive shift models simply address the wrong questions.[28]

[28] To illustrate, suppose that Y_{boys} is a random variable that has a two-component mixture (latent class) distribution. Suppose that Y_{girls} is another random variable that also has a two-component mixture distribution, but one that differs from the distribution for Y_{boys}. Further, suppose that $\mathscr{E}(Y_{boys}) > \mathscr{E}(Y_{girls})$. To be an additive or a shift model, there must exist some constant δ such that $Y_{girls} + \delta$ has the same distribution as Y_{boys}. It is easily seen that this additive property can hold only under very restricted circumstances. For example, the component weights π_r must be the same for both distributions of Y_{girls} and Y_{boys}, and the differences between the *component* means for the boys' distribution must be the same as the difference between the component means for the girls' distribution. This example also suggests how to proceed if restoring an additive model is desirable, namely, partition the sample *before* proceeding with conventional analyses so that latent class membership is controlled.

Correlation

As noted above, the conventional correlational model is based on the assumption of bivariate normality, but that model is not appropriate for interpreting correlation coefficients obtained from latent class settings. The correlational model for Models 1 and 2 (see Chap. VII) is given in Appendix A, but, in the case of Model 2, it is a complicated expression that makes a simple interpretation of r difficult. However, some special cases can be useful in providing the needed intuition concerning how r is to be interpreted within latent class structures. Thus, consider the two-component bivariate mixture model under local independence given by

$$f(x, y) = \pi f_1(x) f_1(y) + (1 - \pi) f_2(x) f_2(y).$$

When f_r $(r = 1, 2)$ are binomial functions, then Model 1 (Eq. [14]) results. Assume further that both marginal distributions are the same and thus that μ_1 denotes the component means of $f_1(x)$ and $f_1(y)$, and similarly for μ_2; and let σ_1^2 denote the variance of $f_1(x)$ and $f_1(y)$, and similarly for σ_2^2. As an example of a setting in which such a structure might sensibly arise, consider the case in which the water-level task is administered twice to the same individuals. With these assumptions, the correlation ρ between X and Y in $f(x, y)$ is given by

$$\rho = \frac{\pi(1 - \pi)(\mu_1 - \mu_2)^2}{\pi\sigma_1^2 + (1 - \pi)\sigma_2^2 + \pi(1 - \pi)(\mu_1 - \mu_2)^2}.$$

Observe that, if $\sigma_1 = \sigma_2 = 0$, then, as long as $\mu_1 \neq \mu_2$, $\rho = 1$ (the correlation cannot be negative under the assumptions specified, as indeed makes sense). In general, however, the correlation ρ depends on the squared difference between the component means, μ_1 and μ_2, with the component parameters weighted by functions of the proportions of individuals in each component, π and $1 - \pi$.

This correlational model is much in the spirit of the more complicated correlational models of Models 1 and 2. The sample correlation coefficient, r, based on random samples computed from $f(x, y)$ above, would be interpreted as estimating ρ given that the assumptions stated above hold. Note that this structure is very different from the correlation in bivariate normal samples where r estimates the correlation coefficient of the bivariate normal distribution, a *single parameter* (not a function of other parameters, as is the case here).

Multivariate Analysis

There is a large body of literature (much of which is reviewed by Eliot, 1987) that takes a psychometric approach to the study of spatial tasks; often these approaches employ factor analysis. These psychometric approaches require that the data be multivariate normal and with certain restricted covariance structures. These requirements will be violated if any of the response variables are univariate mixtures because the joint structure of such variables cannot be multivariate normal. As noted by Lohman (cited in Eliot, 1987, p. 80), the presence of individual differences in response strategies (as we have established for our spatial tasks) can render factor analytic results misleading.

Meta-Analysis

Meta-analyses of spatial tasks that focus on effect sizes, particularly as they relate to sex differences (e.g., Linn & Petersen, 1985), assume a shift model structure. That is, most effect size procedures assume the same kind of structure as the two-sample t test (Hedges & Olkin, 1985). If the latent class structure of the data is to be taken seriously, then conventional effect sizes are not appropriate procedures. New approaches must be developed.[29]

---

[29] Consider the data of Signorella and Jamison (1978) reported in Table 3 above. A test of mean differences favors boys, with $t(91) = 2.85$, $p < .005$, if conventional assumptions are made. However significant this difference might be, it does not account well for the gender differences in the data. Rosenthal (1984) prefers effect sizes to be indexed by $r = \sqrt{[t^2/(t^2 + df)]} = .29$ and $r^2 = .08$. At least in large samples, r^2 will estimate

$$\frac{\frac{(\mu_B - \mu_G)^2}{4}}{\frac{(\mu_B - \mu_G)^2}{4} + \frac{(\sigma_B^2 + \sigma_G^2)}{2}}.$$

This is the between-group variance divided by the between-group variance plus the average of within-group variance, where μ and σ^2 denote the population means and variances, with B and G denoting boys and girls, respectively. What $r^2 = .08$ reveals is precisely what Table 3 above shows, namely, that the shift model does not describe the data well and, in particular, $[(\mu_B - \mu_G)/2]^2$ is estimated at .54, quite small relative to the 6.08 estimate of $(\sigma_B^2 + \sigma_G^2)/2$. A two-component binomial mixture model, however, fits the data in Table 3 well, with over 90% of the variance accounted for in the boys' data and over 98% in the girls' data. A measure that compares the proportion of model variance with total variance in both sexes would seem to provide the kind of measure that is needed. Consider

$$\xi = \frac{\sigma_{MB}^2 + \sigma_{MG}^2}{\sigma_B^2 + \sigma_G^2}.$$

The numerator is the sum of the mixture model variance for boys and girls separately. That is, σ_{MB}^2 and σ_{MG}^2 are each defined by Eq. (8). Letting estimates replace the parameter values in the above equation results, for the data of Table 3, in $\hat{\xi} = .94$. The distribution $\hat{\xi}$ is unknown, but a standard error that can easily be obtained by bootstrap methods is .04. An approximately 95% confidence interval on ξ that can be obtained from the histogram of the bootstrap replications (Efron & Tibshirani, 1986) is .81–.97. With an estimate

Experiments

The data and procedures that we have presented are from two growth studies, not experiments. Conventional experimental design procedures were never intended for latent class populations. When subjects in an experiment arrive "labeled," then latent class differences may be expressed by different values of a factor in a suitable design. Because subjects for experiments in studies of spatial tasks do not typically arrive labeled, procedures different from those conventionally used must be employed if the latent class perspective is to be taken seriously. One solution is to apply mixture decomposition to the various treatment groups and then follow with suitable significance tests if hypothesis testing is the goal. (An illustration of this procedure is provided in App. B.) Another possibility is to use the water-level or a similar task as a screening device to separate subjects beforehand, defining distinct performance groups before subsequent experimentation. Whatever methodology is employed, consideration needs to be given to how experimental effects are to be viewed (e.g., shift models may remain inappropriate).

Comment

The remaining two sections address two issues. The first concerns the assumptions underlying the binomial mixture model. Using data from the present studies along with a simulation study, we will conclude that the assumptions of the model are violated but that the violations do not appear to be sufficiently serious to threaten any of the major findings of the study. The last section considers the binomial mixture model as a general methodological framework useful for the study of structures where latent classes may be suspected. The methodology appears to have the potential for becoming generally useful; its applicability is predicated on a useful theorem that connects binomial mixtures with mixture structures of almost any form. Consequently, the procedure may be useful for solving the general non-parametric mixture problem.

EVALUATING THE BINOMIAL MIXTURE MODEL FRAMEWORK

Are the assumptions underlying the many variations of probability models that have been constructed in this *Monograph* satisfied? Of course

---

of the standard deviation of $\hat{\xi}$, it is possible to provide approximate tests. For instance, is the estimate of .94 significantly different from $\xi = 1$ or 100%? Construct $(.94 - 1)/.04 = -1.5$, which is approximately Z or standard normal, and thus not significant.

not; as Figure 1 indicates, there is always a mismatch between models and data. Models are constructed with an eye to capturing major features of the phenomena under study only approximately at best and with the hope that no major influences are ignored or badly distorted. The present effort is no exception. The substantive question is whether the models that have been proposed provide any further understanding. We think that they do. Lacking some model of behavior, there appears to be no possibility of sorting out such issues as whether development is discrete or continuous, how individual differences are to be characterized, or what sense can be made of the seemingly peculiar joint distributions of van and water-level scores. Thus, in our view, the effort has extended understanding—it has led us somewhere, and we hope not in the wrong direction!

The theory of mixture distributions has been at the heart of our approach. Each time a mixture model was fit, we have provided fit indices that represent a kind of running check on affairs. But checks on specific assumptions have not been made.

The two key assumptions of the binomial mixture model are the same assumptions of independence and equal probability that underlie the binomial model. Curiously, according to Johnson and Kotz (1969, p. 79), it has been rare to provide critical appraisals of the binomial assumptions; we will do so now by using water-level task data from the 11–16-year-old subjects of Study 1.

The Independence Assumption

The independence assumption is used at two different levels. At the most basic level, the assumption states that, on different trials of the same task, the subject's responses are independent of each other (responses are, of course, assumed to be independent among individuals, but this assumption is easily satisfied). At another level, the assumption states that performance on one task is independent of performance on the other. This independence is assumed to hold within each latent water-level or van task performance group. This "local independence" condition was assumed in Models 1 and 2 for the joint water-level and van tasks.

Consideration of the independence assumption is usefully partitioned into two parts: first, our intuition about independence and whether the assumption "makes sense" and, second, whether the data appear to support the assumption.

Intuition about Independence

There are many instances of settings where our reasoning convinces us that *must* be a lack of independence. This conviction, however, can often be erroneous. The elegant work of Brainerd and Reyna (1992) is particularly revealing in this regard. These authors provide a mass of data showing that, in tasks such as transitive reasoning, whether a child remembers the premise underlying transitive reasoning is independent of the child's success on the task. Here is powerful evidence that performance does *not* depend on memory and, more generally, that one might quite reasonably assume trial-to-trial independence on certain tasks. (It does not follow, of course, that this independence extends to independence on the water-level or van tasks, but it makes such a suggestion more palatable.)

A concern that is often raised with regard to the present research comes in the form of statements such as, "Because some children will provide strings of correct responses on the water-level task, it necessarily follows that the trials are dependent." In fact, this does not constitute evidence against independence. Consider a bag of marbles that are all marked with a "1." Draw a marble at random and then repeat the task multiple times. The result is a sequence of 1s that is nonetheless a sequence of independent draws from the bag. This example indicates that our intuition about independence can be misleading; simply reflecting on the matter is clearly not good enough.

Testing the Independence Assumption

Without the independence assumption there would be no theory, at least no simple theory such as has been presented. However, even if the assumption proves to be wrong in our case, that is no prima facie reason for rejecting the theory. The central issue is whether it is wrong in an important way.

As was noted earlier, if responses on different trials are independent, they will be uncorrelated—yet Tables 14 and 22 show that the original, untransformed responses are in fact correlated, and sometimes not negligibly. However, these correlations are not crucial with respect to evaluating the binomial mixture model; what is needed are the correlations between the Bernoulli-scored 0-1 responses on each trial; these are given in Table 36.

These correlations are typically small; for the good performers, the r values average about zero and range from $-.104$ to $.198$. Under the hypothesis that the population correlation coefficient $\rho = 0$ (which is equivalent to independence in this bivariate Bernoulli case), with $n = 142$ individuals, and using Huber's (1977) distribution-free results $\pm 2 \times (141^{-.5}) = \pm .168$, the interval from $-.168$ to $.168$ should contain about 95% of the probability mass about $\rho = 0$. For good performers, all but two of the observed correlations are within this interval; between one and two values

TABLE 36

Intercorrelations among Water-Level Vessel Angle Responses Scored
Correct (1) or Incorrect (0) for the
Good and Poor Performance Groups, Ages 11–16, Study 1

Clock-Hour Position	Vessel Angle Clock-Hour Position							
	10	11	1	2	4	5	7	8
10	. . .	−.052	.063	−.042	−.052	.198	−.036	.080
11	−.037	. . .	−.040	−.074	−.001	−.058	−.064	.060
1	.061	.136	. . .	.182	−.040	.042	−.080	.007
2	.203	.064	.063	. . .	−.074	−.047	.101	.015
4	.220	.016	.016	.215	. . .	.079	.062	−.104
5	−.054	.026	.130	.069	−.022	. . .	−.040	−.066
7	.059	.130	.308	.080	.012	.117	. . .	.042
8	.208	.049	.107	.121	.271	−.078	.035	. . .

Note.—Values in the upper triangle are for good performers (n = 142), the lower triangle for poor performers (n = 263). Means, standard deviations, and ranges of the 28 r's are as follows: upper triangle, .002, .078, and from −.104 to .198; lower triangle, .09, .1, and from −.08 to .308, respectively.

would be expected to fall outside this interval by chance. For poor performers, the range of r values was from −.008 to .308, with a mean of .09. On the basis of 263 individuals, the corresponding interval is ±.124. Nine r values fall outside this interval, and that is a greater number than would be expected by chance. Thus, there is some evidence against independence for poor performers even though the magnitudes of the correlations are still typically near zero; there is, however, little evidence against independence when the good performance group is considered.

For the joint bivariate data that relate the water-level and the van tasks of Model 2, the evidence concerning independence is provided in Figure 18. As noted before, only the r = .17 is reliably different from zero. Moreover, the fact that all four correlation coefficients are small suggests that, while independence does not strictly hold, it does not appear to be an importantly wrong assumption.

Equal Probability Assumption

The equal probability assumption states that the success probabilities remain stationary over different trials with different vessel and van angles. It is not possible to test here the hypothesis of equal probability within individuals for different stimulus angles because replicated trials on the same vessel angle were not obtained in the present study. However, the equal probability assumption may be tested with data for each vessel angle from different individuals within each performance group, as shown in Table 37. If the hypothesis of constant response probability is correct, then

TABLE 37

Proportions of Correct Responses Made at Each Vessel Angle for
11–16-Year-Old Subjects, Water-Level Task, Study 1

| | Vessel Angle Clock-Hour Position | | | | | | | | |
	10	11	1	2	4	5	7	8	Mean
Good	.972	.915	.873	.944	.915	.965	.958	.894	.930
Poor	.205	.388	.350	.194	.198	.298	.335	.163	.265

Note.—Top row, $n = 142$; bottom row, $n = 263$.

the estimates in each row of this table should be constant within sampling error; recall that, if $\hat{p}$ estimates the binomial parameter, $[\hat{p}(1 - \hat{p})/n]^{.5}$ estimates the standard deviation of the estimate.

There is evidence against the hypothesis of equal probability for both performance groups. For the good performers, where an estimated standard error is $.028 = [.873(1 - .873)/142]^{.5}$ or smaller, most of the estimates are significantly different from each other even though the maximum difference among estimates at each angle is less than .1. The assumption is much more strikingly violated for the poor performers; interestingly, the probability of a correct response is greater when the vessel angle is more nearly upright, as the responses to the 11, 1, 5, and 7 o'clock vessel angles indicate.

How Does the Failure of the Assumptions Influence the Results?

There is evidence that both key assumptions have been violated, but more so in the case of the poor than of the good performers. However, the crucial issue concerns whether the results that we have reported would be altered in important ways given these violations.

Violation of the constant probability assumption appears to have negligible consequences. It does mean that estimates of θ_r need to be reinterpreted as being an average value, over different vessel angles, rather than as an estimate of a single fixed value. In this regard, note that the mean proportions shown in Table 37 are .93 for good and .26 for poor performers and hence very close to the maximum likelihood estimates of .91 and .25 obtained under the two-component mixture model (see Table 7). Had these estimates been much closer, the results could have been seriously compromised. The fact that they do not come within shouting distance of each other saves the day and simply reinforces the evidence for striking differences in the success probabilities of the two groups of performers.

Shifts in the success probabilities would be more critical in the construction of confidence intervals and specific tests for the estimates of θ_r; for example, the coverage probabilities for confidence intervals would be expected to be in error.

Evaluating the effect of lack of trial-to-trial independence of the responses—measured here as correlation between different responses—is more problematic because both the signs and the magnitudes of the r values vary over vessel angles, making it difficult to predict how it would influence resulting analyses. The fact that the correlations are typically small (see Table 36) is reassuring; however, it seems that the only way to study the problem is through simulation. We report one "worst-case" simulation here, with correlation between trials much larger than those that we actually obtained, so as to demonstrate that the main results of the mixture decomposition are not likely to be placed in jeopardy.

Mixture Decomposition under Response Correlation: A Simulation Robustness Study

The simulation focused on the correlation between response pairs in a two-component binomial mixture with $\theta_1 = .15 = 2/13$ and $\theta_2 = 1/2$. There were X_i ($i = 1, \ldots, 8$) Bernoulli random variables summed together, to define Y as follows:

$$Y = (X_1 + X_2) + (X_3 + X_4) + (X_5 + X_6) + (X_7 + X_8).$$

Within each pair of X_i in parentheses, the variables were correlated at a constant value within each "binomial" component. For the first component, this correlation was $9/22 = .41$; thus, for each of the four pairs in parentheses, the correlation was .41 for the first component and $5/7 = .71$ for the second. The correlation between the X_i outside the parentheses was 0; thus, for example, X_1 and X_3, and X_6 and X_7, were 0 correlated (which is equivalent to independence). The magnitudes of these correlations are much larger than those typically seen in Table 36; they reflect the fact that there is some correlation between certain pairs of vessel angles but not between others.

The simulation sample size was $n = 30$, with 15 observations sampled from each component. Thus, $\pi_1 = \pi_2 = .5$, and 200 samples were obtained in this way. Each of the 200 samples was subjected to binomial decomposition for $k = 1, 2,$ and 3 components.

The results are easily summarized. For none of the 200 simulations was AIC(1) the smallest; thus, in no case was a one-component model found to fit the data best. AIC(2) was the smallest in the vast majority of cases. On 25 of 200 trials, AIC(3) was found to be smallest, thus prompting in these instances the evidently erroneous conclusion that the population sampled contained three components. Thus, in terms of componential structure, this simulation does not provide evidence that the decompositions that we performed will lead to erroneous conclusions. If anything, there is the tendency to select a too complex rather than a too simple model as the best, at least when AIC is used as the model selection criterion (see also Windham & Cutler, 1992).

Consider next the influence of model violation on the point estimates that were obtained from the data.

The mean of the 200 $\hat{\theta}_1$ was .14, compared with $\theta_1 = .15$; the mean of the 200 $\hat{\theta}_2$ was .57, while $\theta_2 = .5$. Correspondingly, the means of the $\hat{\pi}_i$ were .56 and .44, $i = 1, 2$, respectively, while $\pi_1 = \pi_2 = .5$. The parameter estimates thus appear biased, but precisely how is difficult to answer without additional simulations.

Taken together, the evidence indicates that, although the model assumptions have been violated, there appears little reason to suspect that these violations compromise our general conclusions.

BINOMIAL MIXTURES AS A GENERAL METHODOLOGICAL FRAMEWORK

Our general strategy has been to transform the original responses with the "number correct" scoring rule g_3 (Eq. [3]) and then to regard the number of correct trials as being binomial in distribution. Because different individuals have different values of the success parameter θ, the response distribution for different individuals is a mixed binomial distribution. Once the number of mixture components and their parameters have been estimated, the sample can be partitioned into discrete subgroups for further analyses of the original response data.

Conceptually, mixture distributions can be formed out of any collection of probability distributions. What might be questioned, however, is whether it is sensible to view the problem as a binomial mixture that requires an intermediate data transformation step. At first glance, this approach seems inefficient. Why not view the original data as a mixture distribution and partition it directly, avoiding the transformation step?

Actually, this "inefficient" procedure appears to hold considerable promise as a nonparametric general decomposition strategy. The reason is that it avoids some difficult problems inherent in many mixture frameworks, problems that are nicely illustrated by data from the present study. A second related reason is that there is a very important and congenial conceptual correspondence between the binomial mixture framework and the general mixture or latent class problem.

Should one desire to decompose the original responses of the van or water-level data (be they signed or absolute values), the first issue that must be decided is the distributional form that the individual components should take. For continuous data, the most commonly used mixture framework is a mixture of normal distributions with each component assumed to be a normal distribution. However, as shown by Study 1, the distribution of original error responses (i.e., the degrees off horizontal or vertical) for the good and poor performers comes from very different distributions, particularly in the water-level task. While for the good performers the error distributions appear reasonably normal, for the poor performers a variation of the uniform appears to model the data at least as a first approximation. Thus, to assume that the original data may be viewed as a mixture of normal distributions appears to be an importantly wrong assumption, at least in hindsight.

What the binomial mixture distribution approach does is to allow for an essentially nonparametric approach to the partitioning of the original response distribution. What is being said is that, if the distribution of transformed responses is a binomial mixture, then the original response distribution is a mixture distribution as well. Furthermore, there is a very congenial relation between properties of the binomial mixture and the original response distribution. First, the number of components in the original distribution will agree with the number of components in the binomial distribution. Consequently, if the distribution of binomial responses does not support a mixture, then the original distribution is not a mixture either. Second, the mixture weights (the π_r of the binomial mixture) will be the same as the weights of the original response distribution. Thus, the number of components and weights of the mixture of binomials agrees with the corresponding number of components of the original response distribution, even if the distribution of the components of the original distribution is unknown.

This results in a strong statement: if the original distribution is a mixture, then the binomial distribution will be a mixture, and vice versa. Conversely, an absence of a mixture in either distribution implies its absence in the other distribution.

This result is stated formally in Appendix C; however, the basic ideas can be made intuitively plausible by considering Figure 25. In the foreground, it depicts a hypothetical mixture distribution that models the total population. The two distributions pictured in the background are component distributions and have been weighted by their π_r values ($\pi_1 = 2/3$, $\pi_2 = 1/3$) so that the sum of these distributions is the mixture distribution. In sampling, responses are sampled from one of these two component distributions, but the responses arrive unlabeled: it is not clear which distribution contributed which responses. The problem is to determine the number of components in the original distribution (if more than one exist) and the proportion of observations in each component and, perhaps, to estimate

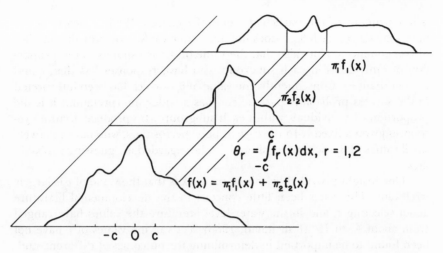

$\pi_1 f_1(x)$

$\pi_2 f_2(x)$

$$\theta_r = \int_{-c}^{c} f_r(x)dx, \ r = 1,2$$

$$f(x) = \pi_1 f_1(x) + \pi_2 f_2(x)$$

−c O c

FIG. 25.—Two-component univariate mixture distribution, $f(x)$, with irregular components. Component 1, $f_1(x)$, and component 2, $f_2(x)$, are shown displaced so that they may be seen. $\pi_1 = 2/3$, $\pi_2 = 1/3$, $\theta_1 = 1/5$, and $\theta_2 = 2/3$. For simplicity, both distributions are shown centered on zero.

the distributions of the components and their parameters as well. It is assumed that responses within the interval from $-c$ to c are assigned a 1 while responses outside this interval receive a 0.

The proportions within the interval from $-c$ to c are different for the two components depicted in Figure 25. In the interval associated with component 1, it is $1/5 = \theta_1 = \int_{-c}^{c} f_1(x)dx$, whereas, in the interval associated with component 2, it is $2/3 = \theta_2 = \int_{-c}^{c} f_2(x)dx$.

Assuming that each subject who is sampled provides m replicated independent responses, each with the same θ_r, then each distribution $f_r(x)$ ($r = 1, 2$) has an associated binomial distribution of Y correct responses for each subject; that is, Y will be $b(y; \theta_r, m)$ in distribution. And, because there are individuals in proportion π_r with $f_r(x)$, there are individuals in the same corresponding proportions with $b(y; \theta_r, m)$; that is, $\pi_r b(y; \theta_r, m)$. This fact leads to the distribution of the transformed scores as a binomial mixture. Thus, the number of components in the mixed binomial matches the number of components in the original mixture designated in Figure 25 as $f(x)$ and shown in the foreground. The component weights of the original distribution match the component weights of the binomial mixture. Note that, if all components had the same $f_r(x)$ (unlike Fig. 25), there would be but one corresponding binomial component. In this sense, there is a one-to-one correspondence between the binomial mixture distribution and the original componentially unknown mixture distribution.

Note that, as Figure 25 illustrates, the number of binomial components is independent of the particular value of c chosen. While c clearly determines the size of each θ_r, it does not determine the size of π_r or the number of components k. Note also that the value of θ_r corresponds to the proportion of individuals in each subgroup who have responses less than c and greater than $-c$. Consequently, the value of θ_r—which has been interpreted as the success probability parameter—has a wider interpretation: it is the proportion of individuals within each subgroup who produce accurate responses given a fixed c. In the case of poor performers, who have relatively small values of θ, such values should not be regarded as "guessing probabilities."

One insight provided by this framework is that the value of c is largely irrelevant. There has been little concern in the developmental literature about selecting c, and in the water-level literature the values have ranged from about 4° to 15° (Kalichman, 1988). Yet varying values of c have not been found to be important in determining the outcomes of different studies; the present framework provides an explanation for this empirical fact.

Once the parameters of the binomial mixture have been obtained, partitioning observations and studying features of the corresponding subgroups, such as their cognitive strategies and features of the original response distribution, are readily achieved. Thus, the general strategy employed here should be useful in addressing issues of individual differences in a variety of settings, particularly in studies where issues of sex and spatial abilities are of concern. The main requirement to permit the application of this methodology is that there be independent replicated responses for each individual and that the replicates have at least approximately the same success or θ probability (as the previous section indicated,

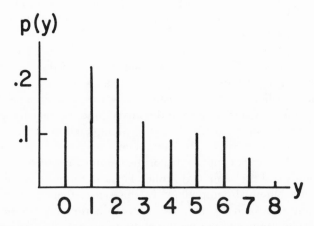

Fig. 26.—Two-component mixture of binomials, $m = 8$, based on the g_3 transformation of distributions $f_1(x)$ and $f_2(x)$ in Fig. 25.

the model framework appears robust against at least some assumption violations, although more research must be done on the matter).[30]

Finally, to illustrate the potential power of the method, consider again the distributions in Figure 25. The marginal mixture distribution, $f(x)$, does not readily reveal either its componential structure or the relative contribution of its components. Furthermore, because the components are of irregular form, it is not obvious how one might decompose the original distribution. But the population model of the discrete binomial mixture distribution, corresponding to Figure 25, is much clearer in this matter. Assume $m = 8$ replicated responses for each individual, each of which is sampled with the same probability θ_r from one of the two individual components $f_r(x)$ $(r = 1, 2)$. Transform these responses by g_3 into frequencies. The binomial mixture distribution $p(y)$ corresponding to Figure 25 is shown in Figure 26. This distribution with its bimodal appearance reveals much more clearly the two-component structure of the original response distribution and, in the proportions of each component, reflects the common π_r weights of both $p(y)$ and $f(x)$.

[30] The general procedure for binomial mixture decomposition is very simple and easily programmed, so computational simplicity is maximized. Computations may be performed on a standard PC; routines are available (from H.T.). In addition, the number of parameters estimated in the k component binomial mixture is $2k - 1$, while a k component normal mixture, the standard default option, has $3k - 1$ parameters. Thus, there are k fewer parameters to estimate. Furthermore, the parameters in the binomial case are probabilities and thus are bounded in the interval 0–1, whereas the mean and variance of the normal are not so bounded, and hence suitable starting values may be more difficult to specify.

Furthermore, for each new family of distributions that might be considered as components for a mixture distribution, the estimation equations must be worked out anew from the likelihood equations and programs written and checked—a nontrivial task. The binomial approach eschews all this effort. The binomial mixture procedure may be inefficient if components of the mixture are known (to be normal, e.g.); in such cases, decomposition based on the known components should be used. In practice, however, it is almost never obvious how best to obtain evidence on the componential character of the data. In fact, specifying the componential form of the components is the major difficulty in applications of mixtures to diverse settings.

APPENDIX A

ESTIMATION IN BIVARIATE BINOMIAL MIXTURES

This appendix provides details concerning the joint van and water-level models, primarily Model 2. Both models are constrained by the desire to preserve marginal two-component binomial mixtures for both tasks. Thus, define the marginals as

$$f(x) = \pi_x b(x; \theta_{x1}) + (1 - \pi_x) b(x; \theta_{x2}),$$

$$f(y) = \pi_y b(y; \theta_{y1}) + (1 - \pi_y) b(y; \theta_{y2}).$$

We write $b(w; \theta, m) \equiv b(w; \theta)$ in most instances.

The posterior probability that observation $W = w$ comes from component r $(r = 1, 2)$ is

$$P(r|w) = \frac{\pi_r b(w; \theta_{wr})}{\pi_1 b(w; \theta_{w1}) + \pi_2 b(w; \theta_{w2})}.$$

Now define the conditional distribution of Y given $X = x$:

$$f(y|x) = \pi_{y|x} b(y; \theta_{y1}) + (1 - \pi_{y|x}) b(y; \theta_{y2}).$$

The conditional weight $\pi_{y|x} = \alpha P(1|X) + \beta P(2|X)$. α and β are state change probabilities. With $X1$, $Y1$, $X2$, and $Y2$ denoting the first and second components of X and Y, respectively, then α is the probability of changing from $X1$ to $Y1$, β is the probability of changing from $X2$ to $Y1$, $1 - \alpha$ is the probability of changing from $X1$ to $Y2$, and $1 - \beta$ is the probability of changing from $X2$ to $Y2$.

The joint distribution of X and Y is given by

$$f(y|x)f(x) = f(x, y) = \alpha \pi_x b(x; \theta_{x1}) b(y; \theta_{y1}) + \beta(1 - \pi_x) b(x; \theta_{x2}) b(y; \theta_{y1})$$

$$+ (1 - \alpha) \pi_x b(x; \theta_{x1}) b(y; \theta_{y2})$$

$$+ (1 - \beta)(1 - \pi_x) b(x; \theta_{x2}) b(y; \theta_{y2}),$$

which is the expression given for Model 2 above.

By summing out X, the marginal distribution of Y, $f(y)$ is given by

$$f(y) = \sum_x f(x, y),$$

with $\pi_y \equiv \alpha\pi_x + \beta(1 - \pi_x)$, so

$$\beta = (\pi_y - \alpha\pi_x)/(1 - \pi_x),$$

eliminating β as an independent parameter.

Note that, if $\pi \equiv \pi_x = \pi_y$, $\alpha = 1$ and $\beta = 0$ give Model 1. In this case,

$$f(x, y) = \pi b(x; \theta_{x1})b(y; \theta_{y1}) + (1 - \pi)b(x; \theta_{x2})b(y; \theta_{y2}),$$

the expression given for Model 1. Also, of course, $f(x, y) = f(x|y)f(y)$. An identical development, with the role of the X and Y interchanged and α' being the probability of changing from $Y1$ to $X1$, with β' similarily defined, reveals that $\alpha/\alpha' = \pi_y/\pi_x$.

The mean and variance of X and Y are given by expressions provided earlier in Equations (7) and (8).

$$\mathcal{E}(Y|x) = \pi_{y|x}[\theta_{y1}(1 - \theta_{y1}) + (m\theta_{y1})^2] + (1 - \pi_{y|x})[\theta_{y2}(1 - \theta_{y2}) + (m\theta_{y2})^2],$$

and similarly for $\mathcal{E}(X|y)$, with the role of X and Y interchanged.

$$\mathcal{E}(XY) = m^2[\alpha\pi_x\theta_{x1}\theta_{y1} + (\pi_y - \alpha\pi_x)\theta_{x2}\theta_{y1} + (1 - \alpha)\pi_x\theta_{x1}\theta_{y2}$$
$$+ (1 - \pi_y - \pi_x + \alpha\pi_y)\theta_{x2}\theta_{y2}];$$

consequently, the model correlation ρ is given by

$$[\mathcal{E}(XY) - \mathcal{E}(X)\mathcal{E}(Y)]/[\mathcal{V}(X)\mathcal{V}(Y)]^{1/2}.$$

Except for α, maximum likelihood estimates are the estimates under the marginal distributions of X and Y. The maximum likelihood estimate of α can be obtained by a simple Newton-Raphson algorithm.

Define functions num_α, $\text{den}1_\alpha$, and $\text{den}2_\alpha$ by

$$\text{num}_\alpha = \pi_x[b(x_i; \theta_{x1}) - b(x_i; \theta_{x2})][b(y_i; \theta_{y1}) - b(y_i; \theta_{y2})],$$

$$\text{den}1_\alpha = [\alpha\pi_x b(x_i; \theta_{x1}) + (\pi_y - \alpha\pi_x)b(x_i; \theta_{x2}, m)]b(y_i; \theta_{y1}),$$

$$\text{den}2_\alpha = [(1 - \alpha)\pi_x b(x_i; \theta_{x1}) + (1 - \pi_y - \pi_x + \alpha\pi_x)b(x_i; \theta_{x2})]b(y_i; \theta_{y2}),$$

$$g(\alpha) = \sum_{i=1}^{n} [\text{num}_\alpha/(\text{den}1_\alpha + \text{den}2_\alpha)],$$

$$g'(\alpha) = \sum_{i=1}^{n} -\text{num}_\alpha/(\text{den}1_\alpha + \text{den}2_\alpha)^2.$$

Then, a Newton-Raphson algorithm for α is given by

$$\alpha_{o+1} = \alpha_o - g(\alpha_o)/g'(\alpha_o),$$

for $o = 1, 2, \ldots$, until α_{o+1} converges.

To estimate a common π under Model 1 when θ estimates from the marginal distributions are available, define

$$\text{num}_\pi = b(x_i; \theta_{x1})b(y_i; \theta_{y1}) + b(y_i; \theta_{y1})b(y_i; \theta_{y1}),$$

$$\text{den1}_\pi = \pi b(x_i; \theta_{x1})b(y_i; \theta_{y1}) + (1 - \pi)b(x_i; \theta_{x1})b(y_i; \theta_{y1}).$$

Then,

$$h(\pi) = \sum_{i=1}^{n} \text{num}_\pi/(\text{den1}_\pi),$$

$$h'(\pi) = \sum_{i=1}^{n} -\text{num}_\pi/(\text{den1}_\pi)^2.$$

Then

$$\pi_{o+1} = \pi_o - h(\pi_o)/h'(\pi_o)$$

is a Newton-Raphson scheme for estimating π.

The posterior probability of pair (x, y) having come from component r is

$$P[r \mid (x, y)] = (\text{weighted component } r)/f(x, y).$$

Thus, the estimate

$$\hat{P}[\text{poor performance on both tasks} \mid (x, y)] = \frac{\hat{\alpha}\hat{\pi}_x b(x; \hat{\theta}_{x1}, m)b(y; \hat{\theta}_{y1}, m)}{\hat{f}(x, y)},$$

where $\hat{f}(x, y)$ is $f(x, y)$ with estimates replacing the parameters.

APPLICATIONS OF DISCRETE MIXTURE METHODOLOGY TO EXPERIMENTS

We illustrate how mixture decomposition procedures may be implemented in experiments by using water-level data from table 2 of Liben and Golbeck (1984). Other approaches might follow Cox (1970). There are two variables of interest: sex and rule (i.e., rule vs. no rule), a manipulated variable. The data are number of correct water-level responses based on a g_3 transformation of the data. There were 40 college students in each condition; histograms of the data are shown in Table B1.

Graphs of the means for each condition appear in Figure B1. From a conventional perspective, the graph suggests a lack of interaction between sex and rule; in fact, the F test reported by Liben and Golbeck (1984) for the interaction was insignificant, but a significant main effect remained.

Within the mixture framework, however, the means are not the quantities on which to focus. Rather, focus on the parameters that define the mean. Under a two-component binomial mixture model with each pair of crossed conditions denoted by $o = 1, 2, 3, 4$, the population means are (from Eq. [7])

$$\mu_o = m[\pi_{1o}\theta_{1o} + (1 - \pi_{1o})\theta_{2o}],$$

with each sample mean $\bar{x}_o$ estimating μ_o; that is, $\hat{\mu}_o = \bar{x}_o$. In this example, $m = 6$.

The analysis begins by decomposing each condition separately. Table B2 shows that a two-component binomial mixture model provides a satisfactory description of the data. All the quantities necessary to explore a number of hypotheses are provided in this table; what is needed are parameter estimates and estimates of their standard errors.

The procedures make use of the approximate normality of the estimates when they are standardized. For example, consider θ_{1o}:

$$Z_{1o} = [\hat{\theta}_{1o} - \mathscr{E}(\hat{\theta}_{1o})]/\hat{S}E(\hat{\theta}_{1o}), \tag{B1}$$

TABLE B1

FREQUENCY HISTOGRAMS FOR MALES AND FEMALES UNDER NO RULE
AND RULE CONDITIONS

Males		Females	Males		Females
No Rule			*Rule*		
.05**	0	******.15		0	*****.13
.13*****	1	*********.23	.03*	1	****.10
.05**	2	*******.18	.05**	2	**.05
.18*******	3	*******.18	.10****	3	*********.23
.10****	4	****.10	.15******	4	*****.13
.15******	5	**.05	.25**********	5	******.15
.35**************	6	*****.13	.43*****************	6	*********.23
n = 40		*n* = 40	*n* = 40		*n* = 40

SOURCE.—Data are taken from Liben and Golbeck (1984).
NOTE.—.05** 0 ******.15 denotes that 5% of the males and 15% of the females had 0 correct. Each * denotes 1 individual.

where $\hat{SE}(\hat{\theta}_{1o}) = [\hat{var}(\hat{\theta}_{1o})]^{1/2}$ are given in Table B2 along with the parameter estimates. Z_{1o} is about standard normal, so it may be referenced to a normal table to obtain approximate p values; similarly, Z_{1o}^2 is about $\chi^2(1)$ in distribution, so, because linear combinations of independent χ^2 random variables are also χ^2, with corresponding addition of the degrees of freedom, it is possible to construct a variety of tests.

First, consider homogeneity tests on the three parameters θ_1, θ_2, and π. For example, to test the hypothesis that the θ_{1o} ($o = 1, \ldots, 4$) are equal against the alternative hypothesis that at least one is different from the rest, form the corresponding Z_{1o} and then construct $\Sigma_{o=1}^4 Z_{1o}^2$, which is about $\chi^2(4)$ in distribution. The expectation in the numerator of each Z_{1o} (Eq. [B1]) is the average of all four $\hat{\theta}_{1o}$ values because, under the null hypothesis, all four values estimate the same quantity.

The three homogeneity tests reveal that the θ_{1o} are not all the same, $P(\chi^2[4] = 20.51) < .002$. A similar finding is revealed for the π_{1o}, $P(\chi^2[4] = 26.1) < .001$, but there is insufficient evidence to conclude that the four θ_2 are different from each other, $P(\chi^2[4] = 2.93) = .43$. These results agree with initial impressions gleaned from Table B2. For example, estimates of θ_2 are very similar except for the female/no rule condition, but both the θ_1 and the π parameters appear quite variable over conditions, suggesting that different parameter values are associated with each condition.

Specific contrasts can be made as well. For instance, is the sum (or average) of the π parameters for the males equal to the corresponding quantity for females? Letting $o = 1, 2$, denote the males in no rule and rule

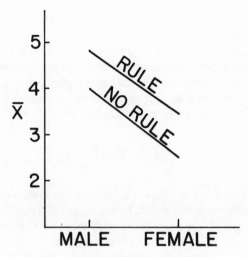

Fig. B1.—Water-level mean values of four conditions, data from Liben and Golbeck (1984).

and $o = 3, 4$, denote females in no rule and rule conditions, respectively, then

$$[(\hat{\pi}_{11} + \hat{\pi}_{12}) - (\hat{\pi}_{13} + \hat{\pi}_{14})]/\left[\sum_{o=1}^{4} \hat{v}ar\,(\hat{\pi}_{1o})\right]^{1/2}$$

is about standard normal in distribution under the null hypothesis of interest. The findings indicate that the two sexes do not have the same π_1 parameters, $P(|Z| > 3.59) < .005$. Because $\pi_1 = 1 - \pi_2$, tests on π_1 are tests

TABLE B2

Binomial Mixture Model Estimates for Sex and Rule Conditions

	$\bar{x}$	$\hat{\theta}_1$	$\hat{\theta}_2$	$\hat{\pi}_2$	$\chi^2(3)$	VAF (%)
No rule:						
Males	4.0	.373	.929	.473	4.65	92
		(.045)	(.023)	(.079)		
Females	2.5	.292	.904	.796	3.75	89
		(.032)	(.042)	(.064)		
Rule:						
Males	4.83	.560	.920	.321	.31	97
		(.057)	(.021)	(.074)		
Females	3.47	.323	.868	.530	12.23	88
		(.041)	(.032)	(.079)		

Source.—Data are taken from Liben and Golbeck (1984).
Note.—Estimated standard errors are in parentheses.

on π_2. Similarly, the θ_{1o} conditions do not have the same θ_1 parameters, $P(|Z| > 3.55) < .005$.

Figures B2 and B3 graph the $\hat{\pi}_1$ and $\hat{\theta}_1$ estimates for the four conditions. A test for parallelism between the curves that is in the spirit of an interaction test in analysis of variance can also be constructed. Are the second-order differences between the rule and the no rule conditions for each sex the same? To answer the question, construct

$$[(\hat{\pi}_{11} - \hat{\pi}_{12}) - (\hat{\pi}_{13} - \hat{\pi}_{14})]/\left[\sum_{o=1}^{4} \hat{var}\,(\hat{\pi}_{1o}) \right]^{1/2}.$$

This statistic is about standard normal under the null hypothesis that the second-order differences are equal. In this case, $P(|Z| > .77) = .22$, so there is no evidence against the lines being parallel. The same test for θ_1 yields $P(|Z| > 1.74) = .08$, marginally significant perhaps.

Overall, these analyses provide more insight into the nature of how the treatment conditions "work" than does a summary figure of means. Briefly, both sexes improved under the rule and no rule conditions with respect to the π parameter: this result says that the proportion of poor responders was reduced by about .2 as a consequence of being told a rule. The rule manipulation appears to influence both sexes about equally. However,

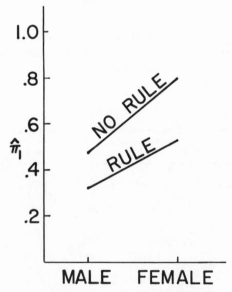

Fig. B2.—Water-level estimates of $\hat{\pi}_1$ for four conditions, data from Liben and Golbeck (1984).

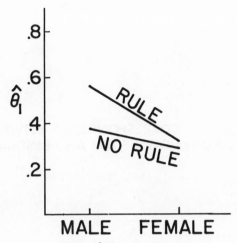

FIG. B3.—Water-level estimates of $\hat{\theta}_1$ for four conditions, data from Liben and Golbeck (1984).

among individuals in the more poorly scoring groups, for both sexes, the proportion of successful responses (the θ_1 parameter) suggests differential effects; at a marginally significant level, males within the poorly performing group are influenced in their accuracy scores more than are poorly performing females. Recall that there is no evidence against the hypothesis that the θ_2 parameter is constant over all conditions (homogeneity was not rejected), which seems quite plausible. θ_2 is the proportion of correct items for subjects in the better performing group who perform accurately, a proportion already about 90%.

It is interesting to view the group means in Figure B1 in light of the present analysis. From the perspective of mixture theory, the figure is, in a sense, an artifact of pooling. The means show "additivity" because of the particular combination of π and θ values; when the means are decomposed, the source of the difference is more readily diagnosed. Note that, when inserted into Equation (7), the parameter estimates give back the sample means, as indeed they should.

Finally, it should be stressed that the p levels given here are all approximate because they were constructed under large sample considerations. If there is concern that the number of statistical tests constructed might result in chance findings, simply require smaller p values for significance.

APPENDIX C

CORRESPONDENCE BETWEEN MIXTURES OF UNKNOWN FORM AND BINOMIAL MIXTURES

This appendix provides the argument that shows that there is a one-to-one correspondence between the components of a binomial mixture distribution and the components of the original score distribution on which binomial mixture is based, given a suitable sampling scheme. That is, both distributions are mixtures with the same number of components, and the corresponding components of the two associated mixture distributions have the same weights:

First, we give some definitions:

CONDITION C1.—Let $\mathscr{F}$ be the set of all density functions ("density" refers to both density and mass functions in the following); $g(x) \in \mathscr{F}$ if $\int_{-\infty}^{+\infty} dG(x) = 1$, $g(x) \geq 0$. Let k be a fixed positive integer and $\pi = (\pi_1, \pi_2, \ldots, \pi_k)$ be a vector of fixed values with $\pi_r > 0$ $(r = 1, \ldots, k)$ and $\sum_{r=1}^{k} \pi_r = 1$.

CONDITION C2.—If $f_r(x) \in \mathscr{F}$ $(r = 1, \ldots, k)$, then $f(x) = \sum_{r=1}^{k} \pi_r f_r(x)$ is a finite mixture, and $f(x) \in \mathscr{F}$. However, only those mixtures with distinct components are of interest, so consider the set of $\mathcal{M} \subset \mathscr{F}$ defined by the following.

CONDITION C3.—$\mathcal{M} = [\sum_{r=1}^{k} f_r(x): f_r(x) \in \mathscr{F}, f_{(1)}(x), f_{(2)}(x), \ldots, f_{(k)}(x)$ are densities of different distributions]. To ensure identifiability of the components through their binomial representation, consider a subset $\mathcal{M}_\pi(\theta) \subset \mathcal{M}$. Mixtures are in $\mathcal{M}_\pi(\theta)$ if, when integrated or summed over a common domain space $\mathscr{C}$, the proportion θ is different for each component.

CONDITION C4.—$\mathcal{M}_\pi(\theta) = [f(x) \in \mathcal{M}: 0 < \theta(\mathscr{C}; f_r) = \int_{\mathscr{C}} dF_r(x) < 1, \theta(\mathscr{C}; f_r), r = 1, \ldots, k,$ are distinct].

CONDITION C5.—Let $\mathcal{P}$ be a population with mutually disjoint sub-populations. Thus, $P_r, r = 1, \ldots, k, \cup_{r=1}^{k} P_r = \mathcal{P}$. Each P_r is in proportion π_r. Associated with each P_r is density $f_r(x)$. Thus, the density associated with $\mathcal{P}$ is the mixture $f(x) = \sum_{r=1}^{k} \pi_r f_r(x)$.

CONDITION C6.—Take a random sample size 1 sampled from $\mathcal{P}$. The probability of the element being selected from P_r is π_r, and the distribution of the sampled X associated with P_r is $f_r(x)$. Define a new random variable $T(X) = W$, where $T(X)$ is $W = 1$ if $x \in \mathcal{C}$ and $W = 0$ if $x \notin \mathcal{C}$.

With these conditions, we have $P(W = 1 | P_r) = \theta(\mathcal{C}; f_r) = \int_{\mathcal{C}} dF_r(x)$. Because $f(x) \in \mathcal{M}_\pi(\theta)$, the $\theta(\mathcal{C}; f_r)$ are all different. Consequently, $T(X)$ defines a distinct binomial distribution for each P_r, $b[w; \theta(\mathcal{C}; f_r), 1], r = 1, \ldots, k$. Furthermore, if there are m independent observations from subpopulation P_r, then associated with P_r is $Y = \sum_{j=1}^{m} W_j$, which is distributed as $b[y; \theta_r(\mathcal{C}; f_r), m]$. Thus, besides an associated $f_r(x)$, P_r has an associated $b[y; \theta_r(\mathcal{C}; f_r), m]$. Therefore, $\mathcal{P}$ has an associated mixed binomial distribution

$$g(y) = \sum_{r=1}^{k} \pi_r b[y; \theta_r(\mathcal{C}; f_r), m] \in \mathcal{M}.$$

To summarize:

THEOREM C1.—Given Conditions C1–C6, a population with an associated distribution $f(x) = \sum_{r=1}^{k} \pi_r f_r(x)$ also has an associated binomial mixture distribution $g(y) = \sum_{r=1}^{k} \pi_r b[y; \theta_r(\mathcal{C}; f_r), m]$.

COROLLARY.—If $f(x) \in \mathcal{F} - \cup_\pi \mathcal{M}_\pi(\theta)$, $T(X)$ leads to a binomial distribution with number of components fewer than k.

REFERENCES

Abravanel, E., & Gingold, H. (1977). Perceiving and representing orientation: Effects of the spatial framework. *Merrill-Palmer Quarterly,* **23,** 265–278.

Abravanel, E., & Gingold, H. (1982). Evidence for perceptual influences in understanding liquid invariance. *Journal of Genetic Psychology,* **140,** 237–247.

Amthauer, R. (1973). *Intelligenz-Struktur-Test.* Goettingen: Hogrefe.

Anderson, N. H., & Cuneo, D. O. (1978). The height + width rule in children's judgments of quantity. *Journal of Experimental Psychology: General,* **107,** 335–378.

Anderson, T. W. (1984). *An introduction to multivariate statistical analysis* (2d ed.). New York: Wiley.

Barlow, R. E., Bartholomew, D. J., Bremner, J. M., & Brunk, H. D. (1972). *Statistical inference under order restrictions.* New York: Wiley.

Barna, J. D., & O'Connell, D. C. (1967). Perception of horizontality as a function of age and stimulus setting. *Perceptual and Motor Skills,* **25,** 70–72.

Barsky, R. D., & Lachman, M. E. (1986). Understanding of horizontality in college women: Effects of two training procedures. *International Journal of Behavioral Development,* **9,** 31–43.

Bisanz, J., Brainerd, C., & Kail, R. (1987). *Formal methods in developmental psychology.* New York: Springer-Verlag.

Blischke, W. R. (1964). Estimating the parameters of mixtures of binomial distributions. *Journal of the American Statistical Association,* **59,** 510–528.

Box, G. E. P. (1976). Science and statistics. *Journal of the American Statistical Association,* **71,** 791–799.

Bozdogan, H. (1987). Model selection and Akaike's information criterion (AIC): The general theory and its analytical extensions. *Psychometrika,* **52,** 345–370.

Brainerd, C. J. (1973). Judgments and explanations as criteria for the presence of cognitive structures. *Psychological Bulletin,* **79,** 172–179.

Brainerd, C. J. (1979). Markovian interpretations of conservation learning. *Psychological Review,* **86,** 181–213.

Brainerd, C. J. (1982). Children's concept learning as rule-sampling systems with Markovian properties. In C. J. Brainerd (Ed.), *Children's logical and mathematical cognition: Progress in cognitive development research.* New York: Springer-Verlag.

Brainerd, C. J. (1985). Structural invariance in the developmental analysis of learning. In J. Bisanz, G. L. Bisanz, & R. Kail (Eds.), *Learning in children.* New York: Springer-Verlag.

Brainerd, C. J., Howe, M. L., & Desrochers, A. (1982). The general theory of two-stage learning: A mathematical review with illustrations from memory development. *Psychological Review,* **91,** 634–665.

Brainerd, C. J., & Reyna, V. F. (1992). Explaining "memory free" reasoning. *Psychological Science, 3, 332–339.*

Brown, J. F. (1936). On the use of mathematics in psychological theory. *Psychometrika, 1, 77–90.*

Chapman, M., & McBride, M. L. (1992). Beyond competence and performance: Children's class inclusion strategies, superordinate class cues, and verbal justifications. *Developmental Psychology, 28, 319–327.*

Coombs, C. H. (1964). *Theory of data.* New York: Wiley.

Coombs, C. H. (1983). *Psychology and mathematics: An essay on theory.* Ann Arbor: University of Michigan Press.

Coombs, C. H., Raiffa, H., & Thrall, R. M. (1954). Some views on mathematical models and measurement theory. *Psychological Review, 61, 132–144.*

Cox, D. R. (1970). *Analysis of binary data.* London: Methuen.

DeLisi, R. (1983). Developmental and individual differences in children's representation of the horizontal coordinate. *Merrill-Palmer Quarterly, 29, 179–196.*

Dempster, A. P., Laird, N. M., & Rubin, D. B. (1977). Maximum likelihood from incomplete data via the EM algorithm. *Journal of the Royal Statistical Society,* Ser. B, 39, 1–38.

Dodwell, P. C. (1963). Children's understanding of spatial concepts. *Canadian Journal of Psychology, 17, 141–146.*

Efron, B., & Tibshirani, R. (1986). Bootstrap methods for standard errors, confidence intervals, and other measures of statistical accuracy. *Statistical Science, 1, 54–77.*

Eliot, J. (1987). *Models of psychological space.* New York: Springer-Verlag.

Everitt, B. S., & Hand, D. J. (1981). *Finite mixture distributions.* London: Chapman & Hall.

Flavell, J. (1963). *The developmental psychology of Jean Piaget.* New York: Van Nostrand.

Flavell, J. H., & Wohlwill, J. F. (1979). Formal and functional aspects of cognitive development. In D. Elkind & J. H. Flavell (Eds.), *Studies in cognitive development.* New York: Oxford University Press.

Geiringer, E., & Hyde, J. (1976). Sex differences on Piaget's water-level task: Spatial ability incognito. *Perceptual and Motor Skills, 42, 1323–1328.*

Golbeck, S. L. (1986). The role of physical content in Piagetian spatial tasks: Sex differences in spatial knowledge? *Journal of Research in Science Teaching, 23, 365–376.*

Guthke, J. (1977). *Zur Diagnostik der intellektuellen Leistungsfaehigkeit.* Stuttgart: Klett.

Halpern, D. F. (1986). *Sex differences in cognitive abilities.* Hillsdale, NJ: Erlbaum.

Hedges, L. V., & Olkin, I. (1985). *Statistical methods for meta-analysis.* New York: Academic.

Hodkin, B. (1987). Performance model analysis in class inclusion: An illustration with two language conditions. *Developmental Psychology, 23, 683–689.*

Hogg, R. V., & Craig, A. T. (1970). *Introduction to mathematical statistics* (3d ed.). New York: Macmillan.

Howe, M. L., Brainerd, C. J., & Kingma, J. (1985). Development of organization in recall: A stages-of-learning analysis. *Journal of Experimental Child Psychology, 39, 179–195.*

Huber, P. J. (1977). *Robust statistical procedures.* Philadelphia: Society for Industrial and Applied Mathematics.

Hull, C. L., Hovland, C. I., Ross, R. T., Hall, M., Perkins, D. T., & Fitch, F. B. (1940). *Mathematico-deductive theory of rote learning.* New Haven, CT: Yale University Press.

Johnson, N. I., & Kotz, S. (1969). *Discrete distributions.* Boston: Houghton Mifflin.

Kalichman, S. C. (1988). Individual differences in water-level performance: A component-skills analysis. *Developmental Review, 8, 273–295.*

Kalichman, S. C. (1989). Sex roles and sex differences in adult spatial performance. *Journal of Genetic Psychology, 150, 93–100.*

Kelly, J. T., & Kelley, G. N. (1977). Perception of horizontality in male and female college students. *Perceptual and Motor Skills, 44, 724–726.*

Kelly, G. N., Kelly, J. T., & Johnson, W. S. (1988). Coordination of perspective by sixth graders and teacher trainees. (1988). *Contemporary Educational Psychology, 13,* 358–370.

Krantz, D. H. (1972). Measurement structures and psychological laws. *Science,* **175,** 1427–1435.

Larsen, G. Y., & Abravanel, E. (1972). An examination of the developmental relations between certain spatial tasks. *Merrill-Palmer Quarterly, 18,* 39–52.

Lazarsfeld, P. F., & Henry, N. W. (1968). *Latent structure analysis.* Boston: Houghton Mifflin.

Liben, L. S. (1975). Long-term memory for pictures related to seriation, horizontality, and verticality concepts. *Developmental Psychology, 11,* 795–806.

Liben, L. S. (1978). Performance on Piagetian spatial tasks as a function of sex, field dependence, and training. *Merrill-Palmer Quarterly, 24,* 97–110.

Liben, L. S. (1991a). Adults' performance on horizontality tasks: Conflicting frames of reference. *Developmental Psychology, 27,* 285–294.

Liben, L. S. (1991b). The Piagetian water-level task: Looking beneath the surface. In R. Vasta (Ed.), *Annals of child development* (Vol. 8). London: Kingsley.

Liben, L. S., & Golbeck, S. L. (1980). Sex differences in performance on Piagetian spatial tasks: Differences in competence or performance? *Child Development, 5,* 594–597.

Liben, L. S., & Golbeck, S. L. (1984). Performance on Piagetian horizontality and verticality tasks: Sex-related differences in knowledge of relevant physical phenomena. *Developmental Psychology, 20,* 595–606.

Linn, M. C., & Petersen, A. C. (1985). Emergence and characterization of sex differences in spatial ability: A meta-analysis. *Child Development, 56,* 1479–1498.

Lohaus, A. (1989). *Datenerhebung in der Entwicklungspsychologie: Problemstellungen und Forschungsperspektiven.* Bern: Huber.

Lohaus, A. (1990). Response scales in developmental psychology: Empirical results of a comparative study. *Journal of Genetic Psychology, 151,* 473–481.

Lord, F. M. (1969). Estimating true-score distributions in psychological testing (an empirical Bayes estimation). *Psychometrika, 34,* 259–299.

Lorge, E., & Thorndike, E. L. (1964). *Lorge-Thorndike intelligence tests.* Boston: Houghton Mifflin.

Maccoby, E. E., & Jacklin, C. N. (1974). *The psychology of sex differences.* Stanford, CA: Stanford University Press.

Marsh, H. W., Balla, J., & McDonald, R. P. (1988). Goodness-of-fit indices in confirmatory factor analysis: The effect of sample size. *Psychological Bulletin, 103,* 391–410.

McAfee, E. A., & Proffitt, D. R. (1991). Understanding the surface orientation of liquids. *Cognitive Psychology, 23,* 483–514.

McLachlan, G. J., & Basford, K. E. (1988). *Mixture models: Inference and applications to clustering.* New York: Dekker.

Meehan, A. M., & Overton, W. F. (1986). Gender differences in expectancies for success and performance on Piagetian spatial tasks. *Merrill-Palmer Quarterly, 32,* 427–441.

Moore, D. S., & McCabe, G. P. (1993). *Introduction to the practice of statistics* (2d ed.). New York: Freeman.

Morris, B. (1971). Effects of angle, sex and cue on adults' perception of the horizontal. *Perceptual and Motor Skills, 32,* 827–830.

Mote, V. L., & Anderson, R. L. (1965). An investigation of the effect of misclassification on the properties of χ^2-tests in the analysis of categorical data. *Biometrika, 52,* 95–109.

Myer, K. A., & Hensley, H. (1984). Cognitive style, gender, and self-report of principle as predictors of adult performance on Piaget's water level. *Journal of Genetic Psychology,* **144,** 179–183.

Piaget, J. (1969). *The mechanisms of perception.* New York: Basic.

Piaget, J., & Inhelder, B. (1967). *The child's conception of space.* New York: Norton.

Randall, T. M. (1980). Training the horizontality concept in a group of nontransitional children. *Journal of Genetic Psychology,* **136,** 213–220.

Reyna, V. F., & Brainerd, C. J. (1990). Fuzzy processing in transitivity development. *Annals of Operations Research,* **23,** 37–63.

Robert, M., & Chaperon, H. (1989). Cognitive and exemplary modeling of horizontality representation on the Piagetian water-level task. *International Journal of Behavioral Development,* **12,** 453–472.

Robert, M., & Tanguay, M. (1990). Perception and representation of the Euclidean coordinates in mature and elderly men and women. *Experimental Aging Research,* **16,** 123–132.

Roberts, F. S. (1979). *Measurement theory.* Reading, MA: Addison-Wesley.

Rosenthal, R. (1984). *Meta-analytic procedures for social research.* Beverly Hills, CA: Sage.

Siegel, S. (1956). *Nonparametric statistics for the behavioral sciences.* New York: McGraw-Hill.

Siegler, R. S. (1981). Developmental sequences within and between concepts. *Monographs of the Society for Research in Child Development,* **46**(2, Serial No. 189).

Siegler, R. S. (1989). How domain-general and domain-specific knowledge interact to produce strategy choices. *Merrill-Palmer Quarterly,* **35,** 1–26.

Signorella, M. L., & Jamison, W. (1978). Sex differences in the correlations among field dependence, spatial ability sex role orientation, and performance on Piaget's water level task. *Developmental Psychology,* **14,** 689–690.

Thelen, E., & Ulrich, B. D. (1991). Hidden skills: A dynamic systems analysis of treadmill stepping during the first year. *Monographs of the Society for Research in Child Development,* **56**(1, Serial No. 223).

Thomas, H. (1982). A strong developmental theory of field dependence-independence. *Journal of Mathematical Psychology,* **26,** 169–178.

Thomas, H. (1985). Measurement structures and statistics. In S. Kotz & N. Johnson (Eds.), *Encyclopedia of statistical sciences* (Vol. 5). New York: Wiley.

Thomas, H. (1987). Modeling X-linked mediated development: Development of sex differences in the service of a simple model. In J. Bisanz, C. Brainerd, & R. Kail (Eds.), *Formal methods in developmental psychology.* New York: Springer-Verlag.

Thomas, H. (1989). *Distributions of correlation coefficients.* New York: Springer-Verlag.

Thomas, H., & Jamison, W. (1975). On the acquisition of understanding that still water is horizontal. *Merrill-Palmer Quarterly,* **21,** 32–44.

Thomas, H., & Jamison, W. (1981). A test of the X-linked genetic hypothesis for sex differences on Piaget's water-level task. *Developmental Review,* **1,** 274–283.

Thomas, H., Jamison, W., & Hummel, D. D. (1973). Observation is insufficient for discovering that the surface of still water is invariantly horizontal. *Science,* **181,** 173–174.

Thomas, H., & Kail, R. (1991). Sex differences in speed of mental rotation and the X-linked genetic hypothesis. *Intelligence,* **15,** 17–32.

Thomas, H., & Turner, G. F. W. (1991). Individual differences and development in water-level task performance. *Journal of Experimental Child Psychology,* **51,** 171–194.

Thurstone, L. L. (1928). The absolute zero in intelligence measurement. *Psychological Review,* **35,** 175–197.

Titterington, D. M., Smith, A. F. M., & Makov, U. E. (1985). *Statistical analysis of finite mixture distributions.* New York: Wiley.

Turner, G. F. W. (1991). *Modeling individual differences in spatial task performance with binomial mixtures.* Unpublished M.A. thesis, Pennsylvania State University.

Tversky, A., & Kahneman, D. (1974). Judgment under uncertainty: Heuristics and biases. *Science*, **185**, 1124–1131.

Walker, J. T., & Krasnoff, A. G. (1978). The horizontality principle in young men and women. *Perceptual and Motor Skills*, **46**, 1055–1061.

Wilks, S. S. (1938). The large sample distribution of the likelihood ratio for testing composite hypothesis. *Annals of Mathematical Statistics*, **9**, 60–62.

Willemsen, E., & Reynolds, B. (1973). Sex differences in adults' judgments of the horizontal. *Developmental Psychology*, **8**, 309.

Windham, M. P., & Cutler, A. (1992). Information ratios for validating mixture analyses. *Journal of the American Statistical Association*, **87**, 1188–1192.

Witkin, H. A., Lewis, H. B., Hertzman, M., Machover, K., Meissner, P. B., & Wapner, S. (1954). *Personality through perception: An experimental and clinical study*. New York: Harper & Bros.

Witters-Churchill, L. J., Kelley, R. R., & Witters, L. A. (1983). Hearing-impaired students' perception of liquid horizontality: An examination of the effects of gender, development and training. *Volta Review*, **85**, 211–225.

Wittig, M. A., & Allen, M. J. (1984). Measurement of adult performance on Piaget's water horizontality task. *Intelligence*, **8**, 305–313.

ACKNOWLEDGMENTS

We offer thanks to the students, faculty, and staffs of the following schools in Muenster, Germany, for making the research possible: Bodelschwinghschule, Hanjo Fleck, director; Dietrich-Bonhoeffer-Schule, Renate Heine, director; Freiherr vom Stein Gymnasium, Ruth Engelbert, director; Paul-Gerhardt-Realschule, Hannelore Bergmann, director; Realschule im Kreuzviertel, Josef Terstiege, director; and Schillergymnasium, Hartmut Hoefermann, director.

We wish to thank Silke Borchardt, Leonore Dinter, Claudia Flake, Johannes Klein-Hessling, Ulrike Krause, Heide Larisch, Silke Mehler, and Andreas Ott for collecting and scoring data for Study 1 and for collecting data for Study 2 and H. M. Trautner, University of Muenster, for his assistance during the planning phase of the research.

This research was supported by Deutsche Forschungsgemeinschaft Research Grant MU 40/73-1 to Hoben Thomas and administered through the University of Muenster.

Correspondence should be addressed to Hoben Thomas, Department of Psychology, Pennsylvania State University, University Park, PA 16802-3105.

COMMENTARY

COGNITIVE DEVELOPMENT IS ABRUPT (BUT NOT STAGE-LIKE)

C. J. Brainerd

Let me begin with a warning. I have been told that *Monograph* readers often turn first to the Commentary. The perception seems to be that a Commentary is a sort of conspectus—that it summarizes and critiques the *Monograph*'s major themes and generally acts as an advance organizer for the principal document. My warning is that this perception is mistaken in the present case. Although Hoben Thomas and Arnold Lohaus have made impressive advances on a number of fronts (e.g., the creation of new techniques for measuring children's understanding of horizontality and verticality concepts, the formulation of an elegant mathematical machinery for modeling developmental and individual differences in these concepts, the segregation of factors that are responsible for such differences into field effects and rule strategy, the gathering of data that are probative with respect to fundamental theoretical questions about spatial development), I shall not touch on most of these advances. Since it will consequently be impossible to gain an appreciation of the scope of Thomas and Lohaus's achievements from my comments, reading this *Monograph* front to back would be far more profitable than reading it back to front.

Getting down to business, this Commentary focuses on a single, thorny question: Are developmental improvements in performance on "cognitive items" abrupt or continuous? Of the many important questions that arise in Thomas and Lohaus's research, this is arguably the most general one inasmuch as its significance would be immediately conceded by everyone. Generality aside, I have chosen to focus on this question for two further reasons. First, an interesting mismatch exists between long-standing theoretical opinions about abrupt versus continuous development and what has actually been found in recent research. Second, by considering Thomas and Lohaus's data in light of other investigators' findings, it is possible to achieve closure on this question, which shows that we have come a long way in our attempts to understand the basic nature of cognitive growth.

I begin with a brief sketch of the history of the abruptness question. Next, three model-based approaches to the question are summarized: absorbing Markov chains, distributional mixtures of the type that Thomas and Lohaus have exploited, and catastrophes. It is stressed that research conducted within each of these traditions has produced the same general outcome—namely, that developmental improvements consist of hops through discrete state spaces. This datum's implications for the stage hypothesis are explored in the concluding section.

A Little History

A quarter century ago, when theoretical and empirical analyses of Piaget's stage construct were in vogue, the possibility that children's acquisition of what were called "cognitive items" (e.g., horizontality, verticality, and other stage-related concepts) could be abrupt, in the sense of zero-order transitions from lower performance levels to higher performance levels, was much debated. Ultimately, we rejected this possibility, concluding that development at the level of cognitive items is normally smooth and continuous (cf. various commentators in Brainerd, 1978). This, in turn, did much to undermine the then-universal influence of Piagetian theory. Given what we knew at the time, the conclusion was right. Given what we have learned since, it was wrong. The latter fact is not widely understood, however, and the belief that cognitive development is smooth and continuous remains the prevailing view.

The linchpin of this view is a series of three papers by Flavell (1970, 1972; Flavell & Wohlwill, 1969) the importance of which can hardly be overestimated. A key objective of the first paper, and the sole objective of the second, was to isolate some properties of cognitive development that everyone could agree were hallmarks of stages in the Piagetian sense. Flavell and Wohlwill (1969) listed two, *abruptness* and *qualitative change*. Flavell (1970) expanded the list to include two others, *concurrence* and *structures*. He summarized them as follows: (*a*) "the development of individual stage-specific items is characteristically abrupt rather than gradual; that is, there is a zero-order transition period between the initial appearance of each item and its stage of functional maturity" (p. 425); (*b*) "stage-to-stage development entails qualitative rather than quantitative changes in thinking" (p. 423); (*c*) "the various items which define a stage develop concurrently, i.e., in synchrony with one another" (p. 435); and (*d*) "stage-specific items become organized and interrelated to form cognitive structures" (p. 443).

Intuitively, abruptness is the most fundamental property, the one that best captures what students of development envision when they think of stage-like development. (Flavell and Wohlwill remarked that there has been an abiding concern among students of development as to "whether cognitive evolution is . . . saltatory, characterized by spurts of intellectual growth. . . . Alternatively, it has been asked whether this evolution is typically 'continuous' or 'discontinuous' in nature" [1969, p. 79].) Insofar as the other properties are concerned, two of them, qualitative change and structure, seem to be more matters of philosophical position than empirical statements about age-change phenomena. The remaining property, concurrence, appears to depend on abruptness in the first instance—abruptness can easily be imagined without concurrence, but it is difficult to imagine the converse.

Flavell (1970) proposed that, whatever else may be true of cognitive development, it is not an abrupt process. Indeed, he maintained that the extant "research literature on the development of Piagetian and other cognitive items strongly indicates that [abruptness] can immediately be ruled out of contention" (p. 428). What was the nature of the evidence to which he referred?

Flavell (1970) observed that, if development is abrupt, plotting performance level on individual cognitive items against age should produce graphs like Figure C1. For purposes of illustration, assume that this graph contains data for one of Thomas and Lohaus's horizontality or verticality tasks and that this task has been administered to a child at 6-month intervals between the ages of 4 and 10. Figure C1 therefore displays the probability of a valid solution as a function of age (in 6-month gradations). Note that the solution probability exhibits a sudden upward explosion at age 6.5. Before that age, this probability remains fixed at a constant low level ($p = .10$). After that, it remains fixed at a constant high level ($p = 1.0$). Flavell argued that then-available data did not conform to this pattern and that, instead, they tended to look like the graph in Figure C2. There, the probability of a correct solution increases gradually from its lowest level to its highest level between the ages of 5.5 and 7.5. Flavell argued that this latter pattern made better theoretical sense than Figure C1 because it was in good agreement with familiar distinctions such as preparation periods versus achievement periods, competence versus performance, and mediation deficiencies versus production deficiencies.

Although the data that motivated the view that Figure C2 is the modal pattern seemed convincing at the time, they are susceptible to other explanations. Again, what were these data? Flavell (1970) relied on cross-sectional results involving *multiple measures of differential difficulty*. Specifically, he relied on data emanating from a dispute over the age at which children solve transitive inference problems (e.g., Braine, 1959; Murray & Youniss, 1968; Smedslund, 1969). The solution age had been found to vary dramatically as a consequence of task variables. It appeared to be age 5 when problems

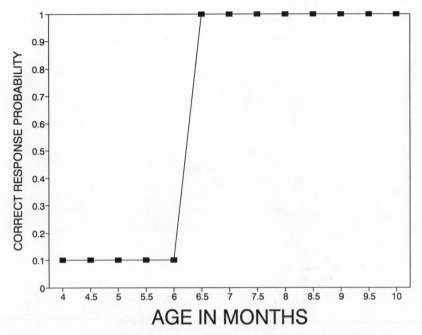

Fig. C1.—Abrupt developmental change in performance on a cognitive item

were presented nonverbally, age 7 when problems were presented verbally, and age 9 when countervailing visual illusions were added to verbal problems. Further, Coon and Odom (1968) found that, when social conformity pressures were included, problems were not solved until after age 11. Flavell added that similar, although less extensive, data were available for concepts such as compensation and conservation.

It turns out that such evidence is guaranteed to produce patterns like Figure C2, even when underlying age changes are strictly abrupt. Recall that Figures C1 and C2 assume that a *single* task has been administered to children on *several* occasions. However, the data that Flavell (1970) relied on came from studies in which *multiple* tasks (which were known to be of differential difficulty) were administered *once* to groups of children from different age levels and mean performance levels were then plotted against age.

To see why such data must produce patterns like Figure C2, suppose that we have five tasks of varying difficulty—say, transitivity problems to conform to Flavell (1970). Suppose that the mean solution ages for the problems are 5.5, 6, 6.5, 7, and 7.5 years, respectively, with a standard deviation of 0.5 years for each problem. Suppose that developmental improvements on each of these tasks are strictly abrupt; solution probability

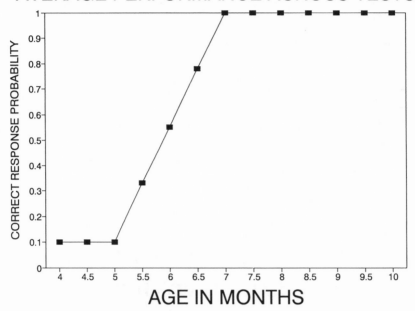

AVERAGE PERFORMANCE ACROSS TESTS

FIG. C2.—Continuous developmental change in performance on a cognitive item

remains fixed at floor level until it suddenly leaps to ceiling level. Now, imagine that these five tasks are administered to a child at 6-month intervals between the ages of 4 and 10. If solution probability on *each problem* is plotted against time of measurement, the outcome will be the five abrupt-change patterns in Figure C3. (These plots are for an ideal child whose solution probability on each problem jumps upward precisely at the norma-tive solution age for that problem.) But what will be the result if mean solution probability across the five problems is plotted against time of mea-surement? The answer is a pattern like Figure C2; a continuous-change function that is produced by averaging across a series of functions that are not continuous.

It is essential to realize that Figure C2 is a general result that is not restricted to circumstances in which solution probabilities are averaged over problems of differential difficulty. Although, to conform to the evidence discussed by Flavell (1970), the problems in the example were assumed to vary in difficulty, averaging will produce the same picture when problems are of identical difficulty. To illustrate, assume that the transitivity tasks all have a mean solution age of 6.5 years and a standard deviation of 0.5 years and that ages of upward jumps vary randomly (but in accordance with the standard deviation). If we repeat the experiment and plot mean solution probability against age, the result will be another continuous-change function like Figure C2.

Model-Based Approaches to Abruptness

The denouement of the discussion so far is that we are still left with the problem of how to dissever abrupt from continuous development. The most reliable method is to use a mathematical model or, better yet, to pit contrasting mathematical models against each other. Such models formalize the core properties of abruptness (or continuity). In their most general sense, they are merely data-generating machines that, given values for their parameters, will manufacture quantitative predictions about what the target data should look like if development follows an abrupt-change scenario. When such models can predict the fine-grain structure of target data to statistically tolerable approximations, the developmental changes that are responsible for those data are abrupt. Q.E.D.

To date, this strategy has been implemented using three distinct modeling technologies: absorbing Markov chains, distributional mixtures, and catastrophes. Although these lines of investigation have been quite separate from each other, they have produced a common outcome—namely, that children's acquisition of concepts such as class inclusion, conservation, horizontality, probability, and verticality is abrupt rather than continuous. I summarize how the abruptness question has been attacked in each instance and review illustrative findings.

Absorbing Markov Chains

About 15 years ago, I noticed that a similar question had once figured in the adult literature on learning and memory (e.g., Bower, 1961; Estes, 1960; Suppes & Ginsburg, 1963). Following a counterintuitive result that Rock (1957) had reported, researchers became interested in the possibility that improvements in performance on standard learning and memory tasks (e.g., concept identification, cued recall, free recall, paired-associate learning) might consist of sudden, all-or-none jumps rather than gradual increments. The result in question was that, when college students studied paired-associate lists, they appeared to learn nothing about an item before they made their first correct response. To illustrate, if, after each study-test cycle, the experimenter replaced all the pairs that had not been remembered with new pairs, learning progressed just as rapidly as if the list remained unchanged; there was no "savings" for the unremembered pairs, even though they had been studied.

To explore this finding, a family of very tractable stochastic models,

PROBLEM #1

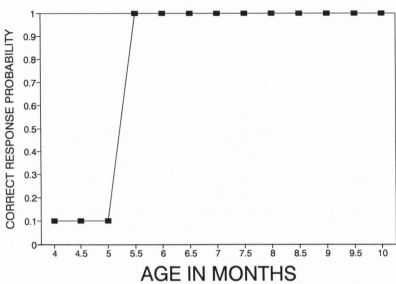

a

PROBLEM #2

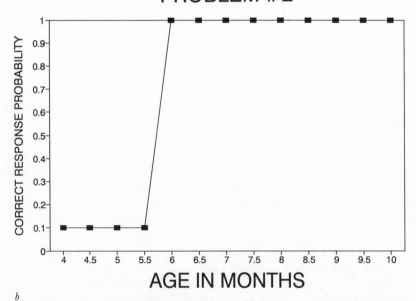

b

FIG. C3.—Abrupt developmental changes in performance on five transitivity problems with different mean ages of solution. Mean ages of solution: *a*, 5.5 years; *b*, 6 years; *c*, 6.5 years; *d*, 7 years; *e*, 7.5 years.

PROBLEM #3

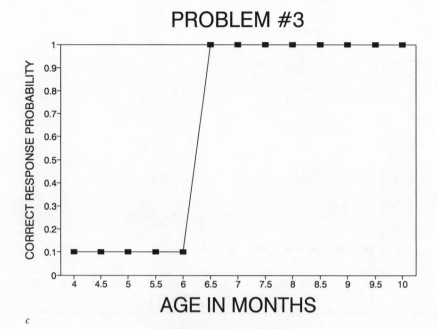

c

PROBLEM #4

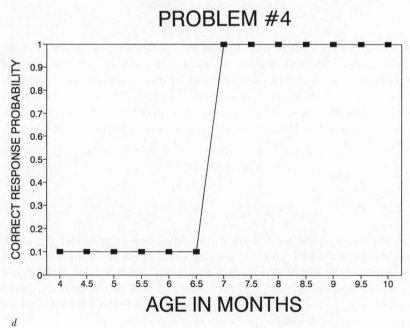

d

PROBLEM #5

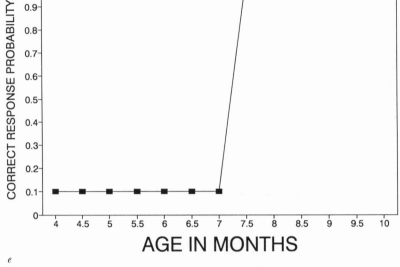

e

absorbing Markov chains, was adapted for application to experimentation. These models assumed that, in learning and memory experiments, the probability of a correct response consists of (*a*) a finite number of values, called *states*, with (*b*) upward all-or-none transitions between states and (*c*) no backward transitions. These assumptions specify the following sequence of models that differ in their respective numbers of performance states, *P*:

$$P_1 = (0, 1),$$
$$P_2 = (0, p_1, 1),$$
$$P_3 = (0, p_1, p_2, 0),$$
$$\ldots,$$
$$P_{k-1} = (0, p_1, \ldots, p_k, 1).$$

The two simplest models are the so-called one-stage model, P_1, which consists of the 0 and 1 probability states and a single all-or-none transition $(0 \rightarrow 1)$, and the so-called two-stage model, P_2, which consists of the 0 and 1 probabilities, an intermediate probability p_1, and two all-or-none transitions $(0 \rightarrow p_1$ and $p_1 \rightarrow 1)$. These models are depicted in Figure C4, along with a four-stage model for purposes of comparison.

An important truth that is conveyed by Figure C4 is that abruptness is a matter of degree and that, crucially, it is not synonymous with Figure

C1. As is apparent from Figure C4, abrupt change corresponds to any circumstance in which developmental improvement consists of all-or-none leaps through a series of performance states. Figure C1 is only the most elementary instance; Figures C4b and C4c qualify, too. Obviously, however, the distinction between abrupt and continuous change breaks down as the number of states proliferates. Thus, while we would regard all the patterns in Figure C4 as depicting abrupt rather than continuous change, we would tend to regard the distinction between a Markov chain with, say, 20 states (and 19 transitions) and a strictly continuous function as a distinction without a difference.

So the practical issue is whether learning and memory data are well fit by Markov chains with *very small* numbers of states. A review of the literature (Brainerd, Howe, & Desrochers, 1982) showed that this was, in fact, the case. Indeed, the two simplest chains, the one- and two-stage models, had been found to give very precise accounts of data from the most commonly studied learning and memory paradigms. The possibility that these models might be equally successful with developmental data immediately suggested itself.

This led to a series of experiments in which absorbing Markov chains were fit to the data of learning experiments involving Piagetian concepts. The initial experiments (Brainerd, 1979a) dealt with the learning of length, number, and quantity conservation. Later experiments (Brainerd, 1979b, 1981, 1982) included class-inclusion and probability concepts. The key finding was that, when children received training on these concepts, improvements in performance were abrupt. In all cases, the data were well fit by either the one- or the two-stage model (Figs. C4a and C4b). An illustration of just how precise the correspondence was is provided in Table C1, where the observed values of some common learning statistics are compared to the values predicted by the two-stage model using data from the Brainerd (1979a) experiments. When the predicted values in this table are subtracted from the observed values, the average difference is only $-.06$.

Distributional Mixtures

Thus, Markovian analyses of children's learning make an optimistic case for the hypothesis that certain concrete-operational concepts are acquired in an abrupt fashion. The case is less than conclusive, however, for two reasons. First, the fitted data were not, strictly speaking, developmental because the concepts had been trained rather than being left to emerge naturally. It is quite conceivable that acquisition might be abrupt when children receive focused training on a concept but continuous when improvements arise from the desultory learning experiences and gradual maturational changes that characterize ontogenesis. Second, the models that were

ONE-STAGE ABRUPT

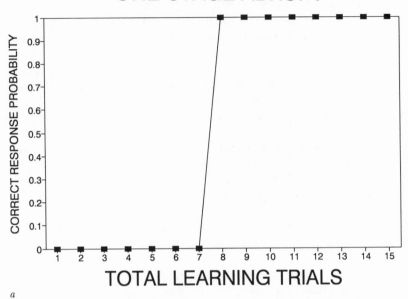

a

TWO-STAGE ABRUPT

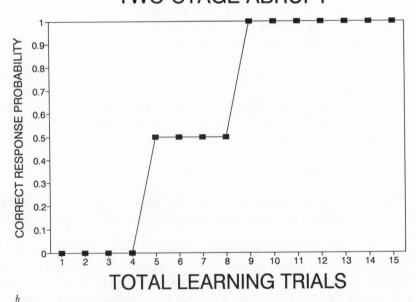

b

Fig. C4.—Absorbing Markov chains for learning and memory. *a*, One-stage model. *b*, Two-stage model. *c*, Four-stage model.

FOUR-STAGE ABRUPT

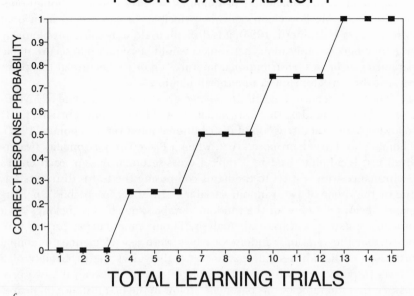

TOTAL LEARNING TRIALS

c

TABLE C1

OBSERVED AND PREDICTED MEAN VALUES OF FIVE LEARNING STATISTICS
IN BRAINERD'S (1979a) EXPERIMENTS

Statistic	Observed	Predicted	Statistic	Observed	Predicted
Errors before			Last error after		
first success:			first success:		
Experiment 1....	2.10	1.98	Experiment 1....	1.27	.97
Experiment 2....	1.80	1.83	Experiment 2....	1.07	.93
Experiment 3....	2.13	2.03	Experiment 3....	.88	.90
Length of			Total errors:		
precriterion			Experiment 1....	2.82	2.53
success runs:			Experiment 2....	2.30	2.32
Experiment 1....	.91	1.09	Experiment 3....	2.93	3.30
Experiment 2....	.81	.74			
Experiment 3....	1.00	.91			
Trials in inter-					
mediate state:					
Experiment 1....	1.33	1.78			
Experiment 2....	1.44	2.00			
Experiment 3....	1.71	2.08			

used made no provision for the measurement of individual differences in development, either qualitative or quantitative differences. Although one- and two-stage Markov chains can, in principle, be applied to individual differences (see Brainerd, 1985), it is difficult to do so because prohibitively large numbers of replications per subject would be required to secure stable parameter estimates. Distributional mixtures enter the picture at this point because they are not subject to either limitation.

The work reported in this *Monograph* greatly expands a line of investigation on such models that was initiated by Thomas and Turner (1991) following a general discussion of distributional mixtures by Thomas (1987). Thomas and Turner proposed that, when a Piagetian horizontality (water-level) test is administered in a typical cross-sectional design, each child's performance with respect to the items composing the test is distributed as one or the other of two random variables.[1] In effect, each child's performance "belongs" to one of the random variables, much as it "belongs" to a probability state in a Markovian analysis. Thomas and Turner further proposed that the relevant random variables were just elementary binomial processes, each with a single parameter θ that gives the probability of a correct response on each item. The only difference between the two processes is that the value of this parameter is low in the first instance (θ_1 nearer to 0 than to 1) and high in the second (θ_2 nearer to 1 than to 0). If the test consists of n items, the average number of correct responses for a child (across multiple administrations of the test) will be the smaller value $n\theta_1$ if performance belongs to the first random variable or the larger value $n\theta_2$ if performance belongs to the second random variable.

Since a child's performance might belong to either random variable, the responses of a group of children are necessarily a mixture of two binomial processes—hence, the name "binomial mixture" or, more generally, "distributional mixture." If π_1 is the proportion of protocols for some group of m children that belongs to the first random variable (and $1 - \pi_1$ is therefore the proportion that belongs to the second random variable), the mean number of correct responses for this group is

$$M = n[\pi_1\theta_1 + (1 - \pi_1)\theta_2].$$

This is an abrupt-change model. In fact, it is easy to see that it is an example of the simplest of such models (Figs. C1 and C4a). The probability of making a correct response can take on only two values. Because no intermediate values are permitted, changes in performance *must* consist of all-or-

---

[1] Another model that assumes that performance is a mixture of two random variables has been devised by Hodkin (1987) for class-inclusion reasoning (see also Chapman & McBride, 1992). However, the statistical machinery for fitting the model to data and for testing hypotheses about its parameter values is not yet fully developed.

none transitions; otherwise, there would have to be correct response probabilities other than θ_1 and θ_2.

Thomas and Turner (1991) fitted their binomial mixture model to the water-level performance of 387 subjects, ranging in age from 6.5 to college. Actually, they fitted different versions of the model that allowed the three parameters to take on different values for different subgroups of subjects. A version that permitted the three parameters to take on different values for different age levels and for different sexes did an excellent job, accounting for more than 90% of the variance on average. Developmentally, age improvements in water-level performance for females were found to involve a *qualitative* shift in the complexity of the underlying distributional structure. At younger age levels (grades 1–4), only the first random variable could be detected. After that, both random variables could be detected, and further age improvements consisted of decreases in π_1, the proportion of protocols that belonged to the variable with the lower performance parameter. For males, on the other hand, both random variables were present at all age levels, although developmental improvements were again a matter of decreases in the proportions of protocols that belonged to the first random variable as opposed to the second.

Finally, sex differences took an especially tractable form. To begin with, the *same two* random variables were detected in the protocols of both males and females. In college students, for instance, the average values of θ_1 were .28 for females and .32 for males, and the average values of θ_2 were .99 for females and .97 for males. Sex differences were confined to the proportions of protocols that belonged to each random variable. The average values of π_1 were .57 for college females and .18 for males. Mature water-level performance was therefore governed by the same two binomial processes in both sexes, but roughly three times as many males as females had made the developmental jump from the first process to the second.

These results have been extended in numerous and fundamental ways in the present *Monograph*—to a new task domain (verticality), to new types of horizontality tests, to a new language group, to individual differences other than sex differences, to the statistical assumptions that we make about what methods of analysis are appropriate for developmental data, to the psychological factors that control the expression of the two random variables (field effects, rule strategy), and to the contributions of verbal understanding to performance. From the perspective of abruptness, however, two outcomes must be emphasized. First, the core finding that the development of certain Piagetian spatial concepts, including sex differences in development, follows the simplest type of abrupt-change function (Figs. C1 and C4a) has been thoroughly replicated, with new tasks as well as with new subject samples.

Second, procedures were implemented *that allowed the abrupt-change pat-*

tern to be preserved when performance was pooled across different tasks (horizontality and verticality in this case). Earlier, I mentioned that, when performance on a given task develops abruptly, a continuous-change function will nevertheless be obtained if average performance is plotted for a series of tasks (Fig. C2). However, Thomas and Lohaus showed that this problem can be overcome by fitting a joint mixture model to pooled data—that is, by fitting a model that assumes that two binomial random variables underlie each task but that the parameters of these variables and the proportions of protocols that belong to each may vary between tasks. Their joint mixture analyses established that the pooled data also conformed to the abrupt-change scenario.

Turning back the pages of history again, this same method of analysis could, of course, be applied to the data that Flavell (1970) used to argue against abruptness. It is true, as Flavell demonstrated, that different tasks yield widely variable age norms for transitive inference. However, it is possible, even likely considering Thomas and Lohaus's findings, that the structure of the pooled data for k such tasks would consist of $2k$ binomial random variables. If so, then, paradoxically, the same data that once spoke eloquently for continuity would now do likewise for abruptness.

Catastrophes

Taken together, Markovian and distributional mixture analyses have provided strong support for the contention that ontogenesis involves abrupt changes at the level of individual cognitive items. Moreover, the types of changes that have been detected are of the most elementary sort inasmuch as they have not yet been found to involve more than two steps. Despite such evidence, there is a potentially annoying technical problem that remains to be dealt with. To see what it is, consider the developmental functions in Figure C5.

Figures C5a and C5b are obtained from Figures C4a and C4b, respectively, by relaxing the constraint that response probabilities must be stationary before and after upward explosions. In Figure C4a, the response probability is fixed at 0 across the first seven measurement occasions, then it jumps upward to 1 without taking on intermediate values, and it remains fixed there on all subsequent measurement occasions. In Figure C4b, the response probability is fixed at 0 across the first four measurement occasions, then it jumps upward to .5 without taking on intermediate values, it remains fixed there across the next four measurement occasions, then it jumps upward to 1 without taking on intermediate values, and it remains fixed there on all subsequent measurement occasions. Figure C5a resembles Figure C4a in that the response probability makes one jump, without taking on interme-

ONE CATASTROPHE

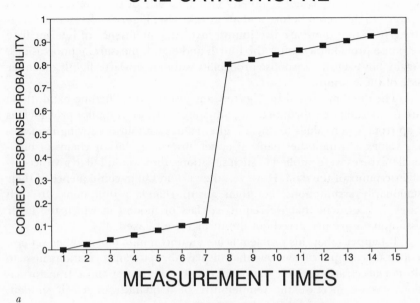

a

TWO CATASTROPHES

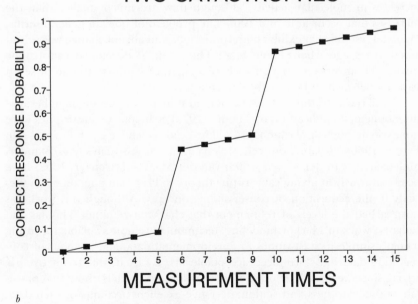

b

Fig. C5.—*a*, A one-stage abrupt-change model with the stationarity assumption re-laxed. *b*, A two-stage abrupt-change model with the stationarity assumption relaxed.

diate values, after the seventh measurement occasion. However, the response probability is not stationary on either side of the jump; it wanders upward slightly both before and after. Likewise, Figure C5*b* resembles Figure C4*b* in that there are two jumps, involving an absence of intermediate response probabilities, after the fourth and eighth measurement occasions. Again, however, the response probability wanders upward slightly on either side of these jumps.

The dilemma posed by Figure C5 is just this. On the one hand, these are unquestionably abrupt-change situations because response probabilities leap from lower values to much higher values without occupying intervening values. On the other hand, if either absorbing Markov chains or binomial mixtures were applied in such situations, they would fail to give acceptable accounts of the data. However, they would fail in consequence of their stationarity assumptions, not their abrupt-change assumptions. In such cases, it is evident that we require a class of models in which the latter assumptions are preserved but the former are relaxed.

It happens that this problem is not an uncommon one in other venues. For instance, physical systems that display abrupt transformations in state do not necessarily exhibit stationarity before and after those transformations. As we increase the temperature of a quantity of ice, it suddenly changes from a solid to a liquid at 0° C and from a liquid to a gas at 100° C. Before and after these changes, however, there are measurable increases in molecular activity, although they are much smaller than the increases that occur at 0° and 100°. The problem of how, in general terms, to model systems that exhibit both continuous and abrupt change was solved a few years ago when Thom (e.g., Thom, 1975) developed catastrophe theory. Thom proved that all such systems must conform to one of seven basic models, which he called "elementary catastrophes."

Until recently, this fact was no help to students of development because developmental applications of Thom's (1975) elementary catastrophes were nonexistent. Such applications are still few and sketchy (e.g., cf. Lewis, 1990; Preece, 1980). Of late, however, Molenaar and his associates (e.g., Stauder, Molenaar, & van der Molen, 1993; van der Maas & Molenaar, 1992) have been vigorously applying catastrophe theory to Piagetian phenomena, especially to the acquisition of conservation concepts. Although this work has not reached the levels of refinement that characterize either Thomas and Lohaus's work or Markov modeling, techniques are now available for fitting Thom's simplest catastrophes to developmental data, and analyses of conservation data have produced acceptable fits. By itself, this result is fairly trivial: since we already know that more restrictive models (those that postulate both abruptness and stationarity) give excellent accounts of such data, less restrictive models (those that postulate only abruptness) should too.

On the latter point, because distributional mixtures and Markov chains have produced such excellent fits, it could be argued that catastrophe models are of purely academic interest. This argument is quite correct if one restricts attention to the extant literature. From that utilitarian perspective, there is no urgent need for catastrophe models. Nevertheless, it is well to be prepared for the possibility that classes of phenomena will eventually be encountered in which distributional mixtures and Markov chains will fail for want of stationarity. With such phenomena, if they can be shown to exist, catastrophe models may prove useful.

Stages Redux?

It is scarcely possible to escape from the toils of a discussion of abrupt-change data without inquiring as to their implications for the stage hypothesis. I remarked earlier that sudden upward explosions in performance are images that immediately come to mind when mediating on the claim that cognitive development is stage-like. Because evidence of such explosions has accumulated from three distinct modeling perspectives, are we not now justified in accepting the stage hypothesis? Thomas and Lohaus, like Thomas and Turner (1991) before them, apparently do not think so because they scrupulously avoid any such suggestion. Others, specifically advocates of catastrophe modeling, are of a different opinion: "The basic tenet of this article is that catastrophes constitute formal analogues of stage transitions in Piaget's theory of cognitive development. . . . It follows . . . that stage transitions constitute the landmark of epigenetic development" (van der Maas & Molenaar, 1992, p. 415).

For various reasons, not the least nostalgia for those simpler days when one theory reigned supreme, it is hard to resist resurrecting the stage hypothesis in the wake of abrupt-change data. The temptation should be resisted, however, for at least two reasons. First, and this is a point that may be easily overlooked, stages are demonstrably *unnecessary* to explain abrupt-change data. We have made theoretical progress in the past quarter century, part of which is the emergence of concepts that can handle such data and that are also more well defined and empirically grounded than stages. Thomas and Lohaus, for example, explain abrupt-change data in terms of the application of distinct response rules—constrained random versus fixed. Rule-based accounts have also proved quite successful in Markovian analyses of developmental data (cf. Brainerd, 1982; Wilkinson, 1982).

Second, succumbing to the stage temptation demands that one be willing to ignore the other formidable lines of evidence against stages, evidence that is not connected to the graininess of development. Here, one must bear in mind that, when the stage hypothesis fell from favor a generation ago, it was not for one reason but for many. Stages did not become unfashionable merely because investigators decided, prematurely it now seems, that cognitive growth is continuous. Instead, there was a gradual attrition process in which stages seemed less and less appealing as more and more arguments against them piled up. Five examples of such arguments (culled from authors in Brainerd, 1978), none of which is addressed by abrupt-change data, are as follows:

1. *Circularity.*—In stage theories, stages are used to *explain* cognitive development—that is, these theories make statements of the form, "Children display concept C because they are in stage S." Such statements have been found to be circular because, although complex theoretical definitions of individual stages may be given, no experimental procedures are provided whereby stage occupancy can be measured independently of the behaviors that stage occupancy supposedly explains.

2. *Measurement sequences.*—Stage theories posit culturally universal orders of emergence for concepts associated with individual stages—so-called invariant sequences. However, the invariant sequences that have received the most empirical support have tended to be trivial by-products of nesting the measurement operations that are required to assess individual concepts. Generally speaking, a measurement sequence exists between two stage-related concepts C_1 and C_2 whenever C_2 consists of C_1 plus some other things. To take a familiar Piagetian example, suppose that C_1 = the child can classify a set of objects that vary along two dimensions (say, color and shape) using one or the other of those dimensions and C_2 = the child can classify the same set of objects using both dimensions. As long as the experiment is competently performed, it would naturally be impossible to find two-dimensional classification before one-dimensional classification.

3. *Typology.*—Stage theories pose that classic problem of personality typologies. Such theories assume that children can be assigned to qualitatively distinct behavioral types, from which it follows that variability between different-stage children will be much greater than variability among same-stage children. As with personality typologies, however, within-stage variability and between-stage variability tend to be similar.

4. *Nonpsychological character of cognitive structures.*—The standard conceptual definition of a stage, which reached its highest form in Piaget's work, is grounded in a set of cognitive structures: fundamentally different cognitive architectures are presumed to regulate the behavior of children who occupy different stages (cf. Piaget, 1949). However, analysis of these architectures has revealed that "cognitive" structures are in fact formalizations of *task structures.* For example, Piaget's familiar INRC cognitive structure was shown to be simply an algebraic representation of the structure of certain scientific reasoning problems.

5. *Stage versus learning.*—Stage theories predict that concept learning will be constrained by stage of cognitive development. That is, training on

a target concept will be much more beneficial if children occupy the stage at which that concept appears during normal development than if they occupy some earlier stage. Learning experiments on Piaget's concrete- and formal-operational concepts repeatedly failed to confirm this prediction.

Although these examples could be multiplied considerably, the result would be the same. On the one hand, abrupt-change data can be explained without resorting to stages. Simpler concepts that are much more closely connected to data, such as rules, do quite nicely. On the other hand, stages suffer from such fundamental difficulties that resurrecting them without first overcoming those difficulties would be a retrograde step. Such a leap of faith would inevitably divert attention from the truly important ramifications of abrupt-change data by driving theoretical discussion down paths that were traveled some years ago. To see what those ramifications are—for nomothetic development, for individual differences, for research design, for statistical analysis—one need search no further than Thomas and Lohaus's *Monograph*.

References

Bower, G. H. (1961). Application of a model to paired-associate learning. *Psychometrika,* **26,** 255–280.

Braine, M. D. S. (1959). The ontogeny of certain logical operations: Piaget's formulation examined by nonverbal methods. *Psychological Monographs, 73*(5, Whole No. 475).

Brainerd, C. J. (1978). The stage question in cognitive-developmental theory. *Behavioral and Brain Sciences,* **2,** 173–213.

Brainerd, C. J. (1979a). Markovian interpretations of conservation learning. *Psychological Review,* **86,** 181–213.

Brainerd, C. J. (1979b). Une modèle neo-Piagetian de l'apprentissage du concept chez l'enfant. *Bulletin de Psychologie,* **32,** 509–521.

Brainerd, C. J. (1981). Working memory and the developmental analysis of probability judgment. *Psychological Review,* **88,** 463–502.

Brainerd, C. J. (1982). Children's concept learning as rule-sampling systems with Markovian properties. In C. J. Brainerd (Ed.), *Children's logical and mathematical cognition.* New York: Springer-Verlag.

Brainerd, C. J. (1985). Three-state models of memory development: A review of recent advances in statistical methodology. *Journal of Experimental Child Psychology,* **40,** 375–394.

Brainerd, C. J., Howe, M. L., & Desrochers, A. (1982). The general theory of two-stage learning: A mathematical review with applications to memory development. *Psychological Bulletin,* **91,** 634–655.

Chapman, M., & McBride, M. L. (1992). Beyond competence and performance: Children's class inclusion strategies, superordinate class cues, and verbal justifications. *Developmental Psychology,* **28,** 319–327.

Coon, R. C., & Odom, R. D. (1968). Transitivity and length judgments as a function of age and social influence. *Child Development,* **39,** 1133–1144.

Estes, W. K. (1960). Learning theory and the new "mental chemistry." *Psychological Review,* **67,** 207–223.

Flavell, J. H. (1970). Stage-related properties of cognitive development. *Cognitive Psychology*, **2**, 421–453.

Flavell, J. H. (1972). An analysis of cognitive-developmental sequences. *Genetic Psychology Monographs*, **86**, 279–350.

Flavell, J. H., & Wohlwill, J. F. (1969). Formal and functional aspects of cognitive development. In D. Elkind & J. H. Flavell (Eds.), *Studies in cognitive development: Essays in honor of Jean Piaget*. New York: Oxford University Press.

Hodkin, B. (1987). Performance model analysis in class inclusion: An illustration with two language conditions. *Developmental Psychology*, **23**, 683–689.

Lewis, M. (1990). Development, time, and catastrophe: An alternative view of discontinuity. In P. Baltes, D. L. Featherman, & R. Lerner (Eds.), *Life span development and behavior* (Vol. **10**). Hillsdale, NJ: Erlbaum.

Murray, J. P., & Youniss, J. (1968). Achievement of inferential transitivity and its relation to serial ordering. *Child Development*, **39**, 1259–1268.

Piaget, J. (1949). *Traité de logique*. Paris: Colin.

Preece, P. F. W. (1980). A geometrical model of Piagetian conservation. *Psychological Reports*, **46**, 143–144.

Rock, I. (1957). The role of repetition in associative learning. *American Journal of Psychology*, **70**, 186–193.

Smedslund, J. (1969). Psychological diagnostics. *Psychological Bulletin*, **71**, 237–248.

Stauder, J. E. A., Molenaar, P. C. M., & van der Molen, M. W. (1993). Scalp topography of event-related brain potentials and cognitive transition during childhood. *Child Development*, **64**, 769–788.

Suppes, P., & Ginsburg, R. (1963). A fundamental property of all-or-none models, binomial distribution of responses prior to conditioning, with applications to concept formation in children. *Psychological Review*, **70**, 139–160.

Thom, R. (1975). *Structural stability and morphogenesis*. Reading, MA: Benjamin.

Thomas, H. (1987). Modeling X-linked mediated development: Development of sex differences in the service of a simple model. In J. Bisanz, C. J. Brainerd, & R. Kail (Eds.), *Formal methods in developmental psychology*. New York: Springer-Verlag.

Thomas, H., & Turner, G. F. W. (1991). Individual differences and development in water-level task performance. *Journal of Experimental Child Psychology*, **51**, 171–194.

van der Maas, H. L. J., & Molenaar, P. C. M. (1992). Stagewise cognitive development: An application of catastrophe theory. *Psychological Review*, **99**, 395–417.

Wilkinson, A. C. (1982). Theoretical and methodological analysis of partial knowledge. *Developmental Review*, **2**, 274–304.

Hoben Thomas (Ph.D. 1963, Claremont Graduate School) is professor of psychology at the Pennsylvania State University. His research interests focus on quantitative theory and methods in various areas of psychology, including cognitive development, psychometrics, psychophysics, and meta-analysis.

Arnold Lohaus (Ph.D. 1982, University of Muenster) is associate professor of psychology at the University of Muenster, Germany. His research interests primarily concern methods of data collection on developmental psychology, cognitive development, and developmental issues of health psychology.

C. J. Brainerd (Ph.D. 1970, Michigan State University) is professor in the Department of Educational Psychology at the University of Arizona. He is the author of fuzzy-trace theory, an intuition-oriented approach to memory and cognitive development. Much of his previous research has involved the formulation of mathematical models and their application to developmental questions. He is editor of Springer-Verlag's Series in Cognitive Development, past associate editor of *Child Development,* and author of *Piaget's Theory of Intelligence.*

STATEMENT OF EDITORIAL POLICY

The *Monographs* series is intended as an outlet for major reports of developmental research that generate authoritative new findings and use these to foster a fresh and/or better-integrated perspective on some conceptually significant issue or controversy. Submissions from programmatic research projects are particularly welcome; these may consist of individually or group-authored reports of findings from some single large-scale investigation or of a sequence of experiments centering on some particular question. Multiauthored sets of independent studies that center on the same underlying question can also be appropriate; a critical requirement in such instances is that the various authors address common issues and that the contribution arising from the set as a whole be both unique and substantial. In essence, irrespective of how it may be framed, any work that contributes significant data and/or extends developmental thinking will be taken under editorial consideration.

Submissions should contain a minimum of 80 manuscript pages (including tables and references); the upper limit of 150–175 pages is much more flexible (please submit four copies; a copy of every submission and associated correspondence is deposited eventually in the archives of the SRCD). Neither membership in the Society for Research in Child Development nor affiliation with the academic discipline of psychology are relevant; the significance of the work in extending developmental theory and in contributing new empirical information is by far the most crucial consideration. Because the aim of the series is not only to advance knowledge on specialized topics but also to enhance cross-fertilization among disciplines or subfields, it is important that the links between the specific issues under study and larger questions relating to developmental processes emerge as clearly to the general reader as to specialists on the given topic.

Potential authors who may be unsure whether the manuscript they are planning would make an appropriate submission are invited to draft an outline of what they propose and send it to the Editor for assessment. This mechanism, as well as a more detailed description of all editorial policies, evaluation processes, and format requirements, is given in the "Guidelines for the Preparation of *Monographs* Submissions," which can be obtained by writing to the Editor designate, Rachel K. Clifton, Department of Psychology, University of Massachusetts, Amherst, MA 01003.